T0321990

Artificial Intelligence for Societal Development and Global Well-Being

Abhay Saxena
Dev Sanskriti Vishwavidyalaya, India

Ashutosh Kumar Bhatt
Uttarakhand Open University, India

Rajeev Kumar
Teerthanker Mahaveer University, India

A volume in the Advances in
Computational Intelligence and
Robotics (ACIR) Book Series

Published in the United States of America by
    IGI Global
    Engineering Science Reference (an imprint of IGI Global)
    701 E. Chocolate Avenue
    Hershey PA, USA 17033
    Tel: 717-533-8845
    Fax: 717-533-8661
    E-mail: cust@igi-global.com
    Web site: http://www.igi-global.com

Library of Congress Cataloging-in-Publication Data

Names: Saxena, Abhay, 1970- editor. | Bhatt, Ashutosh Kumar, 1975- editor.
  | Kumar, Rajeev, 1985- editor.
Title: Artificial intelligence for societal development and global
  well-being / Abhay Saxena, Ashutosh Kumar Bhatt, Rajeev Kumar, editors.
Description: Hershey, PA : Engineering Science Reference, [2022] | Includes
  bibliographical references and index. | Summary: "The book provides
  valuable insights on the best practices and success factors from
  researchers of all fields of study that have an interest in artificial
  intelligence, technology and applications incorporated into our daily
  life routines"-- Provided by publisher.
Identifiers: LCCN 2021052880 (print) | LCCN 2021052881 (ebook) | ISBN
  9781668424438 (hardcover) | ISBN 9781668424445 (paperback) | ISBN
  9781668424452 (ebook)
Subjects: LCSH: Artificial intelligence. | Artificial intelligence--Social
  aspects. | Artificial intelligence--Health aspects.
Classification: LCC Q335 .A78738 2022 (print) | LCC Q335 (ebook) | DDC
  006.3--dc23/eng/20211208
LC record available at https://lccn.loc.gov/2021052880
LC ebook record available at https://lccn.loc.gov/2021052881

This book is published in the IGI Global book series Advances in Computational Intelligence and Robotics (ACIR) (ISSN: 2327-0411; eISSN: 2327-042X)

British Cataloguing in Publication Data
A Cataloguing in Publication record for this book is available from the British Library.

For electronic access to this publication, please contact: eresources@igi-global.com.

Advances in Computational Intelligence and Robotics (ACIR) Book Series

ISSN:2327-0411
EISSN:2327-042X

Editor-in-Chief: Ivan Giannoccaro, University of Salento, Italy

MISSION

While intelligence is traditionally a term applied to humans and human cognition, technology has progressed in such a way to allow for the development of intelligent systems able to simulate many human traits. With this new era of simulated and artificial intelligence, much research is needed in order to continue to advance the field and also to evaluate the ethical and societal concerns of the existence of artificial life and machine learning.

The **Advances in Computational Intelligence and Robotics (ACIR) Book Series** encourages scholarly discourse on all topics pertaining to evolutionary computing, artificial life, computational intelligence, machine learning, and robotics. ACIR presents the latest research being conducted on diverse topics in intelligence technologies with the goal of advancing knowledge and applications in this rapidly evolving field.

COVERAGE

- Machine Learning
- Robotics
- Evolutionary Computing
- Brain Simulation
- Heuristics
- Fuzzy Systems
- Cognitive Informatics
- Synthetic Emotions
- Cyborgs
- Intelligent Control

IGI Global is currently accepting manuscripts for publication within this series. To submit a proposal for a volume in this series, please contact our Acquisition Editors at Acquisitions@igi-global.com or visit: http://www.igi-global.com/publish/.

Titles in this Series

701 East Chocolate Avenue, Hershey, PA 17033, USA
Tel: 717-533-8845 x100 • Fax: 717-533-8661
E-Mail: cust@igi-global.com • www.igi-global.com

Table of Contents

Detailed Table of Contents

Chapter 1

    Shilpi Bisht, Birla Institute of Applied Sciences, India
    Neeraj Bisht, Birla Institute of Applied Sciences, India

Autism spectrum disorder (ASD) is a neurological developmental disorder that results in infirmity in social behaviour and social communication. Autism is identifiable at any stage of life, but symptoms usually appear in the first two years. This chapter deals with ASD at three different levels: child, adolescent, and adult. For this purpose, the authors have used a dataset from the UCI repository submitted by Fadi Fayez Thabtah, which has 20 features. They proposed new supervised machine learning models to predict the possibility of autism disorder at the adult stage through child, adolescent, and adult datasets. The detailed comparative study of various methods developed is supported by performance measures and respective ROC curves.

Chapter 2

    Priyanshi Shah, Thoughtworks Technologies, India
    Ajay Narayan Shukla, DIT University, India

The content of this chapter will start by introducing neuroscience, how the brain communicates with the human body, along with neuroscience's history and research in brief with AI. After that, some of the devices used for gathering brain signals will be explained taking its focus towards EEG signals. The preprocessing techniques and algorithms used will be detailed along with some impactful algorithms which have been proven best till now in some of the real scenarios. It will be followed by the challenges faced in neuroscience (mostly BCI). Next, applications will be discussed under two main categories—(1) medical-related fields for treatment or diagnosis and (2) for global lifestyle change—where it will be further divided into different subfields as stated previously. The chapter will be concluded with its future scope for the well-being of humanity.

Chapter 3

Prof. Abhay Saxena, Dev Sanskriti University, India
Amit Saxena, BIMTECH, India
Aditi Saxena, Banasthali University, India

This chapter will cover the basic problems of women in South Asian countries. For this, a group survey is taken in India, Sri Lanka, Singapore, Malaysia, Thailand, Myanmar, and Nepal covering around 200 women about their basic problems in personal and professional lives and lifestyle and house management routine activities. The chapter will cover the basic segment of artificial intelligence and its support in maintaining the health parametric card for the household makers. The chapter will also assist the women in the kitchen with the help of artificial intelligence, especially in cooking and digital health menu selection. A special segment in the chapter will also address the cleanliness of the house with the help of A.I.-supporting tools and gadgets. Last but not the least, the chapter will also address the security of the household makers especially in day hours when they are alone in the houses. The chapter will be an innovative research to understand the better half of the society and to address their day-to-day problems with technological interventions.

Chapter 4

Chandrashekhar Raghuvanshi, Rama University, India
Hari Om Sharan, Rama University, India

In the current pandemic of COVID-19, artificial intelligence has become crucial and plays a vital role in dealing with and caring for patients because of the infectious nature of the disease. Many research institutions are stressing on new challenges and future issues of AI, and business houses are funding research institutes and scholars as artificial intelligence is transforming every aspect of human life. Artificial intelligence is grooming itself as a multidisciplinary field of study as it borrows concept of machine learning, data analytics, deep learning, neural network, statics, and soft computing. This chapter presents various applications of AI in a variety of fields and shows how it has become essential and significant in the current pandemic of COVID-19 and helps in societal development and global wellbeing. The chapter end with future issues and challenges of artificial intelligence and research prospects.

Chapter 5

Soumili Dey, St. Xavier's College (Autonomous), India
Suchandra Datta, St. Xavier's College (Autonomous), India
Rohan Das, St. Xavier's College (Autonomous), India
Debabrata Datta, St. Xavier's College (Autonomous), India
Anal Acharya, St. Xavier's College (Autonomous), India

Criminal activities in varied forms are present in society, aggravated by social, economic, political, cultural, and religious issues. Crimes can have an impact on a nation's quality of life, economic prosperity, and reputation. The incidence of crime and the modes of criminal activity have grown as technology has advanced, as have the preventive methods. Good quality data facilitates applications of different machine learning techniques and other algorithms which can be used to analyze the data to obtain predictions which would help law enforcement officials to prevent crime at best or to provide sufficient information to guide the police personnel to the appropriate criminal. In this chapter, different approaches that make use of different machine learning algorithms such as linear regression, logistic regression, Naïve Bayes have been proposed for crime analysis in the spatial domain. These algorithms were applied to various datasets and the chosen methodology turned out to be impeccable as the accuracy was quite high.

Chapter 6

Parth Gautam, Uttarakhand Open University, India
Ashutosh Kumar Bhatt, Uttarakhand Open University, India
Anita Rawat, Uttarakhand Science Education and Research Centre, Dehradun, India
Om Prakash Nautiyal, Uttarakhand Science Education and Research Centre, Dehradun, India
Saurabh Dhanik, Pal College of Technology and Management, Haldwani, India

Monitoring of soil elements is essential in characterizing the soil and, therefore, making proper decisions regarding fertilizer application and choice of crops sown. Laboratory soil testing involves the collection of soil samples from different locations and more time and cost. It should upgrade with current technologies like the internet of things (IoT), sensors, and data science. These emerging technologies are smart enough to replace lab testing in real time with minimum effort and with the most accurate results. So, in this research work with a portable IoT device that is coupled with sensors, we can test the soil from wide locations. The system tends to implementation of portable handheld device for soil testing in the Haldwani region.

The system is a microcontroller-based device connected to temperature, moisture, and pH sensor. It takes readings from sensors and shows them on LCD. Finally, the data is used for further analysis and comparison. The main idea behind the system is to make it portable to identify the temperature, moisture, and pH of soil.

Vishal Srivastava, Jain University (Deemed), India
Anni Arnav, Presidency University, India
Neel Rai, NTPC School of Business, India

Social media has been creating a strong presence among youth in making buying decisions. The convenience and the usage perception are also leading the youth to look at different social networking sites for more information. The advertising content on various social networking sites are also witnessing radical changes as per the ever-changing necessities. The integrated marketing communication has been instrumental in taking the marketing communication strategies to a different level. The study gives an insight to the marketing teams of the companies who bank upon the various social media platforms looking at exploring the different opportunities to enhance their business opportunities with reference to youth buying intentions. The findings reveal the influence of social media platforms on youth buying intentions.

Somendra Tripathi, Faculty of Engineering and Technology, Rama
      University, India
Hari Om Sharan, Rama University, India

Diabetes Type-2 is one of the significant medical problems nowadays. Diabetes Type-2 is no longer only a disease of the wealthy; its prevalence is rapidly rising everywhere, particularly in the world's middle class income for different countries. Presently it is not an illness of transcendently developed countries. The pervasiveness of diabetes is consistently expanding all over, most extraordinarily on the planet's center pay countries. The majority of these 3.7 million deaths occur before the age of 70. The number of people who die before they are 70 as a result of high blood glucose or diabetes is higher. There are several computational ways for detecting Diabetes Mellitus, but the major downside is that the patient must undergo several medical tests in order to supply input values to the computer diagnostic system, which is both costly and tedious. There are now a variety of techniques and algorithms in artificial intelligent and machine learning that can be applied to accurately predict and detect a number of diseases.

    Sunil Kumar, Kumaun University, Nainital, India
    Ashutosh Kumar Bhatt, Uttarakhand Open University, Haldwani, India
    Rahul Kumar Mishra, IFTM University, Moradabad, India

History should be preserved so that it can be made available for future generations. Thus arises the need for digitization of cultural heritage. The present chapter discusses digitization of cultural heritage of the temples of the state of Uttarakhand, the one which fall in the Kumaon region of North India. Preserving such heritage with the help of digital technology is a fast-emerging trend in the current century. Digital technologies support the recording, analysis, and management of cultural heritage around the world. The chapter brings forth the multiple ways in which it is done and how the same has helped in the preservation, interpretation, and appreciation of the rich cultural heritage. Undoubtedly, they facilitate accessibility and improve understanding of these sites. At the same time, there are fears too in some quarters that digital technologies undermine the need to conserve the "real thing." The chapter proposes various methods and processes to preserve temples, an important component of cultural heritage.

    Mercedes Barrachina, Universidad Politécnica de Madrid, Spain
    Laura Valenzuela, Universidad Politécnica de Madrid, Spain

Cancer is one of the most common diseases nowadays, and it is a very heterogeneous disease that consists of several different subtypes. According to data from the World Health Organization (WHO), this disease caused death to approximately 10 million people during 2020, and in the same period, 19.3 million new cases were identified. Breast cancer is the most common cancer diagnosed for women, and lung cancer is the most detected cancer in men. Artificial intelligence has many different applications, and specifically, machine learning techniques are used for detecting and treating cancer. The methods associated with machine learning are computer algorithms that are considering different types of logic, and therefore, those types can be classified into supervised, unsupervised, reinforcement learning, self-supervised learning, active learning, etc. The main purpose of this work is to review and evaluate the different techniques associated to machine learning used by medical professionals but also by researchers with the main objectives of detecting and treating cancer.

This work supports a new feature extraction image pre-processing system followed by back propagation-artificial neural networks-based system for class categorization of mango fruit images. For back propagation, scale conjugate gradient (SCG) algorithm is used. The methodology comprises of three parts. First, various external image-based attributes of mango were taken and processed in MATLAB. Size and weight features were also considered as important parameters as only color is not sufficient to judge the quality. Second, features extraction was done at image pre-processing for making the algorithm lighter by focusing only key features. Finally, a single hidden layer BP-ANN (back propagation-artificial neural network) was used with sigmoid activation functions. The result came in terms of a suitable output variable, which is the quality class of the mango, which is chosen A, B, C, and D, respectively. It will also reduce the cost of classification or sorting of the fruits.

Hotels should collaborate with the right technology partner in order to identify gaps in their processes such as customer support, concierge bookings, and in-room technology that can be closed with the help of integrating artificial intelligence and machine learning. AI is doing great for big and established hotel industry brands while, due to the cost barriers, smaller brands in this industry receive less attention from AI. Whether it is the on-season, investing in cloud computing services to facilitate the functioning of the hospitality industry seems unfeasible for smaller organizations. If a hotel provides facilities of automation using AI and ML, then the hotel staff can invest time to focus the quality of service, furnishing full range of hotel facilities to their intended guests, which in-turn results in increased operational efficiency, which may help in remarkable growth by increasing the annual revenue of the organization. It is a good choice to add the latest trends in the processes used in the tourism and hotel industries.

Chapter 13

Umesh Kumar Gera, Rama University, India
Dhirendra Siddarth, Rama University, India
Preeti Singh, Rama University, India

Global population growth and urbanization are ongoing at the same time. Consumption patterns are changing as discretionary money rises. Farmers are under pressure to meet rising demand, so they're looking for new methods to boost productivity. There will be more people to feed in 30 years. Because there is a finite amount of rich soil, it will be necessary to go beyond traditional farming. We need to figure out ways to assist farmers in reducing or at the very least managing their risks. On a global basis, artificial intelligence in agriculture is one of the most fascinating prospects. Artificial intelligence has the potential to change the way we think about agriculture by assisting farmers in achieving greater results with less effort while also bringing a plethora of other benefits. Artificial intelligence, on the other hand, is not a stand-alone technology. As the next step in the transition from traditional to creative farming, AI may improve existing technology.

Chapter 14

Bulu Basak, International Institute of Geospatial Science and
Technology (IIGST), India
Thahira Umar, Bharathidasan University, India
Shahid Gulzar, International Institute of Geospatial Science and
Technology (IIGST), India
Rajeev Kumar, Chandigarh University, India
Biswajit Roy Chowdhury, Vidyasagar College, Kolkata, India

Remote sensing technology provides a spatial-temporal database to track the dynamics of water bodies. Global climatic change has a substantial impact on the dynamic activities of glaciers and glacial lakes and in turn affects the surrounding ecosystem. Thus, monitoring and maintaining an updated database about glacial activity is essential for disaster preparedness. In this study, spatiotemporal analysis of glacial lakes of the Western Himalayas in Chamoli and Pithoragarh District of Uttarakhand during 1994, 2000, 2010, and 2020 were done. These glacial lakes showed significant spatiotemporal changes and an increase in their aerial extent, nearly doubled from 1994 to 2020. GL_A had a sudden tremendous growth in the interim period may tend to many disasters like GLOF (glacial lake outburst floods). The study area holds many tourist pilgrimage attractions, and it needs sufficient monitoring of several factors over the entire fragile region for the construction of any infrastructures, disaster mitigation, and urban development processes.

Manisha Koranga, Kumaon University, India
Pushpa Pant, Motiram Baburam Government Post Graduate College,
India
Tarun Kumar, MIET Kumaun, India
R. P. Pant, Graphic Era Hill University, India
Ashutosh Kumar Bhatt, Uttarakhand Open University, India
Durgesh Pant, Uttarakhand Open University, India

Artificial neural networks have progressed in a rapid way in the field of soft computing, and it is widely used in forecasting. The work presented in this chapter is about the development of artificial neural network (ANN)-based models to forecast the water quality (WQ) in Nainital Lake, Uttarakhand, India. A dataset comprising pH, turbidity, and total dissolved solid (TDS) of time period 2018-2019 has been used and analyzed using MATLAB software. For experimentation purposes, four data partition strategies, 10 learning algorithms of back propagation neural network (BPNN), and different combinations of learning rates and training tolerance were evaluated. The performance of the model was evaluated using statistical methods such as MSE, RMSE, MAD, MAPE. The results of the experiment show the capability of the optimal ANN models to predict the WQ of Nainital Lake.

Preface

It was a bright day and we three Professors—Prof. Ashutosh Bhatt, Prof. Rajeev Kumar, and Prof. Abhay Saxena—were sitting in Bhimtal and talking about Artificial Intelligence. The discussion was how the A.I. is changing our life. Right from the conception of the concept way back in late 40's when John McCarthy had coined this Artificial Intelligence term in 1956, the sojourn of AI is phenomenal. The AI enthusiasm was carried out around two decade and followed by the first AI winter for 7 odd years. 1980 looks to be the turning point for AI and for next 8 years there was lots of work on A.I. Later another winter hit for AI and for around 7 odd years, it looks that there is no murmuring of A.I. and it has lost the interest of Researchers and Labs.

Later with the advent of intelligent systems in 1993 to 2011, followed by Deep Learning, Big Data and Artificial General Intelligence, it looks people are adapting more A.I. in their personal and professional life. This only triggers us, why not come out with a volume on Artificial Intelligence for social development and global well-being. Prof. Rajeev was in touch with IGI Global publication, and this book came into existence.

While looking into societal development, we were concerned more on the practicality of Artificial intelligence. We preferred the term A.I. societal development so that it can reach up to the last mile runners. The societal structure is very typical in nature and we are more concerned for those who are living in high altitudes, rural areas, in the extreme living conditions and especially for those who are even looking for technology in their personal life.

The A.I. Global development is equally important for us, as humanity is in search of the quality of life and it is meant for every individual soul on the earth. The concept of peace and prosperity in everyone's life is the concern and if technology especially A.I. can play a vital role in it, our purpose will be served. The A.I. is playing a vital role in global development. Right from the medical surgery to health diagnosis, recommendations of TV shows, suggesting friends on social media, identifying the faces on the Internet, popular voice assistants like Alexa, Siri, filtering spam mails and many more activities are there in our professional and personal life, where A.I. is pawing way from back door.

Artificial intelligence as an analytical tool is also helping in the global development especially in terms of scrutiny and analyzing voluminous data, providing reports and documentation in taking appropriate decisions, understanding the moods and swings of the users, the A.I. is also helpful in prediction of trends and implication of a particular technology in the market.

Artificial intelligence is often challenged in terms of Ethics and human values. The researchers are now working on these sensitive aspects of technology and many policies have been drafted in order to the usage of technology with an eye on ethics.

While planning this book, we have a thought it will cover the basic aspects of societal development and global well-being like how technology can play a vital role in shaping societal well-being? How the A.I. can make change in the life of an ordinary farmer, a small shopkeeper, household makers, working men & women, children and a common man irrespective of caste, color, creed or sex? How technology can bring smiles for the research community and what are the aspects that A.I. which can be easily implemented to attain the optimum for societal development.

It looks like A.I. Sojourn has taken almost Eight decades and now practicality is the key issue where the people are looking for some concrete solutions from Artificial Intelligence. Our emphasis is on the same as the practical applications of A.I. will be useful for everyone and it will ensure the acceptability among one and all.

There are many aspects that need to be covered as the futuristic A.I. applications and we hope that the various research scholars, eminent laureates, Professors and Industry members who are contributing to this volume will take these challenges and deliver the same in the perspective of A.I. as an effective tool for societal well-being and global development.

We all are a bit sure that A.I. sensible utilization will surely create miracles especially for the society and our upcoming generation is adapting the technology as an integral lesson of life. The changing world does need dynamic Artificial Intelligence and its adaptation in daily life with no prejudices.

Chapter 1 explores autism spectrum disorder (ASD), a neurological developmental disorder that results in infirmity in social behaviour and social communication. Autism is identifiable at any stage of life, but symptoms usually appear in the first two years.

Chapter 2 explores neuroscience, how the brain communicates with the human body, along with Neuroscience's history and research in brief with AI. After that some of the devices used for gathering brain signals will be explained taking its focus towards EEG Signals.

Chapter 3 explores the basic problems of women in South Asian Countries. For this, a group survey is likely to be taken in India, Sri Lanka, Singapore, Malaysia,

Thailand, Myanmar and Nepal covering around 200 women about their basic problems in personal and professional life, lifestyle and house management routine activities.

Chapter 4 explores the current pandemic of COVID-19, artificial intelligence become crucial and play a vital role in dealing and caring of patient because of infectious nature of disease. Artificial intelligence is not a new area of study and not come all of sudden as COVID-19 comes in January 2020.

Chapter 5 explores the criminal activities in varied forms are present in society, aggravated by social, economic, political, cultural and religious issues. Crimes can have an impact on a nation's quality of life, economic prosperity, and reputation.

Chapter 6 explores the monitoring of soil elements is essential in characterizing the soil and, therefore, making proper decisions regarding fertilizer application and choice of crops sown. Laboratory soil testing involves the collection of soil samples from different locations and more time and cost. It should upgrade with current technologies like The Internet of Things (IoT), sensors, and data science.

Chapter 7 explores how social media has been creating a strong presence among youth in making buying decisions. The convenience and the usage perception are also leading the youth to look at different social networking sites for more and more information. The advertising content on various social networking sites are also witnessing radical changes as per the ever changing necessities.

Chapter 8 explores Diabetes Type-2, one of the significant medical problems nowadays. Diabetes Type-2 is no longer only a disease of the wealthy; its prevalence is rapidly rising everywhere, particularly in the world's middle class income for different countries.

Chapter 9 explores how history should be preserved so that it can be made available for future generations. Thus arises the need for digitization of cultural heritage. The present chapter discusses digitization of cultural heritage of the temples of the state of Uttarakhand, the one which fall in the Kumaon region of North India.

Chapter 10 explores that cancer is one of the most common diseases nowadays and it is a very heterogeneous disease that consists of several different subtypes. According to data from the World Health Organization (WHO), this disease caused the death to approximately 10 millions of people during 2020 and in the same period, 19.3 million new cases were identified. Breast cancer is the most commonly cancer diagnosed for women, meanwhile, lung cancer is the most detected cancer in men.

Chapter 11 supports new feature extraction image pre-processing system followed by back propagation- artificial neural networks based system for class categorization of mango fruit images. For back propagation, Scale Conjugate Gradient (SCG) algorithm is used.

Chapter 12 explores how hotels should collaborate with the right technology partner in order to identify gaps in their processes such as customer support, concierge bookings to in-room technology that can be closed with the help of integrating Artificial Intelligence and Machine Learning. AI is doing great for big and established hotel industry brands while due to the cost barriers, smaller brands in this industry receives relatively less attention from AI.

Chapter 13 explores how global population growth and urbanization are ongoing at the same time. Consumption patterns are changing as discretionary money rises. Farmers are under pressure to meet rising demand, so they're looking for new methods to boost productivity. There will be more people to feed in thirty years. Because there is a finite amount of rich soil, it will be necessary to go beyond traditional farming.

Chapter 14 explores how remote sensing technology provides a spatial-temporal database to track the dynamics of water bodies. Global climatic change has a substantial impact on the dynamic activities of glaciers and glacial lakes and in turn, affects the surrounding ecosystem.

Chapter 15 explores how artificial neural networks have progressed in a rapid way in the field of soft computing and it is widely used in forecasting. The work presented in this paper is about the development of Artificial Neural Network (ANN) based models to forecast the Water Quality (WQ) in Nainital Lake, Uttarakhand, India. Dataset comprising pH, turbidity and total dissolved solid (TDS) of time period 2018-2019 has been used and analyzed using MATLAB software.

This will shape the 21st century to more peace, prosperity and perfection in every action. Let us try to build the power of Artificial intelligence as an integral part of societal development and global well-being.

Abhay Saxena
Dev Sanskriti Vishwavidyalaya, India

Ashutosh Kumar Bhatt
Uttarakhand Open University, India

Rajeev Kumar
Teerthanker Mahaveer University, India

Chapter 1

A Machine Learning Approach for Detecting Autism Spectrum Disorder Using Classifier Techniques

Shilpi Bisht
Birla Institute of Applied Sciences, India

Neeraj Bisht
Birla Institute of Applied Sciences, India

ABSTRACT

Autism spectrum disorder (ASD) is a neurological developmental disorder that results in infirmity in social behaviour and social communication. Autism is identifiable at any stage of life, but symptoms usually appear in the first two years. This chapter deals with ASD at three different levels: child, adolescent, and adult. For this purpose, the authors have used a dataset from the UCI repository submitted by Fadi Fayez Thabtah, which has 20 features. They proposed new supervised machine learning models to predict the possibility of autism disorder at the adult stage through child, adolescent, and adult datasets. The detailed comparative study of various methods developed is supported by performance measures and respective ROC curves.

DOI: 10.4018/978-1-6684-2443-8.ch001

INTRODUCTION

Recently, Autism Spectrum Disorder (ASD) has pinched researchers' attention due to its fastest-growing nature and rapidly increasing cases almost all over the world. Autism spectrum disorder (ASD) is a lifelong neurodevelopmental disorder identified by some degree of disabilities in developing social-communicative skills, playing and imagination, and the presence of monotonous or constricted behaviours and interests (American Psychiatric Association, 2013; Ruzich et al., 2015). As per the WHO report (2019), one in 160 children has an autism spectrum disorder (ASD) (Elsabbagh et al., 2012). ASD usually begins in childhood and tends to persist into adolescence and adulthood. However, the conditions are most apparent during the first five years of life.

1. **Categories of Autism Spectrum disorder:** Autism Spectrum disorder is categorized into five childhood-onset conditions. The three most common types are:
   a. **Autistic Disorder:** It is the most common type of ASD whose symptoms are delay in speech, difficulty in social communication, impacting early hearing, learning disabilities, mental retardation and unusual behaviour.
   b. **Asperger Syndrome:** This syndrome's symptoms are mild and do not involve learning disabilities, mental retardation, and speech delay. Patients generally show symptoms of difficulty in social communication and unusual behaviour.
   c. **Pervasive Developmental Disorder:** Patients suffering from PDD involve only a few symptoms of either autistic disorder or Asperger syndrome but not all (Mythili & Shanavas, 2014).
2. **Diagnosis:** Medical professionals like paediatricians or psychiatrists diagnose ASD by taking inputs from various disciplines. Standardized examination tools are at one's disposal, such as Screening Tool for ASD in kids and Younger Children "STAT: a 20 minutes monitoring for young children" and frequently explored "Autism Diagnostic Observation Schedule" (ADOS;16: 45 minutes monitoring done by an expert, available in different styles for persons of distinct degrees of language and ages, from one year to the adult stage) (Lord et al., 2018). Early intervention and diagnosis of ASD may help the subject get the necessary treatment and therapy in time, which certainly reduces the level of difficulties (hyperactivity, irritability, language and attention problems) faced by the patients. A detailed tabular representation of these screening and diagnostic instruments is given in table 1 below (MC, 2013):

Table 1. Screening and diagnostic instruments for ASD detection

	Age	Description
Screening: Young Children		
Checklist for autism in toddlers (CHAT)	18 months	14 - item questionnaire nine completed by parent or caregiver and five by health care provider; takes 5-10 min
Early screening of autistic trails (EAST)	14 months	14 - item questionnaire completed by health practitioner as well as baby visit after interviewing parent or caregiver; takes 5-10 min
Modified checklist for autism in toddlers (M-CHAT)	16-30 months	23 - item questionnaire completed by parent or caregiver; takes 5-10 min
Infant-toddler checklist (ITC)	6-24 months	24 - item questionnaire completed by parent or caregiver; takes 5-10 min
Quantitative checklist for autism in toddlers (Q-CHAT)	18-24 months	25 - item questionnaire completed by parent or caregiver; takes 5-10 min, ten-item short version available
Screening tool for autism in children aged 2 years (STAT)	24-36 months	12 - items and activities assessed by clinician or researcher after interacting with the child; takes 20 min; intensive training necessary; level-two screening measure
Screening: Older Children and Adolescent		
Social communication questionnaire (SCQ)	>4 years (and mental age > 2 years)	40 - item questionnaire; completed by parent or caregiver; takes 10 – 15 min
Social responsive scale first or second edition (SRS, SRS-2)	>2-5 years	65 - item questionnaire; completed by parent, caregiver, teacher, relative, or friends (self-report forms available for adult in SRS-2); takes 15 – 20 min
Childhood autism screening test (CAST)	4-11 years	37 - item questionnaire; completed by parent or caregiver; takes 10 – 15 min
Autism spectrum screening questionnaire (ASSQ)*	7-16 years	27 - item questionnaire; completed by parent, caregiver or teacher; takes 10 min
Autism spectrum quotient (AQ) child and adolescent versions*	Child: 4-11 Adolescent: 10-16	27 - item questionnaire; completed by parent, caregiver; takes 10 - 15 min; 10 item short version available
Screening: Adults		
Autism spectrum quotient (AQ) adult versions*	>16 (with average or above average intelligence)	50 - item questionnaire; self-report; takes 10 - 15 min; 10 item short version available
The Ritvo autism Asperger diagnostic scale- revised (RAADS-R)	>18 (with average or above average intelligence)	80 - item questionnaire; self-report; done with a clinician; takes 60 min
Diagnosis: Structured Interview		

Continued on following page

Table 1. Continued

	Age	Description
The autism diagnostic interview – revised (ASI-R)	Mental age>2 years	93 - item interview of parent or caregiver; takes 1.5 – 3 hr; intensive training necessary
The diagnostic interview for social and communication disorder (DISCO)	All chronological and mental age	362 - item interview of parent or caregiver; takes 2 – 4 hr; intensive training necessary
The developmental, dimensional and diagnostic interview (3D)	>2 years	266 - item computer assisted interview of parent or caregiver; takes 2 hr; 53 item short version available, which takes 45min; intensive training necessary
Diagnosis Observational Measure		
The autism diagnostic observation schedule, first or second addiction schedule (ADOS, ADOS-2)	>12 months	Critical observation via interaction; select one from five available module according to expressive language level and chronological age; takes 40 – 60 min; intensive training necessary
Childhood autism rating scale, first or second edition (CARS, CARS-2)	2 years	15 - item rating scale; completed by clinician or researcher; takes 20-30 min; accompanied by a questioner done by parent or caregiver; moderate training necessary

*Particularly sensitive for high functioning individuals

Unfortunately, this Autism diagnosis process is time taking requires clinical assets and diagnostic methods like "Autism Diagnostic Interview (ADI) and Autism Diagnostic Observation Schedule (ADOS)" (Lord et al., 1994; Lord et al., 2000). This process is tedious and lengthy as it requires answers to many questions from patients, caregivers, parents and teachers.

Hence to speed up the screening process, identify the important features, improving the accuracy of diagnosis, computational techniques play an important role. ASD diagnosis process can be converted to a classification problem to predict whether the subject is suffering from Autism or not (Thabtah, 2019a). Various machine learning methods, classifier ensemble techniques, artificial neural networks and techniques of soft computing can be applied for this purpose. Machine learning is a broad research area that includes mathematics, statistics, artificial intelligence, and classification techniques. The purpose of applying machine learning methods to the field of ASD is to design an automated model which reduces the time of diagnosis and simplifies the process of detecting Autism with better accuracy.

This paper is divided into five sections. Section 1 gives an insight into ASD, its diagnosis and the need for machine learning methods in this area. A brief literature review is given in Section 2. Section 3 discussed details of the data set chosen and machine learning model, which detects Autism with high accuracy. Section 4 covers the detailed analysis of the experiments done. Last section deals with results and future scope in this field.

BACKGROUND

The problem of ASD can be considered a classification problem, and researchers are continuously working on the computational aspects to make the diagnosis faster and more convenient. ADOS-R is a widely used method for ASD diagnosis (Lord et al., 2000). Later, Wall et al. (2012a, 2012b) worked on decision trees to develop a framework that has fewer attributes than those found using "ADOS-R (Module 1)". The shortcomings of Wall et al. (2012b) were identified by Bone et al. (2015).

The ML algorithms on the dataset use the "Childhood Autism Rating Scale" tool for diagnosis used by Pratap & Kanimozhiselvi (2014). Mythili and Shanavas (2014) employed Neural Network, Support Vector Machine and Fuzzy tools with WEKA tools to inspect the student's behaviour and their community interaction for detecting the levels of autism.

Fadi Thabtah has done significant work in this field. Many authors have used his publicly available online datasets (Thabtah, 2017a ; Thabtah, 2017b; Thabtah, 2017c) on the UCI repository for research on ASD.

In 2017, Fadi Thabtah (2017, May) discussed the pros and cons of the methods available in machine learning for ASD classification. He also proposed a screening model using Machine Learning Adaptation and DSM-5.

The imitation method (Li et al., 2017) is used to detect autism in adults. They used a dataset that involved 16 ASC members having a chain of hand movements. Their machine learning model extracted 40 kinematic constraints with eight imitation conditions.

Vaishali and Sasikala (2018) incorporated a sole-objective "binary firefly feature selection wrapper" based on Swarm. Their research declared that just 10 features out of 21 features are sufficient to differentiate between patients who have ASD and those who do not.

Kosmicki et al. (2015), Plittaet et al. (2015), Geetha Ramani and Sivaselvi (2017), Heinsfeld et al. (2018) have also proposed different machine learning and data mining techniques for Autism prediction. Later, Thabtah et al. (2018) developed a new computational method to find features for ASD detection. In another work published in 2019, he proposed an efficient method for screening and prediction of autism (Thabtah, 2019b).

Raj and Masood (2020) proposed a CNN based machine learning model for screening ASD in Children, Adolescents and Adult datasets.

This paper has applied a distinct approach where training and testing data sets are heterogeneous. Authors have modified the currently existing models by hyper tuning their respective parameters, trained on Children, Adolescent and Adult datasets and then applied them to the Adult dataset separately.

Different models have been developed to detect autism, and then these are compared to find better accuracy and sensitivity.

DATASET AND METHODOLOGY

The dataset used for the experiments is taken from the UCI repository. Fadi Fayez Thabtah contributes to it. This research has used three related datasets from the repository, namely:

1. Autistic Spectrum Disorder Screening Data for Children (Thabtah, 2017b)
2. Autistic Spectrum Disorder Screening Data for Adolescent (Thabtah, 2017c)
3. Autistic Spectrum Disorder Screening Data for Adults(Thabtah, 2017a)

Each dataset has 20 attributes in each record; details of the attributes are given in table2: (Thabtah, 2017a)

Table 2. Details of the attributes in available dataset (Thabtah, 2017a)

S.N.	Attribute
1.	Patient's age in years
2.	Sex
3.	Ethnicity
4.	If patient was detected with jaundice by birth
5.	Any family history of PDD
6.	Who is taking test
7.	Domicile Country
8.	If they ever tried any screening app
9.	Type of Screening Test
10-19	Answers of 10 questions of screening test
20.	Screening Score

- **Modified Dataset:** Initially, the number of records in the children dataset are 292, the number of records in the adolescent dataset are 104, and the number of records in the adult dataset are 704. Further, authors have divided the original dataset into two sets. The purpose of creating two groups is to check diversity and to achieve better results. Figure 1 describes the modified dataset.

- ○ **Set One (Training)**
  - ▪ **Children:** 104 records from the original children dataset are randomly selected.
  - ▪ **Adolescent:** All 104 records from the original adolescent dataset are selected.
  - ▪ **Adult:** 104 records are randomly selected and removed from the original adult dataset.
- ○ **Set One (Testing)** The remaining 600 records of the original adult dataset are used to test the models.
- ○ **Set Two (Training)**
  - ▪ **Children:** 104 records from the original children dataset are randomly selected.
  - ▪ **Adolescent:** All 104 records from the original adolescent dataset are selected.
  - ▪ **Adult:** 104 records are randomly selected and removed from the original adult dataset.
- ○ **Set two (Testing)** The remaining 600 records of the original adult dataset are used for testing the models.

Figure 1. Modified dataset

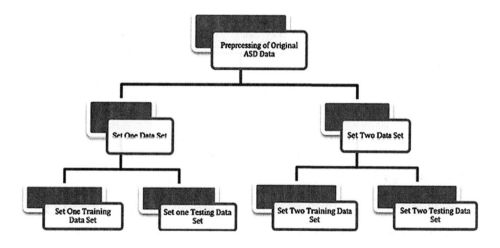

Experiments are conducted with both the derived datasets. Models are trained with training data sets of children, adolescents, and adults and then analysed with a testing dataset that is the only adult dataset. Handling of missing values is done in the modified dataset.

- **Machine Learning Models**

  - **KNN (K-Nearest Neighbours):** KNN is the most straightforward supervised machine learning algorithm which can efficiently perform complex classifications.KNN is a lazy and non-parametric learning algorithm since it does not make any presumptions about fundamental data. Its property of being non-parametric is significant as we know that almost all real-world data does not strictly follow any theory. This algorithm finds the distances (Euclidean or Manhattan) between a fixed data point to all other training data points and then finds the K-nearest data points, where K is an arbitrary integer. Lastly, it decides the class (where the majority of the K data points lie) of the data point. The Euclidean distance, also called L^2 distance, between two points A and B in n-dimensional space is defined as,

The Manhattan distance, also called L^1 distance, between two points A and B in n-dimensional space is defined as,

$$\left\| A - B \right\|_1 = \sum_{k=1}^{n} \left| (a_k - b_k) \right|, k = 1, 2, \ldots\ldots n \, .$$

Since the Autism detection problem is a binary classification problem, i.e. either a sample belongs to Autism class (1) or does not belong to Autism class (0). Then the probability that a sample belongs to the Autism class is given by,

$$P(class = 1) = \frac{N(1)}{N(1) + N(0)}$$

Where, N(1) is the total no of samples belonging to class 1; N (0) is the total no of samples belonging to class 0

- **Gaussian Naïve Bayes (Gaussian NB):** GaussianNB follows Gaussian normal distribution and is a modified form of Naïve Bayes, which is a supervised machine learning algorithm depending upon Bayes theorem, which states

$$P(C_i \mid x) = \frac{P(x \mid C_i) P(C_i)}{P(x)}$$

Here, in this paper C_i, i=1,2 where, C_1 is Autism Class and C_2 is Non autistic class. and $x = (x_1, x_2, \ldots\ldots, x_{20})$ be any data point with 20 attributes. Hence, it can be rewritten as,

$$P(C_i \mid x) = \frac{P(x_1, x_2, \ldots\ldots, x_{20} \mid C_i) * P(C_i)}{P(x_1, x_2, \ldots\ldots x_{20})}$$

Applying, the chain rule on $P(x_1, x_2, \ldots\ldots, x_{20} \mid C_i)$, we get,

$$P(x_1, x_2, \ldots\ldots, x_{20} \mid C_i) = P(x_1 \mid x_2, \ldots\ldots, x_{20}, C_i).P(x_2 \mid x_3, \ldots\ldots, x_{20}, C_i)\ldots\ldots P(x_{19} \mid x_{20}, C_i)$$

Since, all the 20 features in Naïve Bayes are considered independent of each other. Therefore, we have,

$$P(x_k \mid x_{k+1}, \ldots\ldots, x_{20}, C_i) = P(x_k \mid C_i),$$
$$P(x_1, x_2, \ldots\ldots, x_{20} \mid C_i) = \prod_{k=1}^{20} P(x_k \mid C_i)$$

The probability of sample x is belonging to class is given by,

$$P(C_i \mid x) = P(C_i, x_1 \mid x_2, \ldots\ldots, x_{20}), i = 1, 2.$$

Now,

$$P(C_i \mid x) = P(C_i \mid x_1, x_2, \ldots\ldots, x_{20})$$
$$\alpha \, P(C_i, x_1, x_2, \ldots\ldots, x_{20})$$
$$\alpha \, P(C_i).P(x_1, x_2, \ldots\ldots, x_{20} \mid C_i)$$
$$\alpha \, P(C_i).P(x_1 \mid C_i)P(x_2 \mid C_i)\ldots\ldots P(x_{20} \mid C_i)$$
$$\alpha \, P(C_i)\prod_{k=1}^{20}P(x_k \mid C_i)$$

Now, to find the class C whose probability is maximum, we apply 'argmax' function which supplies the maximum value of the input function.

$$C = \underset{i=1,2}{\arg\max} \; [P(C_i)\prod_{k=1}^{20}P(x_k \mid C_i)]$$

Therefore, C becomes the predicted class which contains sample $x = (x_1, x_2, \ldots\ldots, x_{20})$.
The likelihood of the features in Gaussian NB is considered to be Gaussian:

$$P(x \mid y) = \frac{1}{2\pi\sigma_y^{\;2}} \exp\left(-\frac{(x - \mu_y)^2}{\sigma_y^{\;2}}\right)$$

The parameters σ_y and μ_y are approximated using maximum likelihood.

- **Adaptive Boosting (AdaBoost):** Freund and Schapire developed an Adaptive Boosting algorithm in 1996. This general ensemble technique attempts to design a robust classifier from a set of weak classifiers. It gives the weighted combination of N weak classifiers.

The mathematical expression for AdaBoost is given by,

$$F(x) = sign\left(\sum_{n=1}^{N} w_n f_n(x)\right)$$

where f_n stands for the nth weak classifier and w_n is the corresponding weight.

- **Random Forest:** Random Forests is a supervised ML algorithm. It builds the forest of decision tree ensembles, combining Bagging and random subspace.

This algorithm works by creating decision trees on the data samples, and then each tree in a random forest predicts a class, and the class with maximum frequency is denoted as the prediction of model. Usually, Random Forests can handle mislabelled data points better than AdaBoost can.

Scikit-learn calculates Gini Index for deciding how child nodes are branched on a decision tree (assuming binary tree) to apply Random forest on a classification problem. Gini index or impurity is given by,

$$Gini = 1 - \sum_{i=1}^{n} (p_i)^2$$

Where pi denotes the probability of a sample belonging to a specific class. The attribute with the least Gini index is selected as the root node while forming a decision tree. The range of the Gini index is [0,1], where 0 implies that there exists only one class, and 1 implies that the samples are randomly distributed across various classes.

- **Performance Measures:** The analysis is done on the following parameters:

Authors define various parameters to evaluate the performances of various classification techniques.

$$Sensitivity = \frac{TP}{TP + FN} \times 100$$

$$Accuracy = \frac{TP + TN}{n} \times 100$$

where, n= Total number of data points.

- TP signifies count of true positive (Autism is predicted accurately)
- TN signifies count of true negative (Non Autistic is predicted accurately)
- FP signifies count of false positive (Non Autistic is predicted as Autistic)
- FN signifies count of false negative (Autistic is predicted as Non Autistic)

EXPERIMENTS AND DISCUSSIONS

Figure 2. Flow diagram of followed methodology

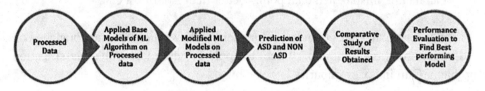

All of the experiments were carried out using the scikit-learn libraries. At first, experiments were carried out with Base models of scikit–learn libraries to train the modified datasets for Children, Adolescents and Adults.

Later on, inbuilt base models are modified to get higher accuracy and better results for predicting ASD in Adults. Each of the applied base models of scikit-learn are modified by hyper tuning their respective parameters using RandomizedSearchCV method from the scikit-learn library. The experiments have been carried out for two types of datasets: Set 1 and Set2 separately. We have considered two essential performance measures for comparing different models- accuracy and sensitivity. All the 20 features of the datasets have been considered for calculating these performance measures. The value of K is 28 in the case of KNN classifier in each case. Flow diagram of followed methodology is presented in Figure 2.

Experimental results of different machine learning models with their respective performance measures are given below in tabular form (Table 3 to 6).

Table 3. Results of base models for set 1 (testing data set adult)

Methods	KNN		Random Forest		Gaussian NB		AdaBoost	
Training Dataset	Accuracy	Sensitivity	Accuracy	Sensitivity	Accuracy	Sensitivity	Accuracy	Sensitivity
Children	86.53	100	86.53	100	82.69	93.33	86.53	100
Adolescent	85.57	98.88	100	100	83.65	90	94.23	97.77
Adult	85.57	98.88	100	100	83.65	90	94.23	97.77

On Autism Adult dataset 1, different machine learning-based models achieve the accuracy of (82.697% - 100%). The least accuracy of 82.69% is observed in Gaussian NB when the training dataset was Children. AdaBoost produces 94.23% prediction accuracy in both the cases when the training dataset was either Adolescent or Adult. Random Forest produced 100% accuracy when the training dataset was Adolescent or Adult.

Table 4. Results of modified models for set 1 (testing data set adult)

Methods	KNN		Gaussian NB		AdaBoost	
Training Dataset	Accuracy	Sensitivity	Accuracy	Sensitivity	Accuracy	Sensitivity
Children	86.53	100	86.53	100	86.53	100
Adolescent	86.53	100	86.53	100	100	100
Adult	86.53	100	86.53	100	100	100

The modified machine ML models on ASD adult dataset 1 produced an accuracy of (86.53% - 100%). KNN classifier with K=28 and Gaussian NB has given the least accuracy of 86.53% in all the cases. AdaBoost produced 86.53% prediction accuracy when the training dataset was Children, while 100% prediction accuracy when the training dataset was either Adolescent or Adult.

Table 5. Results of base models for set 2 (testing data set adult)

Methods	KNN		Random Forest		Gaussian NB		AdaBoost	
Training Dataset	Accuracy	Sensitivity	Accuracy	Sensitivity	Accuracy	Sensitivity	Accuracy	Sensitivity
Children	86.53	100	85.57	98.88	15.38	3.33	85.57	98.88
Adolescent	85.57	98.88	100	100	83.65	90	94.23	97.77
Adult	85.57	98.88	100	100	83.65	90	94.23	97.77

Modified adult dataset 2 produced an accuracy of (15.38% - 100%) through applied machine learning-based models. Gaussian NB produced the least accuracy of 15.38% when the training dataset was Children. AdaBoost produced 94.23% prediction accuracy in both the cases when the training dataset was either Adolescent or Adult. Random Forest produced 100% accuracy when the training dataset was Adolescent or Adult.

Table 6. Results of modified models for set 2 (testing data set adult)

Methods	KNN		Gaussian NB		AdaBoost	
Training Dataset	Accuracy	Sensitivity	Accuracy	Sensitivity	Accuracy	Sensitivity
Children	86.53	100	86.53	100	85.57	98.88
Adolescent	86.53	100	86.53	100	100	100
Adult	86.53	100	86.53	100	100	100

Modified ML models on Autism Adult dataset 2 produced an accuracy of (86.53% - 100%). KNN classifier with K=28 and Gaussian NB has the least accuracy of 86.53%. AdaBoost gave 86.53% prediction accuracy when the training dataset was children while 100% prediction accuracy when the training dataset was either Adolescent or Adult.

A comparative study of various machine learning models is presented with the help of ROC curves of these models for both datasets: Set1 and set2. Also, Area Under Curve (AUC) has been calculated, which is denoted by Δ, and it is mentioned in the ROC curves of each model. Higher the AUC, better the model is distinguishing between positive and negative classes. ROC curves are presented in Figure 3 to 6.

Figure 3. ROC curves of different models for set 1 and set 2 datasets when training set is children

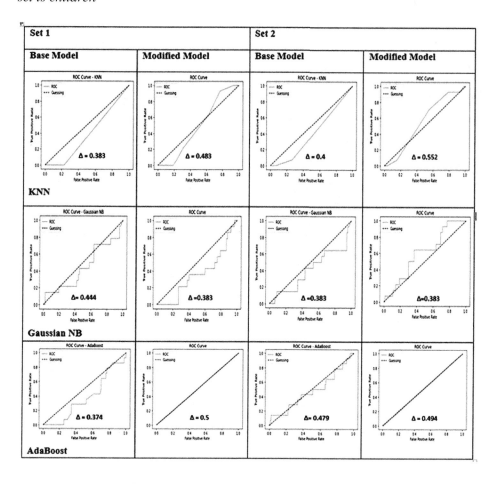

Figure 4. ROC curves of different models for set 1 and set 2 datasets when training set is adolescent

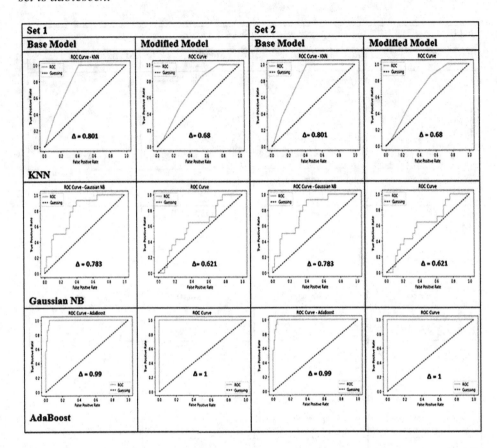

Figure 5. ROC curves of different models for set 1 and set 2 datasets when training set is adult

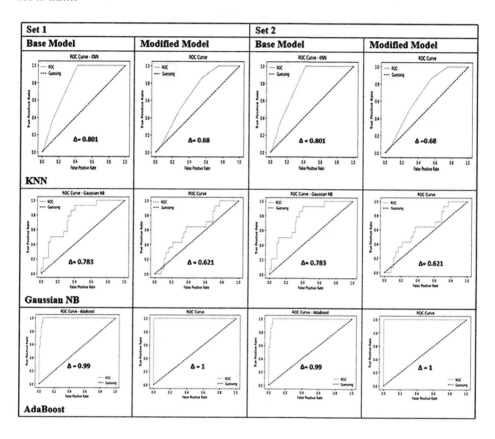

Figure 6. ROC curves for base models of random forest for set 1 and set 2 datasets

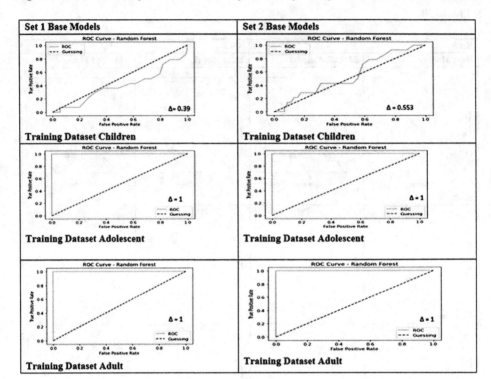

CONCLUSION AND FUTURE SCOPE

It is evident from the results obtained that Random Forest as a Base classifier performed best in all the three training datasets and testing dataset (Adult) of Set 1 and Set 2 (except for the Children dataset where KNN performed better). On the other hand, for modified models, AdaBoost gave the best results in all the three cases of Set 1 and set 2 (except for the Children dataset, where KNN and Gaussian NB performed best). Combining the results for two sets 1 and 2, it can be concluded that Random Forest (as a Base model) and modified AdaBoost model are one of the best machine learning models that can predict Autism Detection Syndrome with higher accuracy in the Adult dataset.

In the future, better performance might be achieved by using feature selection and extraction techniques. Researchers may develop their algorithms for this purpose.

REFERENCES

American Psychiatric Association. (2013). *DSM-5 Task Force Diagnostic and statistical manual of mental disorders: DSM-5*. Washington, DC: American Psychiatric Association.

Bone, D., Goodwin, M. S., Black, M. P., Lee, C. C., Audhkhasi, K., & Narayanan, S. (2015). Applying machine learning to facilitate autism diagnostics: Pitfalls and promises. *Journal of Autism and Developmental Disorders*, *45*(5), 1121–1136. doi:10.100710803-014-2268-6 PMID:25294649

Elsabbagh, M., Divan, G., Koh, Y. J., Kim, Y. S., Kauchali, S., Marcín, C., Montiel-Nava, C., Patel, V., Paula, C. S., Wang, C., Yasamy, M. T., & Fombonne, E. (2012). Global prevalence of autism and other pervasive developmental disorders. *Autism Research*, *5*(3), 160–179. doi:10.1002/aur.239 PMID:22495912

Heinsfeld, A. S., Franco, A. R., Craddock, R. C., Buchweitz, A., & Meneguzzi, F. (2018). Identification of autism spectrum disorder using deep learning and the ABIDE dataset. *NeuroImage. Clinical*, *17*, 16–23. doi:10.1016/j.nicl.2017.08.017 PMID:29034163

Kosmicki, J. A., Sochat, V., Duda, M., & Wall, D. P. (2015). Searching for a minimal set of behaviors for autism detection through feature selection-based machine learning. *Translational Psychiatry*, *5*(2), e514–e514. doi:10.1038/tp.2015.7 PMID:25710120

Li, B., Sharma, A., Meng, J., Purushwalkam, S., & Gowen, E. (2017). Applying machine learning to identify autistic adults using imitation: An exploratory study. *PLoS One*, *12*(8), e0182652. doi:10.1371/journal.pone.0182652 PMID:28813454

Lord, C., Elsabbagh, M., Baird, G., & Veenstra-Vanderweele, J. (2018). Seminar Autism spectrum disorder. *Lancet*, *392*(10146), 508–520. doi:10.1016/S0140-6736(18)31129-2 PMID:30078460

Lord, C., Risi, S., Lambrecht, L., Cook, E. H. Jr, Leventhal, B. L., DiLavore, P. C., Pickles, A., & Rutter, M. (2000). The Autism Diagnostic Observation Schedule—Generic: A standard measure of social and communication deficits associated with the spectrum of autism. *Journal of Autism and Developmental Disorders*, *30*(3), 205–223. doi:10.1023/A:1005592401947 PMID:11055457

Lord, C., Rutter, M., & Le Couteur, A. (1994). Autism Diagnostic Interview-Revised: A revised version of a diagnostic interview for caregivers of individuals with possible pervasive developmental disorders. *Journal of Autism and Developmental Disorders*, *24*(5), 659–685. doi:10.1007/BF02172145 PMID:7814313

MC, L. (2013). Lombardo, Michael V, Baron-Cohen S. Autism. *Lancet*, *383*(9920), 896–910. PMID:24074734

Mythili, M. S., & Shanavas, A. M. (2014). A study on Autism spectrum disorders using classification techniques. *International Journal of Soft Computing and Engineering*, *4*(5), 88–91.

Plitt, M., Barnes, K. A., & Martin, A. (2015). Functional connectivity classification of autism identifies highly predictive brain features but falls short of biomarker standards. *NeuroImage. Clinical*, *7*, 359–366. doi:10.1016/j.nicl.2014.12.013 PMID:25685703

Pratap, A., & Kanimozhiselvi, C. S. (2014). Predictive assessment of autism using unsupervised machine learning models. *International Journal of Advanced Intelligence Paradigms*, *6*(2), 113–121. doi:10.1504/IJAIP.2014.062174

Raj, S., & Masood, S. (2020). Analysis and detection of autism spectrum disorder using machine learning techniques. *Procedia Computer Science*, *167*, 994–1004. doi:10.1016/j.procs.2020.03.399

Ramani, R. G., & Sivaselvi, K. (2017). Autism spectrum disorder identification using data mining techniques. *International Journal of Pure and Applied Mathematics*, *117*(16), 427–436.

Ruzich, E., Allison, C., Smith, P., Watson, P., Auyeung, B., Ring, H., & Baron-Cohen, S. (2015). Measuring autistic traits in the general population: A systematic review of the Autism-Spectrum Quotient (AQ) in a nonclinical population sample of 6,900 typical adult males and females. *Molecular Autism*, *6*(1), 1–12.

Thabtah, F. (2017, May). Autism spectrum disorder screening: Machine learning adaptation and DSM-5 fulfillment. In Proceedings of the 1st International Conference on Medical and health. *Informatics (MDPI)*, *2017*, 1–6.

Thabtah, F. (2019a). Machine learning in autistic spectrum disorder behavioral research: A review and ways forward. *Informatics for Health & Social Care*, *44*(3), 278–297. doi:10.1080/17538157.2017.1399132 PMID:29436887

Thabtah, F. (2019b). An accessible and efficient autism screening method for behavioural data and predictive analyses. *Health Informatics Journal*, *25*(4), 1739–1755. doi:10.1177/1460458218796636 PMID:30230414

Thabtah, F., Kamalov, F., & Rajab, K. (2018). A new computational intelligence approach to detect autistic features for autism screening. *International Journal of Medical Informatics*, *117*, 112–124. doi:10.1016/j.ijmedinf.2018.06.009 PMID:30032959

Thabtah, F. F. (2017a). *Autistic spectrum disorder screening data for adult data set*. UCI machine learning repository.

Thabtah, F. F. (2017b). *Autistic spectrum disorder screening data for children data set*. UCI machine learning repository.

Thabtah, F. F. (2017c). *Autistic spectrum disorder screening data for adolescent data set*. UCI machine learning repository.

Vaishali, R., & Sasikala, R. (2018). A machine learning based approach to classify Autism with optimum behaviour sets. *IACSIT International Journal of Engineering and Technology*, *7*(4), 18.

Wall, D. P., Dally, R., Luyster, R., Jung, J. Y., & DeLuca, T. F. (2012a). *Use of artificial intelligence to shorten the behavioral diagnosis of autism*. Academic Press.

Wall, D. P., Kosmicki, J., Deluca, T. F., Harstad, E., & Fusaro, V. A. (2012b). Use of machine learning to shorten observation-based screening and diagnosis of autism. *Translational Psychiatry*, *2*(4), e100–e100. doi:10.1038/tp.2012.10 PMID:22832900

Chapter 2
Artificial Intelligence for Natural Intelligence

Priyanshi Shah
Thoughtworks Technologies, India

Ajay Narayan Shukla
https://orcid.org/0000-0003-2586-3104
DIT University, India

ABSTRACT

The content of this chapter will start by introducing neuroscience, how the brain communicates with the human body, along with neuroscience's history and research in brief with AI. After that, some of the devices used for gathering brain signals will be explained taking its focus towards EEG signals. The preprocessing techniques and algorithms used will be detailed along with some impactful algorithms which have been proven best till now in some of the real scenarios. It will be followed by the challenges faced in neuroscience (mostly BCI). Next, applications will be discussed under two main categories—(1) medical-related fields for treatment or diagnosis and (2) for global lifestyle change—where it will be further divided into different subfields as stated previously. The chapter will be concluded with its future scope for the well-being of humanity.

INTRODUCTION

In this chapter we will discuss about Neuroscience and how it may be helpful in analysing the brain with the help of AI. We will also go through the devices used for signal acquisitions, some processing techniques and applications which have

DOI: 10.4018/978-1-6684-2443-8.ch002

proven to be the best practices so far. The long term benefits of neuroscience for the well being of humanity expands to unexplored limits. With new tools and rapidly increasing technology, one day AI will contribute to a very large extent.

In recent years with the advancement of technology, researchers and scientists are aiming to achieve human-brain like intelligence and functionalities. While there is still a long way from attaining this goal, the community is working hard to mimic these functionalities in specialized behaviors. Understanding how the human brain works with different parts of our body along with its mental alertness is rather a complex structure to understand. The brain is responsible for memory, speech, visuals understanding, emotions and voluntary actions. The underlying systems behind these mechanisms still lie vague. To gain understanding of these concepts, a combined effort of AI and neuroscience can help in accelerated mechanisms.

Whenever we see an object from our eyes, an image is formed in our retina which is then sent to the brain via neural activity. Then the brain then processes the image and responds accordingly. If we can somehow communicate or send these signals to the brain of visually impaired people, they will be able to perceive the objects. Such mechanisms can be possible in the near future with the collaboration of Neuroscience and Artificial Intelligence. Neuroscience has seen tremendous amounts of research in the past few years. It has the potential to comfort and ease the lives of people and contribute towards the good of humanity.

BRIEF HISTORY

Since the late 1800s there have been a lot of discoveries related to human brain functionalities. Slowly, discoveries related to neurons, brain tissues, psychology and brain surgeries started uncovering the brain functionalities. In the 1900s theories related to the brain's electrical activity started arising. Research related to the brain cognitive and emotional responses began expediting. On the other hand, simultaneous discoveries related to AI like the Turing test(1950s) started evolving. The term artificial intelligence (AI) was coined for the very first time. Since it was the era of technology, efforts to make technology and medical area started to boost up. It was in the early 2000s, when the availability of computational power enabled the coexistence of Neuroscience and AI with the aim to achieve natural intelligence one day.

When it comes to brain signal capabilities, years of experience and training was required to assess the changes and work on them. Even for highly trained experts, it was difficult to analyse the data for insights. It was also very time consuming. With so many opportunities and a wide variety of areas, there has been a lot of enthusiasm in the research community to progress at an exponential rate.

THE BRAIN AND THE NERVOUS SYSTEM

An important aspect of the brain functioning lies in centralized control of the body. To ensure its effectiveness, a network of several neurons help in communication of other parts of the body with the brain. There are billions of neurons with specific functionalities associated with them. The two major types of neurons are sensory and motor neurons. Sensory neurons are responsible for sending information from senses to the brain and motor neurons send signals from the brain to the other parts of the body. There is an adaptive behavior of the brain which is responsible for sensory voluntary actions and command utilizing the nervous system, the primary medium of interaction. Some information is kept within the brain while others are communicated. The brain itself has 4 major lobes (figure 1) which are responsible for different functions like movement, sense, vision, speech, long and short-term memory etc. Thus, depending upon the requirement, the specific lobe gets activated and responds accordingly.

Figure 1. Four major lobes of the brain

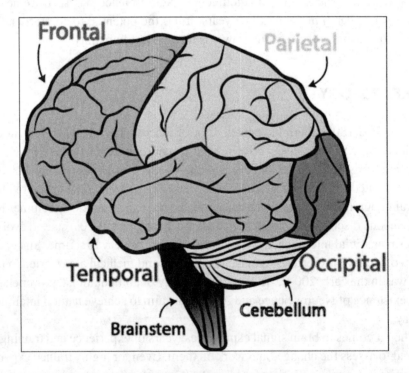

Approximately, there are 100 billion neurons in the brain. Neurons have the capability of transferring information as they differ from most of the cells in the body as they are polarized. The communication between neurons takes place through electrical and chemical signals at a structure called 'synapse'(Figure 2). The electrical events are called 'action potentials', responsible for movement within the neuron. While moving from one neuron to another, chemical processes (or neurotransmitters) are released which in turn activate the action potential of the other neuron. A threshold occurs when the sum of the voltage changes reaches a point of maximum transfer. At this time a neuron triggers a large electrical action potential. In this way information is passed from one neuron dendrite to another.

Figure 2. Neuron structure

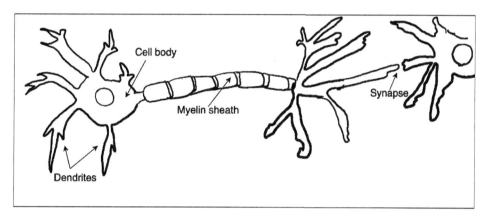

These electrical neuronal signals, if captured properly can help the researchers and neuroscientists to carry out multiple experiments related to the brain functionalities. Over the past few decades, the signal capturing process has progressed tremendously in terms of painless and easy capturing along with being precise. The next section will describe how some of the devices are used for recording the brain potentials

SIGNAL CAPTURING DEVICES

Brain signals or the brain's electrical/neuronal activity is generally captured by the external devices specifically built for the purpose of recording these signals. Since the 1970s, there has been a significant increase in the use of creating the interfaces to capture brain signals to the computer. "A Brain–Computer Interface (BCI), often called a Mind-Machine Interface (MMI), or sometimes called a direct neural interface or a Brain–Machine Interface (BMI), is a direct communication channel between the brain and an external device. Brain-computer interface (BCI) is an upcoming technology which aims to convey people's intentions to the outside world directly from their thoughts, enhancing cognitive capabilities" (J. R. Wolpaw et al). ` BCIs have the ability to regain lost functions like vision, movement or speaking in an indirect substitute method by utilizing extra control devices.

Invasive Devices

These devices can be invasive or non-invasive. Invasive devices are the ones in which BCI devices/electrodes are directly implanted in the gray matter of the brain. These signals are mostly very accurate over the non-invasive techniques provided they are safe to be inserted in a person's brain. One of the successful areas included the role of invasive BCIs in the treatment of non-congenital blindness of a person named Jerry, by creating a light vision sensation, in 1978. Since then, attempts have also been made to extend these towards creating robotic prosthetic controls for paralysed patients. Invasive methods provide quite stable signal acquisition. They are more accurate because they are near to the gray matter and are thus susceptible to even the smallest event in the cortical neural activity.

Partially Invasive Devices

Another type of category, which implant the electrodes inside the skull but outside the brain are the partially invasive BCI devices. The most common monitoring method to measure the signals is Electrocorticography (ECoG). ECoG has a better signal to noise ratio than the non-invasive devices but invasive techniques provide even better signals. An advantage of partially invasive devices is that they are safer than invasive devices because the electrodes are not penetrated inside the brain.

Both the above techniques are an accurate way of measuring the brain activity, however due to a surgical process involved in this, non-invasive techniques are used more often

Non-Invasive Devices

The safest way to acquire the brain signals are the non-invasive techniques. These devices externally take the recordings from the skull by placing a cap or a head band like structure in the desired brain area. These are more popular due to their safe and non-invasive nature. They are also less expensive. However, these are not as effective in signal acquisition because the electrodes cannot be placed directly over the brain. Since these are superficially placed, the skull dampens the high energy signals.

The most effective BCI's are the Electroencephalography(EEG) based devices. The other common devices are Magneto Encephalography (MEG) and functional magnetic resonance imaging (fMRI). In MEG, the electrical signals are measured by the magnetic field through neuroimaging. It can be used in the treatment of seizure detection in epileptic patients. In fMRI, brain activity is measured by using the amount of blood flow in the veins. When some area of the brain is being used, then the blood flow increases in that area, and fMRI can be done.

EEG measures the electrical activity of the scalp. The electrical activity is the result of ionic currents flowing within the neuron which results in voltage fluctuations. Being non-invasive in nature, the most common method used, i.e effective and easily usable in the real world problems.

EEG SIGNALS

The brain cells communicate with each other via electrical impulses. The voltage fluctuations occurring are captured by special electrodes. These recordings are called Electroencephalogram (EEG) signals. These waveforms reflect the cortical electrical activity.

There are 4 major areas of the brain which are associated with specific tasks. These are called lobes and each side of the brain has 4 lobes. The outer part is called the cortex. The Occipital cortex, located at the rear end, is responsible for visual effects. The Parietal cortex is for processing sensory input(feedback) from body movements, like sense of touch or spatial interpretation. The temporal cortex is associated with memory, hearing, language understanding etc. The Frontal cortex located at the front brain is for attention, judgement, emotions, speech expressions and planning. It is enlarged in humans compared to most other species. Since each lobe has different functions involved, electrical activity from these areas can direct to special interpretable wave forms, which can relate to mind states. Therefore, placing electrodes on the skull can detect different waveforms, which can be used by researchers, doctors and scientists to extract meaningful insights from these wave patterns.

These waveforms have different frequencies and amplitudes which help in identifying mind states.

Wave Types

There are five major waves occurring in the brain. These have some different mental states and properties depending upon their frequencies (Figure 3, Table 1).

Delta (1 – 4 Hz)

These waves are detected in deep sleep state. They are the slowest waves with highest amplitude. These are found mostly in adult sleep states indicating high relaxation and healing sleep states. They are also dominant in infants. During some abnormal states like, Attention Deficit Disorder or brain injuries, these waves are commonly found.

Figure 3. Brain wave frequency representation

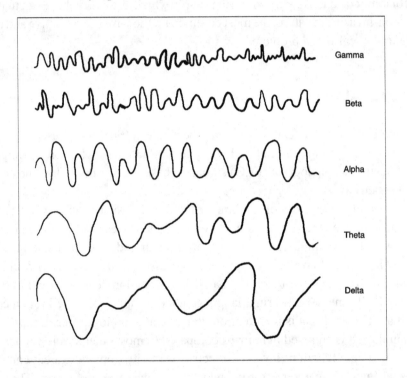

Theta (4 – 7 Hz)

Theta is also a slow wave, with an amplitude slightly lower than Delta waves. These are found while daydreaming, deep relaxed, creative or fantasy or states. These also appear while meditation or when a person is mentally awake but physically inactive. Young children possess these very commonly. These can become intense while critical thinking tasks or can be related to increased tiredness.

Alpha (7 – 12 Hz)

Alpha waves are medium slow and have a lower amplitude than Theta waves. Alpha waves indicate a calm and light relaxed state. These indicate awake state and attentive state. These indicate body concentration and inner awareness. It shows alertness but not an information processing state. These are mostly concerned with a positive mind state. These can be present in more than one lobes but are very strong near the occipital lobe

Beta (12 – 30 Hz)

Beta is faster and smaller in amplitude. The frequencies tend to become stronger whenever there is movement of any body part. They can range from an active calm state to a mild stressed state. They are common during active thinking, anxiousness, calculation stress and high alert states.

Gamma (>30 Hz)

These are the fastest and the smallest amplitude waves. It is mostly concerned with internal information transmission tasks.

Table 1. Frequency bands and brain states

Band	Frequency	Brain states
Delta	1-4 Hz	Deep sleep
Theta	4-7 Hz	Deep relaxation and meditation
Alpha	7-12 Hz	Calm and passive awareness
Beta	12-30 Hz	Alertness, anxiety, active thinking
Gamma	>30 Hz	Internal transmission

It is challenging to extract meaningful information from the EEG signals, especially while identifying it manually, it requires a lot of expertise. There are many physiological changes that might affect the EEG data. During signal acquisition, even blinking of the eye, muscular activity or even noise of electrical power communication line can affect these signals. Thus, it becomes very important that before analysing the data, there must be removal of any unnecessary artifacts. The data must be converted to require form and should go through a process of feature extraction, outlier removal and then classification.

The equipment used for recording consists of an electrode based cap mounted over the skull. These electrodes are placed at special predefined positions to measure EEG signal activity from multiple areas (Figure 4). The electrode discs are fixed onto the scalp with a gel to reduce artifact generation through electrode movement. The gel also maximizes skin contact.

Figure 4. Electrode placement like in 10-20 system

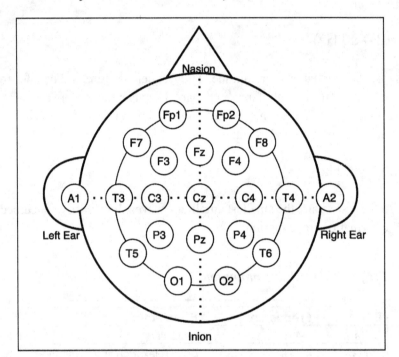

The positioning points are symmetrically divided and placed on each hemisphere of the brain. A commonly followed nomenclature includes naming the electrode channels as odd numbers in the left side and even on the right. Furthermore lobe regions also have special coding like, Temporal(T), Central(C), Frontal pole(Fp), occipital(O) and Parietal (P). So the channel names are labelled as C3,O2, P4 etc. This system is called the international 10-20 system.

A basic EEG procedure works from taking raw recorded signals to its classification state(Figure 5). The preprocessing and classification techniques can vary according to the use case. Broadly the techniques or algorithms might not work for all, but, in general the procedure remains the same. Cleaning/preprocessing of input raw signals is followed by, feature extraction, feature selection and then the final classification.

Figure 5. EEG signal processing pipeline

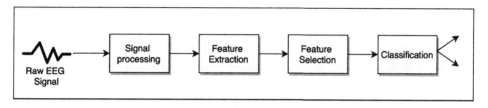

EEG TECHNIQUES/PROCESSING TECHNIQUES

The common patterns found in EEGs are mostly noise and/or outliers, high dimensional features and non-stationary signals. To solve these, classifiers, transforms and dimensionality reduction techniques must be applied. In the processing state, mostly outliers occurring in the form of artifacts are removed. These can be due to ocular, muscle, cardiac and extrinsic effects (Urigüen, Jose Antonio, and Begoña Garcia-Zapirain et al).

In a traditional approach, a regression method is used for artifact removal. This method requires readings from other devices like ECG(electrocardiogram), EOG(electrooculogram), and EMG (electromyogram). Based on the reading frequencies of these signals, the artifacts from the original signals are estimated and removed by regression techniques.

Other techniques include frequency and time domain filters like Fourier Transform, Wavelet transformation and band pass filters. These can also be used as a feature extraction technique as explained further in detail.

FEATURE EXTRACTION

Time frequency analysis is widely used because the signals are non-stationary in nature, this means that their property changes over time. Hence, they need to be localised. This can be done with many methods like eigenvectors, autoregressive techniques (Khamis et al., 2009), time-frequency domain filters and many more. Out of these, most commonly Fast Fourier Transform (FFT) Method and Wavelet Transform (WT) Method is used.

Fast Fourier Transform (FFT) Method

In simple words, Fourier Transform means that any wave signal can be broken down into a set of sine waves. On adding the components back, the original signal can be restored. Thus, the actual signal is not lost. The EEG signals are complex, thus breaking them into smaller frequencies gives it the ability to interpret multiple bands like alpha, delta etc.

Fourier transform is one of the most common methods used. The technique is called Fourier analysis. It changes a signal from time domain to frequency domain. The smaller components of the original wave are plotted to a power frequency spectrum, from where the peaks and troughs can be detected.

Fast Fourier Transform shares spectral information only in the frequency domain and the details about time domain are lost. Also, FFT cannot analyse short duration signals. To resolve this, Wavelet transform was introduced which has varying window sizing. It can also handle different frequency ranges.

Wavelet Transform (WT) Method

A wavelet is a wave-like oscillation with an amplitude that begins at zero, increases or decreases, and then returns to zero one or more times(Wavelet (2014); In Wikipedia) Wavelet analysis plays an important role for analyzing time domain signals. WT can give multi-resolution information of the signals as it does not depend on the constant size.

The wavelet possesses two types of properties; scale and location. Scale defines how much a wave is dilated or compressed, whereas the location shows the position in time(or space). In WT, signals are broken down into different frequency components after which a frequency range is assigned to each component. It can then be studied with a matching scale resolution. If there is discontinuity in a signal, then FT will give a lot of coefficients but WT will only give a few relevant coefficients which are easier to analyse sharp spike times in the signal.

Wavelet analysis is usually applied in two ways, Continuous Wavelet Transform (CWT) and Discrete Wavelet Transform (DWT). CWT includes infinite ranges of location and scales whereas DWT uses a finite set of range for location and scales.

WT is the most common method for epileptic seizures(Sartoretto and Ermani, 1999).

FEATURE SELECTION/ DIMENSION REDUCTION

EEG signals are mostly more than 2 dimensional signals. If we take EEG data of 10 volunteers, for a 20 channel data and take 1000 voltage recordings each, the data would be 3 dimensional data. Similarly, for an increased number of volunteers, channels, voltage values depending upon the usage, the data would still be more than two dimensions in almost all the recordings. Also, apart from the pure EEG data, researchers might also have some physiological data which can make the overall process quite complicated. FFTs, SDFTs, WTD and Autoregressive methods can also be used sometimes for feature extraction and feature selection combined. However, Independent Component analysis and Principal component analysis are the best ones suited for any multidimensional data.

Independent Component Analysis

While the EEG signals are being recorded, it is natural for humans to blink their eyes as the recordings can go on for very long durations. This can lead to disruptions in the signals. ICA comes to the rescue when it helps in separating out eye blinks from the original signal. This is analogous to the famous "Cocktail party problem", where people are trying to converse in a noisy room but only want to hear one person's voice. In this case ICA has the ability to separate out mixed audio waves to two individual waves. Similarly, in EEG eyeblink can be separated using ICA.

ICA tries to decompose a multivariate signal into independent non-Gaussian signals. It follows two assumptions

1. independence of source signals from each other
2. source signal values should have non-Gaussian distributions

Often ICA-based algorithms are capable of handling almost all kinds of artifacts occurring in EEG recordings.

Principal Component Analysis

Principal Component Analysis (PCA), is a dimensionality-reduction method that is used to reduce the dimensionality of large data sets. If the data set contains n dimensions, then after PCA there will be smaller than n dimensions. We need to reduce the high dimensionality feature vectors because any Machine learning model's performance will start degrading with large features (Curse of Dimensionality effect). It becomes very crucial in EEG analysis to perform PCA on the data.

PCA(Wold et al. (1987))is a computationally expensive process of calculating the covariance, then eigenvectors, followed by choosing the Principal (or the main) features with reduced dimensionality. PCA reduces data to uncorrelated data, which means almost all features hold their own importance. PCA can help in improving algorithm performance and reduce overfitting.

ALGORITHMS

There are some commonly used algorithms in typical scenarios and real world problems. Many algorithms under supervised, unsupervised, deep and reinforcement learning have been used in BCIs. Supervised learning techniques were a very common approach specially in EEG based emotion detections. Recently many deep learning algorithms have performed better.

There are broadly two types of decision boundaries on which the classification happens for supervised and unsupervised learning. These are linear and non-linear boundaries. The linear models, linear support vector machine (SVM) and linear discriminant analysis (LDA) are the most popular.

For a non-linear decision boundary, k-nearest-neighbor (kNN) algorithm, non-linear Bayesian classifiers, Hidden Markov Models(HMM) are mostly used. SVM and HMM have proven to be a very robust classifier, mostly for high dimensional data.Occasionally, RBMs, DBNs, or AEs were also used in unsupervised learning to create labels.

Recent popularity in End to End(E2E) networks have attracted the researchers towards it. With the use of Artificial Neural networks (Roy et al. (2019)), E2E might even accept minimally processed data and still give a decent result. This is because neural networks can itself extract features and classify accordingly. The only concern is that the model loses explainability with E2E networks, as it is unclear due to its "black box" nature(Gemein, Lukas AW, et al.).

In deep learning based approaches CNNs, RNNs and AEs have also played a major role. Success and popularity of CNNs on computer vision tasks shifted the community to work on direct spectrogram images of signals. Some architectures also use CNNS along with a combination of RNNs. These also achieve end to end functionalities capable of working in the real world. Due to its robust architecture, CNNs like VGG-16(Simonyan, K., & Zisserman, A. (2014)), ResNet-18(He, Kaiming, et al.) offers a flexibility of extracting feature vectors of raw EEG data.

Generative adversarial networks (Goodfellow, I. (2016)) have also helped in augmenting synthetic data. This resulted in carrying out experiments easily with more readily available data.

Hence, many types of machine learning and deep learning architectures have been used by various researchers with different processing techniques depending upon the use cases. It also means that immense efforts are being made to develop a working product which is effective in the real world.

CHALLENGES

A lot of effort is required to create error free BCI systems. There can be a lot of challenges while improving these systems, some of them are described below.

Restriction in Environment

There have been numerous researches carried out in this field. On one hand, there have been tremendous efforts to work on multiple areas but at the same time, not every progression has the ability to scale up to the real world. This is because most of the research is carried out in a controlled environment in a small room. The EEG recordings are usually taken in a sophisticated area but this is a problem when it comes to the real-world problem. When we talk about the real world scenarios, we know that the real world will be very noisy having people around having different types of sounds and movements. This means there would be far more artifacts in the data. Normal data is trained on a restricted environment; thus, it is possible that it will not work on the real case scenarios that means the model will not be a generalized model. Therefore, the experiments should be carried out in such a way that it is able to scale up and people are able to use the technology.

Data Collection

Collecting data for EEG is a very tedious task. Firstly, it is difficult for people to volunteer easily, it is not easy to convince people to take their brain till related data. Especially, in medical related data it is difficult to identify a group of people and identify the subset of people willing to donate their data within that subset. For example, in epileptic seizure patients, there are less number of people suffering from elliptic seizure, and out of those it is laborious to collect data even from a subset of patients. Creating a balanced age grouped data is also a tedious task. Secondly, data collection usually happens in special laboratories where each person has to wear an EEG cap and it should be ensured by the practitioner that all the equipment is placed accurately for proper recordings. Thus, it is a resource consuming task in terms of time and energy.

Lack of Standard Norms

As mentioned earlier there has been a lot of research that has taken place in the BCI area. Comparing two or more BCI research is difficult because of a lack of similar performance metrics. In general, two results can only be compared when they have been measured with the same matrix metrics. Therefore, we might not always know which performance is better. Another problem is lack of well-designed Universal testing data(i.e. a benchmarking dataset). Reporting results every year on a universal testing data will ensure the improvement of performance in the models. This challenge can be solved with a well-designed single performance metric and a benchmark test set creation.

Recording Limitations

EEGs mostly measure the recordings from the outer structure of the brain thus it has a very limited ability to record data from the deeper parts of the brain. Also, the neurons are connected with each other throughout the brain, thus even if the electrodes are placed at some specific region there can still be overlap from the surrounding neurons as it is not a discrete structure but spread out over the entire brain. Therefore, there will mostly be some kind of interference in the channel recordings.

High SNR

A very big challenge is the presence of artifacts in the recordings. Before EEG signals are passed for training, it must be ensured that the signals have a high sound to noise(SNR) ratio. The noise or the artifact should be as minimal as possible. The artifacts can occur due to biological or environmental interference, this can be due to eye blinking, external noises or even equipment loss. Thus, there may be variation in the actual and the recorded signal. Hence, processing and feature extraction becomes very important for a high SNR data which should have high quality and low noise to obtain continuous clean signals.

BCI Technology Integration

Capturing the signals and building the model alone is not enough for a full-fledged product. What we ideally want is a use case product which can work in a multisensory environment and is capable of performing its desired functions. For example, in detecting drowsiness in a person, the EEG headband should be capable of analyzing the person's level of tiredness and also alert the person, which involves technology usage much more than just EEG. Similarly in many cases, use of AR and VR might also need to be integrated like in game systems. Thus, for widespread usage, the end product will have to integrate far more than just EEG signal models. End product should be portable also for anywhere usage.

APPLICATIONS

Nowadays EEG and BCI devices are used for a lot of clinical, diagnostic purposes, physical movement aiding, sleep analysis and even in entertainment like gaming or consumer research for neuromarketing. The role of AI becomes so important to enhance existing human capabilities and come up with problem solving products.

This is a generation of out of the box thinking, thus as every day we are generating more and more data, we are expanding the human limits that are beyond imagination for many. With computational power and research increasing at an exponential rate, it becomes important that we as humans give something back to society. This era of change is continuing to enhance technology towards a better lifestyle. Here are some use cases that have evolved to some extent and continuous efforts are being made to enhance these areas better. Broadly these have been classified into medical related fields and areas for global lifestyle change.

Medical Related Fields

Epilepsy

Seizure detection (Alotaiby, Turkey N., et al. 2014) in epilepsy has been used for a long time. Earlier they used to be a manual check but with the increase in use of AI epileptic seizure detections have become easier for doctors to identify. It is possible to determine which hemisphere of the brain is experiencing epileptic seizures. The intensity of the seizures can also be identified with the help of EEG graphs. Any abnormality occurring due to neuronal changes indicate an unusual behavior. Within a particular time frame the frequency of seizure occurrences can also be detected and diagnosed accordingly the doctors also take help of the pre existing data from agile past patients to treat this condition. EEG is also recommended for children diagnosed with autistic spectrum disorder (ASD).

Brain Dysfunctionalities

Whenever there is damage to the brain, the neuronal activity in that particular area is limited/ceased. This can be due to temporary or permanent brain dysfunction, encephalitis, brain damage/injury (2016), brain tumor, brain trauma or in worst cases brain death. Previous experimental data can help in detecting these listed issues with greater accuracy than manual prediction. With the coming of AI there has been a tremendous increase in life saving diagnosis, as each moment becomes important when it comes to dysfunctioning of the brain. When it comes to accidental brain injuries, the affected area of injury needs to be treated right away. Medical EEG equipments have provided this functionality and has proven to be effective in many scenarios. Sometimes anesthesia levels can also be detected, especially during large, time taking operations to estimate the anesthesia effect. Coma states can also be identified and adequate treatment can be started.

Sleep EEG

Active delta waves indicate a deep sleep state. EEGs can help in detecting abnormalities in the delta and theta waves thereby by helping in the treatment of conditions like insomnia, sleepwalking etc. A network called SLEEPNET (Biswal, Siddharth, et al. "SLEEPNET: automated sleep staging system via deep learning.") was created with data of 10,000 patients to annotate sleep staging. This network helped in scaling up to the real world scenario.

Vision Capabilities

This is an emerging field which has the capability to give visual insights to a blind person. For example, If a band-like device, capable of perceiving objects with the help of computer vision and communicating directly with the brain could possibly give artificial vision-like environments to the person and will help in easing their lives.

For Global Lifestyle Change

Emotion Detection

This is the most common field that has been boosted with AI and neuroscience. The DEAP (Koelstra et al., 2012) dataset is built for emotion detection through subjects watching 1-minute-long video. Emotion states of subjects were marked for each video. Many models with different architectures have been trained with accuracies greater than 70%. This is a very important field as it provides extensive capabilities of emotion detection apart from videos. Depression (Cai et al. (2016)) and consciousness disorders can also be treated (Engemann et al. (2018)) by detecting brain states of a person and knowing the intensity of effect on a person's life.

Neuromarketing

Neuromarketing combines neuroscience with consumer marketing. Consumer behavior is analyzed with the brain states of people. Neuromarketing is very important for the retail sector as it helps in maximizing the profits. Eye tracking, gaze, pupil dilation, muscle movements are important factors in determining consumer behavior. It can also help in branding through advertisements.

Classroom Attention Analysis

An experiment was conducted in a school, where the students wore a harmless EEG headband device. It captured the mental states, like attention levels of students through their classes. This data was shared with the teachers and parents, which helped them understand which subject the student was struggling to understand, or how much interest they had in attending classes. This was also analyzed during outdoor game activities to see their emotional states. On one hand this field could help in understanding children's behavior, it could also pressurize students regarding their emotional health.

Robotic Control

Prosthetic robot arms, legs, movable cursors without arms and robotic wheelchairs are some sub applications of robotic control systems. The movement of these can be associated by special devices to work effortlessly. These systems can tremendously help people with natural or accidental disabilities.

Gaming Applications and Virtual Reality

Devices have been made that move the game forward with increasing concentration levels. A recent game developed for children showed stimulating positive visuals using an AR/VR band. The more the concentration, the better the deep dive visuals. Similarly, games were introduced which increased the weapon strength with concentration levels. Another game was created using controls from an eye blink. All these are possible by combining multiple technologies like game development, AR/VR etc.

Driver Fatigue

Many road accidents take place every year due to driver fatigue. Factors affecting driver fatigue include lack of sleep and long drives. In such a situation, drivers might fall asleep and become prone to accidents. Some experiments using Bayesian networks (Yang et al), ICA(Chai, Rifai, et al.) and PCANet (Yuliang Ma, C.Ma et al)have been carried out for driver fatigue. The main challenge faced is the ability to work in the real world.

Security: Identification and Authentication

Experiments are being carried to incorporate EEG features as a new form of Biometrics for users. Till now retina scans, face detection and fingerprint recognition have been the most common utilities for authentication. EEG research has triggered the idea of EEG related biometrics like single channel authentication (Zeynali, M. and Seyedarabi, H., 2019) or by performing motor imagery tasks (T.Pham, W. Ma et al).

CONCLUSION

The desire to comprehend natural intelligence just like in biological species can be compared with the desire to create intelligent robots, which is the focus of artificial intelligence (AI). The procedures and applications discussed in this chapter take us to the first steps of building naturally intelligent systems. AI has shown the capability of scaling the current research to a next level of naturally intelligent systems.

The long-term benefits of neuroscience for the well-being of humanity expands to unexplored limits. It would enable a new revolution if we could create synthetic brains with the same abilities as their counterparts. With new inventions and rapidly increasing technology, one day AI will contribute to a very large extent. Academicians, researchers, scholars and scientists have joined hands to make this growing technological world a better place. It is pretty clear that with the recent inventions, humans will start unlocking their potentials and capabilities in the new AI world. Devices that replicate human intellect have been thought for a long time. Even though we are far from achieving this, the new tools and technologies are bridging the gap between humans and machines. A world with utility robots like surgical, emotional and security robots will become quite common in the upcoming years. Conditions of mental and physical disorders related to the human nervous system will be treatable to a large extent. This is a rapidly increasing exponential curve which is set to bring out the best of humanity. The world is set on a never-ending path of inventions!

REFERENCES

Albert, B., Zhang, J., Noyvirt, A., Setchi, R., Sjaaheim, H., Velikova, S., & Strisland, F. (2016). Automatic EEG processing for the early diagnosis of traumatic brain injury. *Procedia Computer Science*, 96, 703–712. doi:10.1016/j.procs.2016.08.253

Alotaiby, T. N., Alshebeili, S. A., Alshawi, T., Ahmad, I., El-Samie, A., & Fathi, E. (2014). EEG seizure detection and prediction algorithms: A survey. *EURASIP Journal on Advances in Signal Processing*, *2014*(1), 1–21. doi:10.1186/1687-6180-2014-183

Biswal, S., Kulas, J., Sun, H., Goparaju, B., Westover, M. B., Bianchi, M. T., & Sun, J. (2017). *SLEEPNET: automated sleep staging system via deep learning*. arXiv preprint arXiv:1707.08262.

Cai, H., Sha, X., Han, X., Wei, S., & Hu, B. (2016, December). Pervasive EEG diagnosis of depression using Deep Belief Network with three-electrodes EEG collector. In *2016 IEEE International Conference on Bioinformatics and Biomedicine (BIBM)* (pp. 1239-1246). IEEE.

Chai, R., Naik, G. R., Nguyen, T. N., Ling, S. H., Tran, Y., Craig, A., & Nguyen, H. T. (2016). Driver fatigue classification with independent component by entropy rate bound minimization analysis in an EEG-based system. *IEEE Journal of Biomedical and Health Informatics*, *21*(3), 715–724. doi:10.1109/JBHI.2016.2532354 PMID:26915141

Engemann, D. A., Raimondo, F., King, J. R., Rohaut, B., Louppe, G., Faugeras, F., Annen, J., Cassol, H., Gosseries, O., Fernandez-Slezak, D., Laureys, S., Naccache, L., Dehaene, S., & Sitt, J. D. (2018). Robust EEG-based cross-site and cross-protocol classification of states of consciousness. *Brain*, *141*(11), 3179–3192. doi:10.1093/brain/awy251 PMID:30285102

Gemein, L. A., Schirrmeister, R. T., Chrabąszcz, P., Wilson, D., Boedecker, J., Schulze-Bonhage, A., Hutter, F., & Ball, T. (2020). Machine-learning-based diagnostics of EEG pathology. *NeuroImage*, *220*, 117021. doi:10.1016/j.neuroimage.2020.117021 PMID:32534126

Goodfellow, I. (2016). *Nips 2016 tutorial: Generative adversarial networks*. arXiv preprint arXiv:1701.00160.

He, K., Zhang, X., Ren, S., & Sun, J. (2016, October). Identity mappings in deep residual networks. In *European conference on computer vision* (pp. 630-645). Springer.

Khamis, H., Mohamed, A., & Simpson, S. (2013). Frequency–moment signatures: A method for automated seizure detection from scalp EEG. *Clinical Neurophysiology*, *124*(12), 2317–2327. doi:10.1016/j.clinph.2013.05.015 PMID:23786794

Koelstra, R. A. L. (2012). *Affective and Implicit Tagging using Facial Expressions and Electroencephalography* (Doctoral dissertation). Queen Mary University of London.

Ma, Y., Chen, B., Li, R., Wang, C., Wang, J., She, Q., Luo, Z., & Zhang, Y. (2019). Driving fatigue detection from EEG using a modified PCANet method. *Computational Intelligence and Neuroscience, 2019*, 2019. doi:10.1155/2019/4721863 PMID:31396270

Pham, T., Ma, W., Tran, D., Nguyen, P., & Phung, D. (2014, July). Multi-factor EEG-based user authentication. In *2014 International Joint Conference on Neural Networks (IJCNN)* (pp. 4029-4034). IEEE. 10.1109/IJCNN.2014.6889569

Roy, Y., Banville, H., Albuquerque, I., Gramfort, A., Falk, T. H., & Faubert, J. (2019). Deep learning-based electroencephalography analysis: A systematic review. *Journal of Neural Engineering, 16*(5), 051001. doi:10.1088/1741-2552/ab260c PMID:31151119

Sartoretto, F., & Ermani, M. (1999). Automatic detection of epileptiform activity by single-level wavelet analysis. *Clinical Neurophysiology, 110*(2), 239–249. doi:10.1016/S0013-4694(98)00116-3 PMID:10210613

Simonyan, K., & Zisserman, A. (2014). *Very deep convolutional networks for large-scale image recognition.* arXiv preprint arXiv:1409.1556.

Urigüen, J. A., & Garcia-Zapirain, B. (2015). EEG artifact removal—State-of-the-art and guidelines. *Journal of Neural Engineering, 12*(3), 031001. doi:10.1088/1741-2560/12/3/031001 PMID:25834104

Wolpaw, J. R., Birbaumer, N., Heetderks, W. J., McFarland, D. J., Peckham, P. H., Schalk, G., Donchin, E., Quatrano, L. A., Robinson, C. J., & Vaughan, T. M. (2000). Brain-computer interface technology: A review of the first international meeting. *IEEE Transactions on Rehabilitation Engineering, 8*(2), 164–173. doi:10.1109/TRE.2000.847807 PMID:10896178

Yang, G., Lin, Y., & Bhattacharya, P. (2010). A driver fatigue recognition model based on information fusion and dynamic Bayesian network. *Information Sciences, 180*(10), 1942–1954. doi:10.1016/j.ins.2010.01.011

Zeynali, M., & Seyedarabi, H. (2019). EEG-based single-channel authentication systems with optimum electrode placement for different mental activities. *Biomedical Journal, 42*(4), 261-267.

Chapter 3
Artificial Intelligence for the Comprehensive Development of Household Makers (Especially in South Asian Countries)

Prof. Abhay Saxena
Dev Sanskriti University, India

Amit Saxena
BIMTECH, India

Aditi Saxena
Banasthali University, India

ABSTRACT

This chapter will cover the basic problems of women in South Asian countries. For this, a group survey is taken in India, Sri Lanka, Singapore, Malaysia, Thailand, Myanmar, and Nepal covering around 200 women about their basic problems in personal and professional lives and lifestyle and house management routine activities. The chapter will cover the basic segment of artificial intelligence and its support in maintaining the health parametric card for the household makers. The chapter will also assist the women in the kitchen with the help of artificial intelligence, especially in cooking and digital health menu selection. A special segment in the chapter will also address the cleanliness of the house with the help of A.I.-supporting tools and gadgets. Last but not the least, the chapter will also address the security of the household makers especially in day hours when they are alone in the houses. The chapter will be an innovative research to understand the better half of the society and to address their day-to-day problems with technological interventions.

DOI: 10.4018/978-1-6684-2443-8.ch003

1. INTRODUCTION

This human world consists of two basic pillars – Man and Women. Although both are different in nature, physical appearance and strengths but compliment and comprehension of both of them makes the world perfect. Women are better half of men and take the responsibility of household makers especially in South Asian Countries. The men are supposed to perform outhouse jobs and women are supposed to take household activities (Megan, 2020).

Although the women are the basic pillar of the society but they are not getting the equal importance in their personal and professional life. To understand the basic problems of women especially in the South Asian Countries better and on the realistic environment, the authors have conducted a group survey conducted virtually in India, Sri Lanka, Singapore, Malaysia, Thailand, Australia and United States covering around 100 women about their basic problems in personal and professional life, lifestyle & house management routine activities.

Figure 1. The house hold makers problems

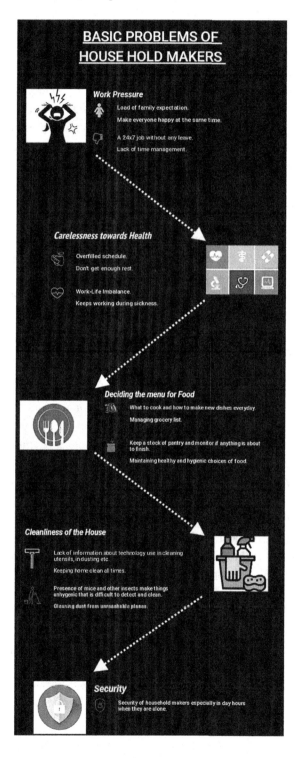

2. THE HORIZONS OF ARTIFICIAL INTELLIGENCE

Artificial intelligence is a big term where the knowledge and intelligence of human being is being articulated. In simple words we can understand it as man-made machine thinking power. Right from the bots who can play chess effectively to answering the question on customer services. The self-driven car is a good example of Artificial intelligence where the car is governed by the datasets, algorithms and sensors technology all combine together to replace regular drivers in the car (Nilesh, 2021). The robots based surgery, recommendations based on the user's likes, e-commerce, google map (for navigation), facial recognition (finger print / face pattern to open mobiles), smart assistants (Siri, Alexa, Google Assistant), spam filters in mails are the amazing uses of Artificial intelligence in our day to day life (Gupta, 2017).

If we look around the Artificial intelligence components, they are Learning (Gaming, language and words), Reasoning (drawing inferences), problem solving (image classification, task assignment and completion), perception (self-controlled car or bike) and language understanding (traffic sign, strong AI). (Beller & Clark, 2018)

3. THE WOMEN'S PROBLEMS ON GLOBAL BASIS

The world is facing many problems in terms of well-being of an individual, society and even on nations basis and this situation looks worse when we are not able to cater the need and respect of half of the society i.e. women. The gender gap in India is roughly around 62.5%, all because of women's lesser representation in business, leadership, politics, business and technical startups (Sharmita, 2021). The global scenario is mostly dominated by Males. There are no clear opportunities or position for women so as to lead the society. The Lack of women in positions of power is a major challenge. Whether it is a court room or corporate boardrooms, research center to the policy makers, in most of the cases we found the Patriarchy is everywhere. The decision making authorities are mostly males (Mishra & Jagdish, 2021).

Sexism, racism and economic inequality is also forcing the women to the wall. Trauma centered feminism is creating havoc for the women. The young women are taught in colleges that they are fragile, vulnerable and in danger. Genital mutilation, acid attacks, honor killing are making the things worst enough for women. Another aspect where the women are facing challenge is to prioritize between the professional growth and motherhood.

4. THE HOUSEHOLD MAKERS PROBLEMS ESPECIALLY IN INDIAN SCENARIO

The Household Maker's Problems

Human beings are the most complicated species in the world. He or she includes numerous physical, emotional, behavioral and societal needs and it varies from society, community and nation. Here, identifying the household maker's problems is a big tough job. However, it is being tabulated on the generalized perspective (Rajeev, 2020).

Table 1. Basic problems of household makers

Physical Problems...	House Space Problems...	Emotional Problems...
Sprain – excessive working or by twisting ligaments	**Mess making kids –** family members and kids are making the life and cleanliness havoc.	**Neglected or less valued-** often treated as a less valued or non-important member of the house.
Back injuries – bending, lifting or straining the body on a daily basis.	**Overfilled schedule –** there is no end of the work and the whole day is just work and work.	**Loneliness & Boredom-** No one is there to share thoughts and emotions.
Joint compression – hip, hand, neck, legs, knees joints are giving pain dues to excess amount of work	**Priority –** the family is priority, the kids, grandparents, husband comes first then the household makers.	**Emotional Imbalance-** the hitch of how the people will react keeps the things within self.
Tiredness – The heavy occupancy is leading towards a 24 hour tiredness.	**Grocery and food menu selection –** with so many demands and time constraints the cooking and food menu is a serious concern.	**Psychological outburst –** often the work stress is affecting the life balance resulting in unnecessary outburst.

5. SURVEY FINDINGS

A survey was conducted on 100 women across the globe especially South Asian countries to know how about the basic problems of Household makers. It was through a questionnaire, designed to have a real time understanding about the technology usage and its impact on household makers personal and professional life.

The women were from various south asian countries like Singapore, Malaysia, Thailand, India, Bangladesh, Vietnam, United states, Gulf countries and out of them 70.15% were in the age group of 15 to 30 years and 29.85% were in the age group of 30 to 70 years.

Figure 2. The technology usage of household makers

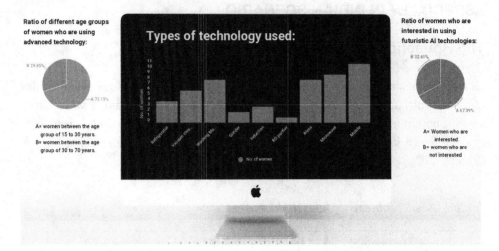

As from the (figure 2), 67.39% household makers are interested in using futuristic A.I. This clearly indicates that the women are keen to adapt and adjust with the futuristic technologies and they are well aware about the recent development of tools and gadgets which are in the market and they are also using it in their day to day life.

5.1 Interview Part

In a telephonic interview with 30 odd participants, there was a conscious on usage of technology. Some of the interview opinions are as follows:

- **Ms. Swarnima Bisaria,** 20 year old from Lucknow, India emphasized on the key issues that household makers faces is the time management and non-stop working. She is using Alexa in her daily life and her suggestion is the usage of Robots in the daily life.

Figure 3. The technology comfort and unawareness of house hold makers

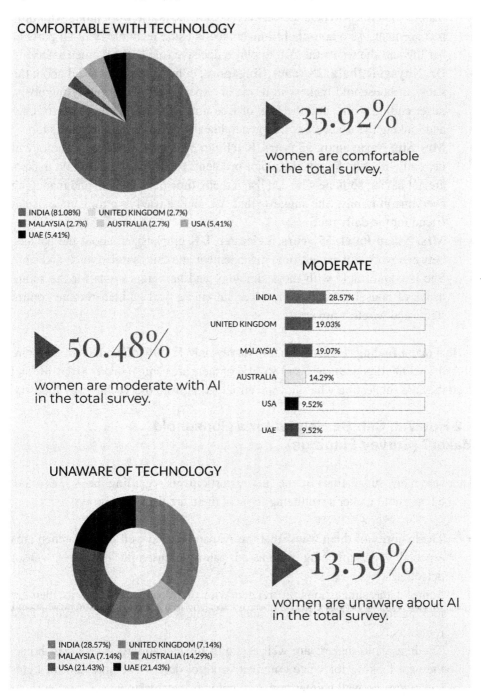

COMFORTABLE WITH TECHNOLOGY

35.92%

women are comfortable in the total survey.

- INDIA (81.08%)   UNITED KINGDOM (2.7%)
- MALAYSIA (2.7%)   AUSTRALIA (2.7%)   USA (5.41%)
- UAE (5.41%)

MODERATE

INDIA	28.57%
UNITED KINGDOM	19.03%
MALAYSIA	19.07%
AUSTRALIA	14.29%
USA	9.52%
UAE	9.52%

50.48%

women are moderate with AI in the total survey.

UNAWARE OF TECHNOLOGY

13.59%

women are unaware about AI in the total survey.

- INDIA (28.57%)   UNITED KINGDOM (7.14%)
- MALAYSIA (7.14%)   AUSTRALIA (14.29%)
- USA (21.43%)   UAE (21.43%)

- **Mrs. Meenakshi Gaur**, **60 years, from Sydney, Australia** is finding the major problems is to balance between health and house work along with time management. As a household Maker, she is using technology in all parts of her life and she wants the A.I. to play a decisive role in the women safety.
- **Dr. Nityagini Jhala**, **28 years, Singapore**, in her interview talked about the stress of household makers in terms of expectations from family members, never ending works and the lack of free time. She is a medical practitioner and looking the usage of A.I. in general health checkup and diagnosis too.
- **Mrs. Sita Narayanan, 55 years, Kuching, Malaysia,** is using technology in her daily life. She founds the major problems related with household makers are not having somone who can listen them, time management and managing everyone in family. She suggests that A.I. can be used as a tool, an assistant friend for the daily routine.
- **Mrs. Nilam Patel, 55 years, Leicester, UK** emphasized about the balance between work and career, time management and things to be quick and easy. She is comfortable with the technology and her suggestions for the future usage of household makers are like automatic wall painter, remote control lights and wireless hovers.

In a major finding (Figure 3) in this survey only 13.59% of women are unaware of Artificial Intelligence usage and 86.41% of them are using it in day to day life and even they are suggesting what they are anticipating from the Technology Industry.

5.2 How A.I. Can Be Helpful for a Household Maker? (Survey Findings)

There are many suggestions by the survey participants regarding the A.I. as a tool for the household maker's wellbeing. Few of them are listed as follows:

- The majority of them wants that the AI can be used well in the kitchen area especially strengthening automated pantry, household inventory, sensor detection.
- Some of the suggestions are related with the cleaning devices as they are looking for automated floor cleaners, Wireless hoover and automated Dust removers.
- The household makers are well aware of the technology. As a smart home, they are looking for voice command control devices, remote control lights and automatic wall painter and to monitor safety threats.
- Bots as a friend is also a suggestion for AI for household makers as it will help them in lifting heavy weights, managing schedule and an intelligent assistant.

Figure 4. A.I. can be helpful for household makers

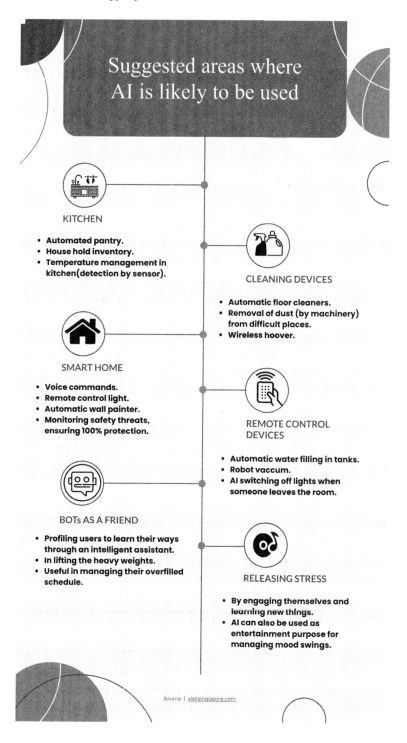

- The AI can also be used a tool for releasing stress by engaging household makers in learning new things, entertainment and to control mood swings.

6. A.I. AS A SOLUTION PROVIDER FOR HOUSEHOLD MAKERS

The Artificial Intelligence can play a pivot role in the personal life of household makers. We are herewith suggesting some of the usages of artificial intelligence for the comprehensive development of the women's.

6.1 A.I. Based Health Card for Household Makers

The health card of an individual is equally important in terms of understanding the health and other relative matters for the quality of the life. It must have the routine checkups, health status, diseases if any, remedies or medicines that he or she is taking and the diseases comprehensive details (Brassy & Price, 2019). This is a desire for every human being and Artificial intelligence is playing an active part in it. The A.I. is being utilized in the health care system as a virtual nursing assistant in the surgery and hospital management, Robotic surgery, image processing of a particular segment, neuro analysis, clinical judgement or disease diagnosis and so many aspects. (Jiang & Jiang 2017)

We are proposing that if Artificial Intelligence can be used to prepare the health card of the person or exclusive for the household makers, it will be a sheer help to the society. The live health improvisation or detonation, the surmounting stress and its complication, the health checkup reminders, the human organs status on the live basis will surely be a help for mankind and it will be an effective societal use of Artificial Intelligence.

A.I support in maintaining the Health Parametric card for the household makers. The Health card will provide the insight of the women right from the conception of the baby to the delivery. It will also address the various health issues during and after the pregnancy. Moreover, this health card will connect to the nearest Doctor and the family members in case of any Emergency.

6.2 A.I. for Kitchen Management and Grocery Inventory

The kitchen management is a serious problem for the household makers. The grocery selection and their timely management is the need of the hour (Thomas, 2016). The important aspect of every household maker is to prepare the meals based on the taste and needs of the individual members in the house. It is the most typical job where one has to deal with the taste of the family members. The likes of one is not suited for another member in the family and this only increases the stress of household makers. What to cook and when to cook is crucial as everyone in the family is on the run. It may vary from the kids to adults and if the grandparents are with the family, then it will be an additional responsibility.

Here Artificial intelligence can play a crucial role. If the A.I. assistant can pick the various health parameters from the health card, then it can suggest the menu and the cooking of the dishes with the available grocery. This will help the household maker job and even the cooking and distribution of the food can be divided with the A.I. assistant.

Artificial intelligence can also be used to manage the grocery and their regular management. It will reduce the stress of household makers who often complain about the no or less stock of a particular grocery element. Artificial intelligence can be helpful in maintaining the day to day need of the grocery elements and the utilization status and if these A.I. Based grocery assistants are connected to nearly departmental stores, it will be a great help. The A.I. based grocery assistants can place a direct order to the department stores, so as to provide the grocery well in time and it will surely reduce the day to day stress of household makers along with providing a healthy diet to all the family members.

6.3 A.I. for Loneliness, Boredom and Counseling

The human society is a close-netted structure and there is importance for everyone in the family. It is often found that once the kids and the male members are occupied in their respective studies or jobs, there is often the feeling of loneliness in the household makers. It may be a scenario where the household maker is not having anyone in the house to share the emotions, and feelings and this often leads towards anxiety, stress, depression and in some occasion's suicide. (Kannan, 2021)

This is a bit crucial especially in South Asian countries' communities, where the household managers are restricted to their respective houses and often they are confined to their own surroundings. Here loneliness is a critical issue and it needs to be catered to effectively. We can use A.I. over here as an assistant. Siri, Alexa and other digital assistants are in the market but they are yet to be in reach of a common man family.

The fine tuning of these digital assistants in the local and native languages, attached with emotional and behavioral support systems will surely help the household makers to better perform and to improvise the quality of the life. The A.I. based assistant can keep track of the household maker's emotional and behavioral imbalance and can provide needful information to near and dears well in time. They can also be connected with the nearest psychiatrist or health center, so as to provide the real time emotional health status and to provide immediate assistance in case of any emergency or untoward situation.

7. A.I. ROLE IN SECURITY OF HOUSEHOLD MAKERS

Security is the important aspect of an individual and it is a must for the household maker as she may be alone in the house or in some cases with the old members. It is often a concern to ensure the safety of the house and the person. The CCTV installations and various safety measures are already in use and it has given them even more confidence. The usage of Artificial Intelligence in the safety aspects of household makers will be an asset for them. A.I. can be used in three levels for the household makers. (Max, 2016)

- **Security of the smart devices**: The A.I. based laundry and washing machine, A.I. based refrigerator, A.I. based chimney, A.I. based water filters, A.I. based lights, A.I. based geezer and all the day to day utility equipment are if connected to a smart board, it will be easy for the household makers to keep track of the equipment's functionalities and working. This will also be helpful in checking out the maintenance and wear and tear factor more effectively.
- **Security of the kin and kids:** This is also a big concern for the household maker. The kin and kids are moving around and their safety is a big factor of household maker stress. An A.I. base security measures to keeping track of the kin and kid can be helpful and handy. Many wearable A.I. based gadgets are in the market to keep track of individuals but they are yet to be in the affordable region of a common man. A lost cost, effective A.I. based Digital tracer can be helpful for the household maker to ensure the safety of their kin and kids in a more efficient way.
- **Security of the Individual:** The least priority safety is of the household makers but that is equally important as the household makers are the backbone of the family. They must be equipped with security devices, traceable and cost effective, so that they can ensure safety of the self as well as all the smart belongings they own.

8. CONCLUSION

Artificial intelligence is playing a crucial role in terms of improvising the quality of life of a common man. The household makers are back bone of the family and it can be easily visualized from their sheer commitment and continuous efforts.

We find herewith in the survey that the women's are welcoming technology and they want to imbibe the same into their personal and professional life. Now, it is our responsibility to develop certain sets of devices & gadgets for the household maker's wellbeing such as A.I. based house cleanliness, food menu selection and health based food preparations, A.I. supported health card etc. This will surely help them in minimizing their day to day stress and this energy can be channelize in more efficient and constructive way for improvising the quality of life of household makers.

REFERENCES

Becker, A. (2019). Artificial intelligence in medicine: What is it doing for us today? *Health Policy and Technology*, *8*(2), 198–205. doi:10.1016/j.hlpt.2019.03.004

Beller, E., Clark, J., Tsafnat, G., Adams, C., Diehl, H., Lund, H., Ouzzani, M., Thayer, K., Thomas, J., Turner, T., Xia, J., Robinson, K., & Glasziou, P. (2018). Making progress with the automation of systematic reviews: Principles of the International Collaboration for the Automation of Systematic Reviews (ICASR). *Systematic Reviews*, *7*(1), 77. doi:10.118613643-018-0740-7 PMID:29778096

Brassy, J., Price, C., & Edwards, J. (2019). Developing a fully automated evidence synthesis tool for identifying, assessing and collating the evidence. *BMJ Evid Based Med*.

Cui, C., Chou, S. S., Brattain, L., Lehman, C. D., & Samir, A. E. (2019). Data engineering for machine learning in women's imaging and beyond. *AJR. American Journal of Roentgenology*, *213*(1), 216–226. doi:10.2214/AJR.18.20464 PMID:30779668

Gupta, N. A. (2017). *Literature Survey on Artificial Intelligence*. https://www.ijert.org/research/a-literature-survey-on-artificial-intelligence-IJERTCONV5IS19015.pdf

Jiang, F., Jiang, Y., Zhi, H., Dong, Y., Li, H., Ma, S., Wang, Y., Dong, Q., Shen, H., & Wang, Y. (2017). Artificial intelligence in healthcare: Past, present and future. *Stroke and Vascular Neurology*, *2*(4), 230–243. doi:10.1136vn-2017-000101 PMID:29507784

Kannan, A. (n.d.). *What are the different therapeutic interventions for depression?* https://www.whiteswanfoundation.org/disorders/mood-disorders/what-are-the-different-therapeutic-interventions-for-depression

Max, T. (2016). *The Future of Life: Benefits and Risks of Artificial Intelligence*. The Future of Life Institute. https://futureoflife.org/background/benefits-risks-of-artificial-intelligence/

McCarthy, J., Minsky, M. L., Rochester, N., & Shannon, C. E. (2006). A Proposal for the Dartmouth Summer Research Project on Artificial Intelligence. *AI Magazine*, 27, 12.

Megan, B. (n.d.). *Women still handle main household task in US*. Gallup Mag. Politics. https://news.gallup.com/poll/283979/women-handle-main-household-tasks.aspx

Mishra, P., & Jagdish, S. (2021). *How India fared in Global gender gap report*. Mint. https://www.livemint.com/news/india/how-india-fared-in-global-gender-gap-report-2021-11617726598143.html

Moore, A. (2017). *Carnegie Mellon Dean of Computer Science on the Future of AI*. Available online: https://www.forbes.com/sites/peterhigh/2017/10/30/carnegie-mellon-dean-of-computer-science-onthe-future-of-ai/#3a283c652197

NileshB. (n.d.).Self Driving Cars with Convolutional Neural Network. https://neptune.ai/blog/self-driving-cars-with-convolutional-neural-networks-cnn

Politico Magazine. (2019). *What are the biggest problems women faced today*. https://www.politico.com/magazine/story/2019/03/08/women-biggest-problems-international-womens-day-225698/

Rajiv, M. (n.d.). *Common Problems Faced By Homemakers Who Stay Indoors - How Physiotherapy Can Be Of Help?* Lybrate Mag. https://www.lybrate.com/topic/common-problems-faced-by-homemakers-who-stay-indoors-how-physiotherapy-can-be-of-help/de3def568eb692f805b619e3d53ff7a3

Sharmita, K. (2021, Nov. 19). Women entrepreneurs in India boosting start-up ecosystem amid challenges, gender inequality. *The Hindustan times*.

Thomas, J. (2016). *Making the kitchen a women place*. https://www.livemint.com/Leisure/VZTcuPvgxIymhqJe4FKkDP/Making-the-kitchen-a-womans-place.html

Chapter 4
Artificial Intelligence Technology and Applications in the Current Scenario

Chandrashekhar Raghuvanshi
Rama University, India

Hari Om Sharan
Rama University, India

ABSTRACT

In the current pandemic of COVID-19, artificial intelligence has become crucial and plays a vital role in dealing with and caring for patients because of the infectious nature of the disease. Many research institutions are stressing on new challenges and future issues of AI, and business houses are funding research institutes and scholars as artificial intelligence is transforming every aspect of human life. Artificial intelligence is grooming itself as a multidisciplinary field of study as it borrows concept of machine learning, data analytics, deep learning, neural network, statics, and soft computing. This chapter presents various applications of AI in a variety of fields and shows how it has become essential and significant in the current pandemic of COVID-19 and helps in societal development and global wellbeing. The chapter end with future issues and challenges of artificial intelligence and research prospects.

INTRODUCTION

Since the invention of machine or computer system, efficiency, accuracy and processing speed is growing exponentially and span of performing variety of task

DOI: 10.4018/978-1-6684-2443-8.ch004

is also growing. AI is about to study of how human brain thinks, learn, decide and solve a problem and applies the study result in making intelligent machine or computer system (Sternberg, 2019).

Now AI is considered as a very special branch of computer science engineering and its main aim is to study principal of intelligence, that can be equally apply on machine as well as on animal. AI is trying to make intelligent machine or software program that can analyze, behave, think and react as human being. Majority of work in AI is mathematical or computational in nature and AI literature is technique oriented.

Father of Artificial Intelligence *John McCarthy* said it is "The science and engineering of making intelligent machines, especially intelligent computer programs" (McCarthy & Minsky, 2006).

In general sense, word artificial intelligence includes applications that resemble human cognitive behavior and define as a machine that imitate intelligent human behavior such as visual perception, speech recognition, decision-making, and translation between languages (Moore & High, 2017).

John McCarthy, said "once defined the field as getting a computer to do things which, when done by people, are said to involve intelligence." It is considered as an endeavor to replicate or simulate human intelligence in machines.

With the tremendous growth in computing technology, high speed of processing, capacity of storing and handling large volume of data, and advancement in machine learning and deep learning, human is moving toward to think "Can a machine think and behave like humans do?". This assumption made AI so broad and popular that the areas of AI are now classiðed into 16 categories (Becker, 2000; Chen & Van, 2001; Hong, 2001; Singer & Gent, 2000; Stone et al., 2001) includes programming, reasoning, belief revision, artiðcial life, data mining, expert systems, distributed AI, genetic algorithms, systems, machine learning, knowledge representation, neutral networks, natural language understanding, theorem proving, theorem of computation and constraint satisfaction(Peng & Zhang, 2007; Zhou et al.,2007; Wang et al.,2007). In the 21st century, it has become a significant vicinity of research in all fields: Science, engineering, medicine, education, business, finance, accounting, marketing, economics, stock market, and law (Halal, 2020; Masnikosa, 1998; Metaxiotis et al., 2003; Raynor,2000; Stefanuk & Zhozhikashvili, 2002; Tay & Ho,1992; Wongpinunwatana et al.,2000)

Goals of AI are to make the following systems.

- **To Create Expert Systems** – The systems which exhibit intelligent behavior, learn, demonstrate, explain, and advice its users.
- **To Implement Human Intelligence in Machines** – Creating systems that understand, think, learn, and behave like humans.

Before getting connotation of Artificial Intelligence, we should get intuition of Intelligence, what is intelligence? After then we will be able to gain insight of Artificial Intelligence.

INTELLIGENCE

In general, Intelligence can be defined as ability to quick response to the action, or the ability to understand, and apply human mind in solving problem (Larrañaga, 2006). *Sir Francis Galton* (the cousin of Charles Darwin) was the first person who studied intelligence as measurable attribute in late 1800 and established a laboratory to test his hypothesis that intelligence is a general mental ability that is a producer of biological evolution and operationalized intelligence as reaction time.

It becomes base for future research of proving and defining intelligence from immeasurable phenomenon (such as intelligence) to measurable terms (such as reaction time).

Human Intelligence vs. Artificial Intelligence

Intelligence can be considered as a human intelligence and machine intelligence, machine intelligence is considered as artificial intelligence. Human intelligence indicates and points to human ability to think, learn, decide, solve mathematical complex problem and communicates with fellow human being.

Some of the basic difference between the human intelligence and machine intelligence are as follow.

1. By nature, human intelligence revise the process by using a cognitive procedures, whereas artificial intelligence intends to create devices that can mock human behavior and conduct human-like actions.
2. Human being use their brain while AI machine depends on the data given to them.
3. It is obvious to all that human learn through experience or past mistakes while AI system improve its performance by the information and through regular training and can never attain thinking procedure unique to human(Terrence, 1997).
4. AI system take much more time to adjust the new changes where as human beings can adapt to change easily and make human able to learn different skill easily.
5. Computer system normally works on 2 watt of memory where as human mind take 25 watts of energy.

6.   Machine can handle large volume of data and can process at higher speed than to human.

7.   Machine is not as good as human in social interactions.

HISTORY OF ARTIFICIAL INTELLIGENCE

Artificial intelligence is not a new born baby; it has a history of more than 70 years of ups and downs but after 1997 when IBM deep blue computer defeated world chess champion Gerry Kasprow, starts gaining attention of students, researchers and investors(Cassel, 2017). Goal of AI is to imitate the cognitive ability of human. AI is initiated in the breath of Second World War and its development led to computing complex tasks which could previously reserved for human minds. From the year 2010, Artificial Intelligence is grooming and booming with the advancement in computing technology and access ant storage of massive volume of data.

Table 1 shows the step by step development of AI from its generation to till today's development.

Table 1.

Year	Particular
1943	Evolution of Artificial Neurons
1950	Turing Machine
1956	Birth of AI: Dartmouth Conference
1966	First Chat boat: Eliza
1972	First Intelligent Robot: Wabot 1
1974-80	First AI Winter
1980	Expert System
1987-1993	Second Winter
1997	Deep Blue computer Defeated World Chess Champion
2002	AI in Home: Roomba
2011	IBM Watson: Wins a Quiz Show
2012	Google Now
2014	Chat boat Eugene Goostman: Wines a Turing Test
2015	Amazon \echo

History of Artificial Intelligence starts in 1943 with the concept of first computer and mathematical model of the biological neuron known as artificial neurons proposed by McCulloch and Walter pits (Council of Europe, n.d., LiveScience, 2014, business-standard, n.d.) . MCP artificial neurons exhibit the functioning of human neurons how it takes multiple signals as input and take action accordingly. MCP neurons are connected with directed weighted input signals. The weights associated with input signal can be of two types either positive (excitatory) or negative (inhibitory). MCP neurons is of binary nature means either it will fire or not depending on the values activation function. If activation function determines value more than the given threshold values, means neurons will fire otherwise it will not.

Figure 1. Activation Function for MCP Neurons

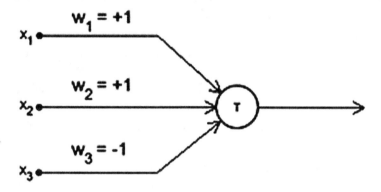

Figure 2. Where b is a threshold value.

$$y = 0 \text{ if any } x_i \text{ is inhibitory, else}$$

$$g(x_1, x_2, ...x_n) = g(x) = \sum_{i=1}^{n} x_i$$

$$y = f(g(x)) = 1 \text{ if } g(x) \geq b$$

$$= 0 \text{ if } g(x) < b$$

In 1949 Donald Hebb proposed a ruled called Hebbian learning for adjusting the connection strength between two neurons. In MCP neurons, there is single neuron getting input and firing if the activation function value is greater than threshold values other not fire. Donald Hebb proposed a learning method to adjust the weight of connection between two neurons. Weight between the neurons is a neuronal activity function . The classical rule says "neurons that fire together, wire together". In simplest form of Hebb's rule wij represents the weight of the connection between neurons j to neuron i.

In the year of 1950 Alan Turing who was a famous mathematician and pioneered Machine learning publishes a "Computing Machinery and Intelligence" in which he proposed a test to check whether a machine having the capability of exhibit intelligent behavior equivalent to human intelligence, called a Turing test. Alan Turing was not the first person who coined the term Artificial Intelligence but they proved that computer can be transformed to deal with values from 0 to 9 and rely on Boolean algebra, dealing with chains of 0 or 1. Alan Turing formalized the base of modern computer system and shown that computer is a versatile machine, capable of doing anything that can programmed.

American scientist John McCarthy, first coined the name 'Artificial Intelligence 'at Dartmouth Conference organized and funded by the Rockefeller Institute. This conference considered as the founder of the discipline. Only six people, including McCarthy and Minsky, remained consistently present till last day of conference which relied essentially on developments based on formal logic).

At this time high level programming language were invented such as COBOL, LISP, and FORTRON and enthusiasm for AI was at very high that time. Researchers were attracting toward new field of AI and developing algorithm which can solve mathematical problems. In the year 1966 first chatbot "ELIZA" were created by Joseph Weizenbaum. In the year of 1972, the first intelligent humanoid robot named WABOT-1 was built in Japan.

While the field of AI remained charming and promising, popularity of technology fell back because the machined had very limited memory and making it very difficult to use computer language.

One of the famous sociologist and economist Herbert Simon prophesied in 1957 that AI would succeed in beating a human at the chess in the next 10 years but then the AI entered a first winter. Simon vision proved to be right 30 years later.

Time between 1974 and 1980 was considered as the first winter of AI. Here winter is representing the downfall and recession in technology because of relentless shortage of funding from government for AI researches. This shortage in funding of AI research project results in diminish in publicity in artificial intelligent.

After the first AI winter duration, in the year 1980, AI started getting attention again with the proposal of expert system. Expert system programmed to exhibit the decision making ability of a human expert.

Concept of expert system was first proposed in 1965 at MIT with DENDRAL an expert system specialized in molecular chemistry, and in 1972 at Stanford University with MYCIN specialized in diagnosis of blood diseases and prescription drugs. These expert systems were based on inference engine programmed to be a logical mirror of human reasoning.

These systems gave answer of high level of expertise by analyzing historical data entered to the system and system was programmed to be a logical mirror of human reasoning.

But the craze will fall again because the programming of such expert system actually required a lot of effort and development and maintenance thus became extremely problematic and - above all - faster and in many others less complex and less expensive ways were possible.

In the 1990s, artificial intelligence had almost become proscribed and much more advanced variation had introduced such as advanced computing.

AI experienced another major winter from 1987 to 1993 because of Expert System computers, seen to be slow and clumsy. At the same time desktop computer were becoming very popular and replacing the bulky and less user friendly computers. Expert systems simply became too expensive compared to the desktop computer. At the same time, DARPA (Defense Advanced Research Projects Agency) announced about AI that it has no future and redirected its fund to other projects likely to provide good results. These consequences cut funding for AI project and create the second AI winter.

In the year of 1997, IBM Deep Blue (IBM's expert system) defeated world chess champion Garry Kasparov. Deep Blue actions were based on a systematic brute force algorithm where all possible moves were evaluated and weighted. In the year of 2002, AI entered in the home through a vacuum cleaner named Roomba.

Presently a number of big software companies like Microsoft, Google, IBM and Facebook are investing and researching on a number of AI projects including virtual assistants. They all are working on creating digital assistant such as Facebook's M, or Cortana from Microsoft, or Apple's Siri.

The goal of AI is now shifted from creating an intelligent machine capable of imitating human conversation to the next evolutionary step, software programs capable of speaking in a natural language like English and act as virtual assistant. These virtual assistant is the future of AI and may take form of robots for physical help or housed in laptops and help in business decision.

The advancement in storage of massive volume of data and computing power has boosted funding in AI projects in 2011. Watson, IBM's IA (understand natural language and solve tricky questions), won jeopardy, a quiz show, where it had to answer complex questions and riddles.

In the year of 2012 Google has launched an android app named "Google Now", which was able to provide information as prediction.

In the year of 2016 AlphaGo, a Google's AI specialized in Go games, defeated European champion (Fan Hui) and the world champion (Lee Sedol) then herself (AlphaGo Zero). Game of Go has a combinatorics much morte than game of chess.

In the year of 2018 IBM made an intelligent system named "Project Debater" who can participate in debate on complex topics with two master debaters and also performed extremely well.

Google as made an AI program named "Duplex" is a virtual assistant which could take an appointment on phone and person at other side cannot understand that he is talking with machine.

In present AI is at boom and concept of Deep Learning, Big Data, Machine Learning, Data Science are supporting AI to proof as a miracle technology. Many of the giant technical companies such as Google, Facebook, IBM, and Amazon are investing in AI project and working with AI and creating amazing devices. AI future is inspiring and will come with high intelligence.

KEY COMPONENTS OF AI APPLICATIONS

AI system or AI application is the technology of future or we can take it as an inspiration of future researcher. AI application generally involves algorithm, data and feedback and is far away than to the simple concept of simple computer program in the sense that AI system continuously improves its performance with time as input data is growing and feedback is getting from user. Its true AI system have the algorithm in background but nature of algorithm is to improve performance with growing data, experience and feedback exactly like human improve its performance with time and feedback.

- **Data:** With the invention and advancement in technology our capacity of storing massive amount of data and have the improvement in computing power also, data is driving business and lead to the business decisions making approach and also reveal amazing prediction and results. Service Sector and Financial Service Sector industries are growing exponentially over the decade due to the use of mobile technology and digitization.

Cloud technology is helping industry to shift their business on cloud infrastructure and record each business activity in digital form and make use of it in business planning and decision making. Business organization are collecting data through their online business application like on line shopping portal and social media platform such Face book, Google, Instagram and You tube to gain insight of customer interest and trends.

Data play a decisive role in making AI application as it works as fuel in igniting AI. AI applications are generally designed to analyze data and make prediction on that basis. AI applications continuously and iteratively learn from inaccurate prediction identified by human review and improve the output consequently. AI applications yield meaning result when the underlying data is large, valid and accurate.

- **Algorithm:** Algorithm is a well defined set of steps in order to perform or achieve desired output by computing machine. In general output of algorithm is same for same set of input data, but in AI application algorithm uses the machine learning approach to improve its performance or result with new input data, user review and experience.

AI application is not object to perform a specific and same task but object to learn from the task and new set of input. Availability of open source AI algorithms has helped fueled AI innovation and made technology available to the business.

- **Human Interaction:** This is the human working behind the AI projects and trying their best to make machine intelligent and intellectual more than to human.Human is implicitly involved throughout the life cycle of AI project. Human decide making the AI project and specify the functions and accordingly collect and prepare data set, write algorithm and implement and deploy the AI project. After deploying and implementing project, verify the output and give feedback accordingly to the AI system and again check its improvement and keep in touch with AI system for forever. Absence of such human interaction may lead to the inaccurate prediction or result and business using this inaccurate AI system may lead to big loss or may be demolish.

TYPES OF ARTIFICIAL INTELLIGENCE

Artificial Intelligence can be divided in many categories or classes. But here we are studying its type by classifying on the basis of its capabilities and functionality.

1. **Based on Capabilities:** Artificial Intelligence is divided into following class.
   a. Weak AI or Narrow AI: AI or Narrow AI is able to perform some set of dedicated work. Most common and currently available AI comes under

the category of weak or narrow AI. It can work well in the specific field for it designed and beyond its specific field it can fail in unpredictable ways (McCarthy, 2006). The best example of weak AI is Apple Siriis, it operates with a limited pre-defined range of functions. Another example of weak AI is IBM's Watson supercomputer, as it uses an approach of an Expert system combined with natural language processing and Machine learning.

b. General AI: General AI system can perform any intellectual task with the accuracy of human mind(Council of Europe, n.d.) . The purpose of such AI system is to make machine smarter and think like a human by its own. In present no AI system is present which can perform all tasks with human intelligent. Current AI research is concerning on making General AI system.

c. Super AI: Super AI is about to make AI system that can super pass the level of human intelligence and can accomplish task with more accuracy and cognitive properties (McCarthy, 2006; Mülle & Bostrom, 2016). It is an outcome of general AI. Some characteristic of super AI are ability to think, to reason, solve puzzle, make judgments, plan, learn and communicate by its own. In present super AI is still a virtual concept and still world changing task.

2. **Based on Functionality:** Artificial Intelligence is divided into following class

a. Reactive Machines Reactive machine focuses only on the current state and take best possible action on that basis. It's most basic type of AI does not have any memory or past experience for future action. Google AlphaGo and IBM Deep Blue computer are the best example of reactive AI system.

b. Limited Memory These AI systems have very limited memory to store data for very limited time period and take action based on current state and past data. Self driving are is best example of limited memory AI system, store speed of nearby car, the distance of others car and other related information that help to take quick decision while driving.

c. Theory of Mind This kind of AI system are not present now but researchers are working on this type of AI system, that encompasses the ability of interacting with human and can understand human emotion, people belief, and be able to have social interaction like human.

d. Self-Awareness These AI systems are the future of AI and will have the intellectual more than the human and will have their own consciousness, sentiments and self awareness.

AI AS AN INTERDISCIPLINARY APPROACH

AI is globally defined as a technology working to make machine intelligent or intellectual as human being. For doing such big miracles, miracle of making machine capable of doing complex task that requires cognitive process of human being, a one technique or subject knowledge is not having ability to make machine like human. Achieving goal of making such AI system, different technologies or subject concepts need to assist and come together. Machine Learning, Deep Learning, Statics and Sift Computing are the key technologies and subjects proving a great milestone in the history and development of artificial Intelligence(Becker, 2000; Chen & Van, 2001; Hong, 2001; Singer & Gent, 2000; Stone et al., 2001).

- **Machine Learning (ML):** It is a branch of computer science that takes large amount of data as input called training data and learns from it. After learning, a testing process is accomplished on another set of data called test data. After reaching to satisfactory level of accuracy of prediction or result final project is deployed. The intelligent behavior of ML system is that it improves its performance with new set of data and users feedback. ML system is classified in two major categories.
- **Supervised Learning:** Supervised machine learning system take input data and match it with the labeled output. For example we have a dataset of animal and output is animal is cat or not cat. In such scenario machine learning will analyze the input data (animal photos) with respect to animal characteristic and identify them as cat or not cat. This machine learning model continuously improves its accuracy as new input data is provided for training and get the user feedback. Supervised learning model is classified again in two class as classification and regression. Regression deal with numeric input as classification deal with the nonnumeric values.
- **Unsupervised Learning:** In unsupervised model input data as well as output data are not labeled. In this model is fed with large volume data and ML system identify the commonality between the data and classify them on the basis of similarity. For example a time series of trade is given and unsupervised model classify similar trades as well as outliers. Result of such model is interpreted by humans in order to check whether result is accurate and relevant.
- **Reinforcement Learning:** Reinforcement learning model improve its performance or result by trial and error. In this model is deployed and result is observed to see it is as per expectation or not. If the result is as per our expectation then system is rewarded otherwise it is penalized. This way system is continuously improve its performance by trial and error.

- **Deep Learning:** A deep learning borrows concept of neural network, process massive amount of unlabeled or unstructured data through multiple layer of learning in a manner how neurons work in brain. Deep learning model works in case of large data collected from dissertate sources may have different format such as text, video, and voice. Deep learning algorithms can be supervised, unsupervised and reinforcement based.

- **Natural Language Processing (NLP):** Natural Language Processing is a one of the AI technique enable machine to read or recognize text and voice, retrieve value from it, and convert into a desired output format, such as text or voice. For example in security industries NLP application ranges from keyword extraction from legal document and language translation to more complex task such as providing relevant information through chat-boxes and virtual assistants. and sentiment analysis.

- **Computer Vision (CV):** Computer vision is also referred to as machine vision, is a branch of computer science that enable machine to see, identify and process images in the same way that human vision does and result appropriate output. Computer Vision uses machine learning model to interpret what it sees and predict or determine result. CV based application are used in finger print recognition facial recognition, optical character recognition and other biometric tools to verify user identity.

- **Robotics Process Automation:** RPA refers to the use of preprogrammed tools to automate labor intensive tasks result in increased accuracy, speed and cost saving. RPA tools are used for repetitive processes involving structured data such as account reconciliation, accounts payable processing, and depositing of checks. Some AI experts do not consider RPA as AI because it concern only on automation of process and other consider it to be a simple form of AI, when it is combined with other technologies such as ML.

APPLICATIONS OF AI

Now a time no field is untouched to artificial intelligence. AI is contributing every aspect of life by making things easy and processed at the high speed that is much beyond the human speed. Main goal of AI is to assist by incorporating human intelligence in machine. Robotics surgery is an amazing contribution of technology to the health care. AI started its journey with automating the process that iterate itself very frequently but is ready to replace human where accuracy and speed is more important because it can store massive amount of data and can process at the speed and accuracy that is beyond the human limit. Here are the some applications of AI are as follow.

- **AI in Marketing:** Marketing add sugar coat to our product to attract customer and increase sales and profit. With the advancement in data storage, computing and web technology mean of business is changed and business is very different than to business of one decade before. Now every business is on web and we have option of purchasing everything on single click by e commerce websites such as Amazon, Flit cart, Alibaba, and many more. E commerce changed the wary of promotional and marketing strategy by using AI technology. AI systems are assisting business by providing customer buying pattern, payment capacity and also analyzing customer emotions and reviews in order to help management in business decision making and planning(Anshari et al., 2018 ; Wirt, 2018).

We are continuously under observation by AI system on web to provide accurate prediction and probability of customer to have particular product like health care and life insurance policy and possibility to watch movie.

In the near future, with the advancement and research in AI technology it is supposed to be possible for customer to buy a products by snapping a photo of it. Many of the companies like CamFind and their competitors are experimenting this already.

- **AI in Healthcare:** Most of the health care companies are relying on AI to save patient live(Jiang et al., 2017). AI is contributing to health care system in saving patient live by alerting the dangerous well in advance. Cambio Health Care developed an AI system for stroke prevention by alerting physician a warning when there I s patient at risk of having a heart attack.

Robotic surgery is a great invention of AI for very complex and risky surgery with great care and observation of patient, Robotics in nursing services are also helping health care by observing patient health.

- **AI in Education:** AI is also doing miracle in education sector in assessing student performance and automate student grading based on their performance. Teacher can save their time of assessing and examine student and can consume more time in class room with student.

In the future, it is going to be happen very soon to have virtual tutor to teach student with more accuracy than to human and will available at any place and any time(Zawacki et al., 2019; Tang et al., 2021).

- **AI in Banking:** Banking sector is relying on AI day by day as AI assisting banking by automate customer support, detect anomalies and fraud. AI system is also analyzing loan risk and predicting the behavior of customer (Aazhvaar, 2019). HDFC Bank has a AI system named EVA (Electronic Virtual Assistant) support customer query by collecting information from different sources and able to answer in seconds. Multiple AI solutions are addressing security issues and by tracing card usage and endpoint access, security specialists can effectively prevent fraud.

- **AI in Finance:** Personnel in finance sector are relying on AI system to analyze the market trends and trading is mainly depends on the future prediction. An AI system is capable of storing and analyzing large volume of data at very high speed and predicts accurate future possibility than to human (Alam & Khokhar, 2006).

Stock market is using AI system to trace the record of trading and boost profit. In Japan one organization named Nomura Securities has been analyzing the insights of experienced stock traders with the help of computers. After years of research, Nomura is set to introduce a new stock trading system. This new system stores massive amount of data in its computer and make assessment such as current market condition is similar to the condition of two weeks ago and predict how price of share will be changing in coming gone day or two days. This help in better trading decision and predict market prices.

- **AI in Gaming:** AI has started gaining attention of researchers and investors after defeating world chess champion Gerry Kaspro in 1997 by IBM Deep Blue Computer. We can say one of the important accomplishments of AI is in gaming industry (Karlsson, 2003). AI based AlphaGo game software named **DeepMind's d**efetated the world champion in the game of GO, Lee Sedol is one of the most significant accomplishment in the field of AI than to chess. Other examples of Artificial Intelligence in gaming include the First Encounter Assault Recon, popularly known as F.E.A.R, which is a first-person shooter video game.

- **AI in Space Exploration:** Space research and discovery require analyzing large volume data and Artificial Intelligence and Machine Learning are best fitted in such requirement(Adetunji, n.d.).

AI is being used by NASA's rover mission to Mars, the Mars 2020 Rover. AEGIS, which is an AI based mars rover is already to launch The rover is responsible for autonomous targeting of cameras in order to perform investigation on Mars.

- **AI in Chatbot:** Main goal of AI is to make virtual assistance means virtual device that can understand human command given in human language like English and accomplish the task accordingly(Adam et al., 2021). Almost everyone has virtual assistant that control the appliances, such as Siri recognize the natural human language and play the required song.

Amazon's Echo is another popular example of virtual assistant uses speech recognition and NLP to perform a wide range of tasks on your command. It can do more than just play your favorite songs like make phone call, order food, check the weather conditions and so on.

Virtual Assistant devices use Natural Language processing and machine learning algorithms to process human language and performs task.

- **AI in Social Media:** Ever since social media has become a part of our life, large immeasurable amount data has been generating through chats, tweets, posts and so on. In social media platform like face book AI is used for face verification wherein machine learning and deep learning are used to detect facial features and tag your friends (Liu et al., 2021).

Deep learning is used to extract every minute detail from an image and on other hand machine learning algorithms is used to design your feed based on your interest.

In twitter's AI is used to identify hat speech and terroristic language in tweets. . AI makes use of use Deep Learning, Machine Learning and Natural language processing to filter out disgusting content. AI system expelled 300,000 terrorist-linked accounts, 95% of which were found by non-human, artificially intelligent machines.

- **AI in Automotive Industry:** Many of the automobile industries are working on providing virtual assistant to their user for better performance and security while driving. Suc as Tesla has introduced TeslaBot, an intelligent assistant to help drive.

Many of the automotive companies are making self driving car to make our journey more safe and comfort.

- **AI in Entertainment:** Now a time most of us are using AI based application with some entertainment services like Amazon and Netflix which recommend movies or programs based on our interest with the help of ML and AI.
- **AI in Agriculture:** Ai is an area that employs lot of labor, money and care for best result. With the advancement in technology agriculture is becoming

digital and AI is emerging in this field. AI is applying itself in agriculture as agriculture robotics, solid and crop monitoring, predictive analysis.

AI CHALLENGES

Artificial Intelligence is considered as one of the key technology that transforming business as well as world to the new heaven or work environment. With the time nothing is untouched using artificial intelligence. Healthcare, Banking, Security, Finance, Gaming and many other sectors are using AI as a great technology boost for accuracy and efficiency in business. Apart from number of advantages and solution of complex problem, following challenges seems unending (RSNA, n.d.; Marr, 2021; aiforgood, 2018)).

- **Workforce Challenge:** A major challenge in implementation of technology (Artificial Intelligence) is the possibility of elimination of jobs as AI improving its ability to takeover human work. It is very hard to calculate the exact impact of technology on job market but employees are scared about their job certainty.

A study by McKinsey & Company said that 60% of all job have some duties that could be automated to some level. Subset of duties does not directly correlate to job eliminations but no doubt that some jobs are at risk where as some of market expert believe that digital economy will feature new job roles working in concert with intelligent systems.

Employee psychology and thinking about job elimination is one of the biggest challenge in technology implementation.

- **Shortage of AI talents:** AI is continuously growing at a steady rate as most of the businesses are adopting AI and AI product in their daily business routine and according to the reports of IDC in 2019 predicted that in 2023 97.9 billion USD will be spent on AI technology. This tremendous growth demands technically sound IT professional having enough skill and experience on AI technology and product. But AI professionals who are having skill o create fully-functional systems are still lacking.
- **Supporting IT Systems**: Information Technology works to fulfill the need of the fast growing world and business demand. It facilitates business as well human by providing system that can store, retrieve and process information.

Apart from the tremendous growth in IT infrastructure, still AI supporting IT systems are a challenge. For example in creating layered security systems, help identify security threats and breaches, help programmers write better code, ensure quality, and optimize servers are still challenge.

- **Infrastructure Challenge:** AI based system need high level of computation speed and storing capacity of large volume of structured and unstructured data. Replacing traditional set up with new AI enabled infrastructure is not easy and feasible form business houses.
- **AI Integration into Existing Systems:** It is one of the most common challenge for business houses, that are implementing AI system. For integration of AI system with existing IT infrastructure, will require AI solution providers having expertise and enough experience in the field of AI, from conception to deployment.
- **Cloud Integration:** Cloud technology is also impacting today's business as it lessen the burden of storing large volume of structured and unstructured data and make available globally. Integration of AI system with Cloud result tremendous outcome but still face some technical issues and demand expertise and experience professional.
- **Processing Unstructured Data:** Unstructured data may have important values for business, but organization may not be able to retrieve in sight because traditional system is not able to process unstructured data. Unstructured data cannot be stored in traditional relational database management system thus it is challenge to process and analyze. Unstructured data include video files, audio files and, images, web content, texts etc. For this to make easy task, implementation of AI system need high speed computation and storage of massive data and IT infrastructure support.
- **Data Security and Storage:** Most of the AI applications use a massive amount of data for prediction, learning and intelligent decision. The problem in utilizing large volume of data is that it may create storage issues for business and security issues.
- **Complex Algorithms and Training of AI Models:** The function and performance of AI system heavily rely on AI algorithms. AI system is not programmed system; it is a trained system and need massive amount of past data and feedback to improve its performance. Once AI system is implemented and for better result, it must be trained continuously. This may be quite challenging to provide data and require expertise and experienced manpower.

Apart from the challenges, AI is growing at very high speed and most of the business houses are relying on AI system for accuracy, efficiency and digital assistant. AI is continuously transforming world and business.

AI: FUTURE

Artificial intelligence is impacting the future of almost of industry and human being (deloitte, n.d.; nextgov, 2021). It has gone from fiction to reality in a couple of years. AI is acting as a main driver of emerging technologies like big data, robotics, and IoT and will continue to act as a technological innovator for expected future. I have realized that AI is one of the most in demand technology of expertise for job seeker. Future of AI looks quite promising and eventful. In business, future of AI has cemented the way for smart monitoring, quicker feedback and improved business line. Robotics will reduce the time taken to complete repetitive tasks, and make the process less cumbersome and more effective. Future AI will be able to get clear view of customer's mind and business to take real time decision to improve their experience. Data driven insight lead to personalized solution and improve interaction.

It is not enough to adopt AI, we also need to prepare organization and boost employees to cooperate new technology. If we plan to use AI solution, we should get data and experience from those who have pioneered this technology. Understand how they managed for success and what did not work for them. This technology helps you to get success and engage your customer better. We can customer problem in better way, we tend to understand them better. It helps us to accumulate more customers and build a good customer base. It also help us to aware of the issues faced by customer which is essential for growth.

CONCLUSION

As the researchers are working and investors are investing, we hope AI will reach to super intelligence stage in the couple of year. However new technology transition has begun and majority of business houses are using this fixture. AI is not only expecting business in better sale and forecast but also offer companies new growth opportunity. AI comes with its ethical and security issues which need to be minimized if we want user to stay for a while.

We also need to work on employees training and enhancement so that the employee who are with us for years can feel job surety and safe. The concept is to transforming future of AI technology without harming the goodwill of loyal employees. This concept will help we introduced overall changes to build a robust AI induced enterprise. No doubt that AI future is exciting and extremely promising.

REFERENCES

Aazhvaar, V. (2019). Artificial Intelligence in Indian Banking Sector: Challenges and Opportunities. *International Journal of Advanced Research, 7*(5), 1581–1587.

Adam, M., Wessel, M., & Benlian, A. (2021). AI-based Chatbots in Customer Service and their Effects on User Compliance. *Electronic Markets, 31*(2), 427–445. doi:10.100712525-020-00414-7

Adetunji, J. (n.d.). *The Conversation.* https://theconversation.com/five-ways-artificial-intelligence-can-help-space-exploration-153664

Airforgood. (2018). https://aiforgood.itu.int/challenges-and-opportunities-of-artificial-intelligence-for-good/

Alam, M., & Khokhar, R. (2006). Impact of Internet on Customer Loyalty in Swedish Banks. *Journal of Economic Psychology, 16,* 311–329.

Anshari, M., Almunawar, M. N., Lim, S. A., & Al-Mudimigh, A. (2018). Customer Relationship Management and Big Data-Enabled: Personalization & Customization of Services. *Applied Computing and Informatics, 15*(2), 94–101. doi:10.1016/j.aci.2018.05.004

Becker, A., Bar-Yehuda, R., & Geiger, D. (2000). Randomised Algorithms for the Loop Cutset Problem. *Journal of Artificial Intelligence Research, 12,* 219–234. doi:10.1613/jair.638

Business-Standard. (n.d.). https://www.business-standard.com/about/what-is-artificial-intelligence#collapse

Cassel, D. (2017). *Remembering Shakey: The First Intelligent Robot.* SRI International Artificial Intelligence Center.

Chen, X., & Van Beek, P. (2001). Conflict-Directed Backjumping Revisited. *Journal of Artificial Intelligence Research, 14,* 53–81. doi:10.1613/jair.788

Council of Europe. (n.d.). https://www.coe.int/en/web/artificial-intelligence/history-of-ai

Deloitte. (n.d.). https://www2.deloitte.com/us/en/pages/consulting/articles/the-future-of-ai.html

Halal, W. E. (2003). Artificial intelligence is almost here. *On the Horizon*, *11*(2), 37–38. doi:10.1108/10748120310486771

He, J., Baxter, S. L., Xu, J., Xu, J., Zhou, X., & Zhang, K. (2019). The Practical Implementation of Artificial Intelligence Technologies in Medicine. *Nat.*, *2019*(25), 30–36. doi:10.103841591-018-0307-0 PMID:30617336

Hong, J. (2001). Goal Recognition through Goal Graph Analysis. *Journal of Artificial Intelligence Research*, *15*, 1–30. doi:10.1613/jair.830

Jiang, F., Jiang, Y., Zhi, H., Dong, Y., Li, H., Ma, S., Wang, Y., Dong, Q., Shen, H., & Wang, Y. (2017). Artificial Intelligence in Healthcare: Past, Present and Future. *Stroke and Vascular Neurology*, *2*(4), 230–243. doi:10.1136vn-2017-000101 PMID:29507784

Karlsson, B. F. F. (2003). Issues and Approaches in Artificial Intelligence Middleware Development for Digital Games and Entertainment Products. *CEP*, *50740*, 540.

Larrañaga, P., Calvo, B., Santana, R., Bielza, C., Galdiano, J., Inza, I., Lozano, J. A., Armañanzas, R., Santafé, G., Pérez, A., & Robles, V. (2006). Machine Learning in Bioinformatics. *Briefings in Bioinformatics*, *7*(1), 86–112. doi:10.1093/bib/bbk007 PMID:16761367

Liu, R., Gupta, S., & Patel, P. (2021). The Application of the Principles of Responsible AI on Social Media Marketing for Digital Health. *Information Systems Frontiers*. Advance online publication. doi:10.100710796-021-10191-z PMID:34539226

MarrB. (2021). https://bernardmarr.com/the-7-biggest-ethical-challenges-of-artificial-intelligence/

Masnikosa, V. P. (1998). The fundamental problem of an artificial intelligence realization. *Kybernetes*, *27*(1), 71–80. doi:10.1108/03684929810200549

McCarthy, J., Minsky, M. L., Rochester, N., & Shannon, C. E. (2006). A Proposal for the Dartmouth Summer Research Project on Artificial Intelligence, August 31, 1955. *AI Magazine*, *27*(4), 12. doi:10.1609/aimag.v27i4.1904

Metaxiotis, K., Ergazakis, K., Samouilidis, E., & Psarras, J. (2003). Decision Support through Knowledge Management: The role of the Artificial Intelligence. *Information Management & Computer Security*, *11*(5), 216–221. doi:10.1108/09685220310500126

Moore, A., & High, P. (2017). Future of AI. *Forbes*. https://www.forbes.com/sites/peterhigh/2017/10/30/carnegie-mellon-dean-of-computer-science-onthe-future-of-ai/#3a283c652197

Mülle, V. C., & Bostrom, N. (2016). Future Progress in Artificial Intelligence: A Survey of Expert Opinion. In Fundamental Issues of Artificial Intelligence (pp. 555–572). Springer.

Nextgov. (2021). https://www.nextgov.com/emerging-tech/2021/10/future-artificial-intelligence/186123/

Peng, Y., & Zhang, X. (2007). Integrative Data Mining in Systems Biology: From Text to Network Mining. *Artificial Intelligence*, *41*(2), 83–86. doi:10.1016/j.artmed.2007.08.001 PMID:17888638

Raynor, W.J. (2000). The International Dictionary of Artificial Intelligence. *AMACOM, 14*.

RSNA. (n.d.). https://www.rsna.org/education/ai-resources-and-training/ai-image-challenge

ScienceL. (2014). https://www.livescience.com/49007-history-of-artificial-intelligence.html

Singer, J., & Gent, I.P., & Smaill. (2000). A Backbone Fragility and the Local Search Cost Peak. *Journal of Artificial Intelligence Research*, *12*, 235–270.

Stefanuk, V. L., & Zhozhikashvili, A. V. (2002). Productions and Rules in Artificial Intelligence. *Kybernetes*, *31*, 817–826.

Sternberg, R. J. A. (2019). Theory of Adaptive Intelligence and Its Relation to General Intelligence. *Journal of Intelligence from MDPI*, *7*(4), 23. doi:10.3390/jintelligence7040023 PMID:31581505

Stone, P., Littman, M. L., Singh, S., & Kearns, M. (2001). ATTac-2000: An Adaptive Autonomous Bidding Agent. *Journal of Artificial Intelligence Research*, *15*, 189–206. doi:10.1613/jair.865

Tang, K. Y., Chang, C. Y., & Hwang, G. J. (2021). Trends in Artificial Intelligence-Supported e-Learning: A systematic Review and Co-Citation Network Analysis 1998-2019. *Interactive Learning Environments*, 1–19. doi:10.1080/10494820.2021.1875001

Tay, D. P. H., & Ho, D. K. H. (1992). Artificial Intelligence and the Mass Appraisal of Residential Apartments. *J. Prop. Valuat. Invest*, *10*(2), 525–540. doi:10.1108/14635789210031181

Terrence, W. D. (1997). *The Co-Evolution of Language and the Brain-The Symbolic Species*. W. W. Norton.

Wang, S., Wang, Y., Du, W., Sun, F., Wang, X., Zhou, C., & Liang, Y. (2007). A Multi-Approaches-Guided Genetic Algorithm with Application to Operon Prediction. *Artificial Intelligence, 41*(2), 151–159. doi:10.1016/j.artmed.2007.07.010 PMID:17869072

Wirt, N. (2018). Hello Marketing, What Can Artificial Intelligence Help You. *International Journal of Market Research, 60*(5), 435–438. doi:10.1177/1470785318776841

Wongpinunwatana, N., Ferguson, C., & Bowen, P. (2000). An Experimental Investigation of the effects of Artificial Intelligence Systems on the Training of Novice Auditors. *Managerial Auditing Journal, 15*(6), 306–318. doi:10.1108/02686900010344511

Zawacki-Richter, O., Marín, V. I., Bond, M., & Gouverneur, F. (2019). Systematic Review of Research on Artificial Intelligence Applications in Higher Education – Where are the Educators? *International Journal of Educational Technology in Higher Education, 16*(1), 39. Advance online publication. doi:10.118641239-019-0171-0

Zhou, X., Liu, B., Wu, Z., & Feng, Y. (2007). Integrative Mining of Traditional Chines Medicine Literature and MEDLINE for Functional Gene Networks. *Artificial Intelligence, 41*(2), 87–104. doi:10.1016/j.artmed.2007.07.007 PMID:17804209

Chapter 5
Crime Analysis on Spatial Domain Using Machine Learning

Soumili Dey
*St. Xavier's College (Autonomous),
India*

Debabrata Datta
*St. Xavier's College (Autonomous),
India*

Suchandra Datta
*St. Xavier's College (Autonomous),
India*

Anal Acharya
*St. Xavier's College (Autonomous),
India*

Rohan Das
*St. Xavier's College (Autonomous),
India*

ABSTRACT

Criminal activities in varied forms are present in society, aggravated by social, economic, political, cultural, and religious issues. Crimes can have an impact on a nation's quality of life, economic prosperity, and reputation. The incidence of crime and the modes of criminal activity have grown as technology has advanced, as have the preventive methods. Good quality data facilitates applications of different machine learning techniques and other algorithms which can be used to analyze the data to obtain predictions which would help law enforcement officials to prevent crime at best or to provide sufficient information to guide the police personnel to the appropriate criminal. In this chapter, different approaches that make use of different machine learning algorithms such as linear regression, logistic regression, Naïve Bayes have been proposed for crime analysis in the spatial domain. These algorithms were applied to various datasets and the chosen methodology turned out to be impeccable as the accuracy was quite high.

DOI: 10.4018/978-1-6684-2443-8.ch005

INTRODUCTION

Crime analysis is a field of study that practices systematic research methods and analysis that identifies and analyzes patterns and trends in crime and disorder (Boba, Rachel (2005)). This supports the mission of police agencies and provides valuable information to wide range of audience and investigators. Parameters like, social environment, ecological factors, presence of certain community and demographics of an area are taken into consideration to predict possible crime and its rate in future (Yadav, Timbadia, Yadav, Vishwakarma and Yadav (2017)). This predictive data will help police department to come up with efficient policing strategies that can mitigate the crime whereby minimizing causalities, destruction. It will also enable to find at what time the police should be patrolling, or maintain a presence, in order to make efficient use of resources. Spatial analysis is one of the essential techniques of crime analysis which is concerned with how a certain community, ecological factors or the social environment affects the criminal activities of a given location (Kawthalkar, Jadhav, Jain and Nimkar(2020)).The proposed work aims to provide close to accurate prediction results in finding the crime type and crime rates of the crime prone locations by means of crime analysis in the spatial domain.

The main ingredient of crime analysis is a crime. Crime analysis, as a process, revolves around the commission of a crime including both reported and unreported offences. The observations and analysis of the data in crime analysis are relevant to the perpetrators, victims, evidence, arrest etcetera which are the fundamental keywords related to crimes. Crime is something that people tend to commit voluntarily or non-voluntarily, unlike war, disease, natural calamities crime cannot be prevented completely. In this universe there is nothing perfect but with our constant evolution of cutting edge technology we can achieve almost perfect scenarios. With the help of data extracting previous useful information from an unstructured unknown data, solving criminal activities becomes faster; we have an approach between computer science and criminal justice. The history is everything in this manner; it provides us the required data and the required crime pattern to pin down possible crimes from happening and capturing them. If in the past if something occurs following a certain pattern then with the help of the technology it is evident that event can be retaliated. But nowadays not everything follows the past, with the rise of technology it gives birth to iniquitous dark web, corrupt social media platforms and foul websites. These types of things are becoming hard to dig up and handle. From trading weapons, smuggling humans, drug selling every ungodly thing happen here. Most of the countries did not have strong cyber judiciary laws to punish them. But still the cyber security personnel are doing their best to deal with the situation. The crime analysis process is one such mechanism that is essentially a part of the criminal act of any country and is the intellectual property of law enforcement agencies. The law enforcement officer and their insight and perceptibility in any undertaken crime are the main factor in any crime curtailment and its prevention. Though these procedures are not commonly mentioned in all the criminal laws and investigation guidelines, according to the necessity of surrounding the crime and circumstances various crime analysis techniques are used. The government, powers, and jurisdiction of the police, other law enforcement agencies, and laws established in the country have their own crime analysis method. The subject of crime analysis dives much deeper than what can be found in the surface of theoretical approach as the exploration of crime and the interrogation of the criminal, in practice, is dissimilar in most of the time.

In order to obtain the best possible results from crime analysis, the data set should be large enough so that the number of features which we want to take into consideration can be increased, facilitating usage of machine learning algorithms which primarily require a large quantity of data. Moreover, it is important to choose appropriate datasets based on the characteristics of the particular crime problem. When an investigation has already started and the investigation team has started gathering data from the actual crime scene, the suspects in person, and the crime scene attributes itself such as location, the collection of all such data in publicly available sources such as Kaggle aids in procuring data for performing crime analysis using machine learning. Causality and the relationship between variables are a vital aspect in analyzing crime patterns from data. The nature of crime can be considered as randomness arising from several factors, each with its own effect on the whole crime situation. Crime is influenced by factors which are difficult to quantify in a deterministic manner, such as the social environment in which an individual is associated with, which influences the execution of crimes in deep, subtle manners which are elusive to primary investigation. Predicting the future crime is difficult, subject to the inherently complex nature of crime and varied techniques, motives and mechanisms that are employed to perpetrate crimes. The phenomenon needs to be better understood which can help in predicting it. The improvement in technology helps criminals to do their misdeeds more efficiently without even being caught. Policemen are trying to predict the crime to minimize the effects on victims but it cannot be perfectly predicted since it is neither systematic nor random. Crime when taken as a cumulative entity it becomes difficult to isolate and understand which attributes are responsible for which aspects of the crime. Each new dimension introduces further complexities that make accurate prediction even more difficult. It is likely that a factor not accounted for in the hypothesis will result in the prediction being inaccurate.

When analyzed along different dimensions, such as spatial analysis or location of the crime, the focus on each individual dimension and analysis of the features that influence crime for that dimension helps to refine crime analysis and makes predicting future crime feasible to some certain extent. The usage of machine learning algorithms helps to carry out robust analysis of criminal data.

A crime in a place is not totally a random occurring; it can occur when a pedestrian breaks traffic rule while walking on wrong side or it can be some type of aggravated assault on a specific target on a specific place (Curtis-Ham,Walton(2017)).For prediction of crime this type of patterns should be recognized, because a murderer cannot be same as a bystander breaking a traffic rule by mistake. It is indeed a debatable topic. People supporting this fact may not consider that as a real crime but people defending that may state this behavior to be abused voluntarily to get past the hands of law enforcement system. In the eye of law, both of them are guilty and should be punished but if is thought in terms of resource, then, any type of aggravated assault, murder, and rape etcetera should be given more priority than traffic rule breakers or any sneaky theft. As an example, in the United States of America (USA), according to the Uniform Crime Reports (UCR) published by the Federal Bureau of Investigation (FBI) (FBI, Crime in the United States 2013 (n.d.)), violent crimes implies the use of force or threat of using force, such as rape, murder, robbery, aggravated assault, and non-negligent manslaughter. In 2013, it was reported 1,163,146 violent crimes, with an average of 367.9 per 100k inhabitants. This was equivalent to one violent crime every 27.1 seconds. In 2012, according to the United States Department of Labor (B. Labor-Statistics, United States Department of Labor - Bureau of Labor Statistics: Police and detectives (n.d.)), there were 780,000 police officers and detectives in the USA, with a median salary of $56,980 per year. Therefore, the optimizations of police officers are often useful to optimize costs, while guaranteeing the security of the population.

Spatial analysis is one of the fundamental approaches of crime analysis, and it is concerned with how a specific community, ecological elements, or the social environment impacts the criminal activities of a certain place. The proposed study attempts to give near-accurate prediction results in determining the kind of crime and crime rates in a crime-prone region.

The proposed study also enables crime mapping that focuses on understanding the geographic aspect of a crime prone area. In addition, crime patterns can also be found by examining situations in which victims and offenders come together in time and space. Such circumstances may be investigated by taking into account land features such as residential lands, the existence of significant landmarks, employment centers and highways.

Various studies have addressed crime control issues and suggested various crime-prediction algorithms, and it has been observed that the accuracy of such predictions is dependent on the attributes chosen and the dataset used as a reference.

RELATED WORK

In paper (Kim, Joshi, Kalsi and Taheri(2018)), crime prediction is done with the help of machine learning. Vancouver crime data for the last 15 years was analyzed with the help of machine learning predictive models like k-nearest-neighbor and boosted decision tree. The dataset was processed using two different approaches: In the first approach whenever a certain crime occurred in a certain neighborhood, each neighborhood and crime category was given a number or unique ID. Classification algorithm was used as the machine learning technique to find the crime type or crime category for a given neighborhood. Crime type was chosen as target to train the machine learning model. In the second approach, the neighborhood where the crime was committed and the day of the week when the crime was committed was given a binary number 0 or 1. 0 meant the crime was not committed in the neighborhood given a day of the week and 1 meant the crime was not committed. This dataset can now be used to train the model to find if a given place is crime prone or not. Moving average was employed to find the average number of crimes per month.

In paper (Toppireddy, Saini & Mahajan, 2018) proposes various visualization-based crime prediction tool and web mapping to show crime trends and various ways that can predict crime using machine learning. These visualizations will generate various reports and maps for diagnosis and analysis process. Various R libraries were used for developing the visualization modules. In model building phase classification of crime type that can happen in a particular location is made using machine learning algorithms. The dataset is obtained from official site of U.K. police department. The first module that was designed was to visualize crime data using Google maps. This module extracted recent crime data and tagged the latitude and longitude where the crime occurred along with type of crime can occur in that place. The second module was to visualize based on crime type which can help law enforcement to analyze the frequency of crimes happening in the area and hence improve security measures. Third module helps to visualize crime hotspot that is the place where there is high crime density. The fourth module generates crime report based on number of crimes happening every month and different crime category enabling crime analysts to check which type of crime has increased or decreased. Module 6 is based on Interactive Crime Frequency Report Using Graph and Bar chart which generates a video representation of trend of the type of crimes every month enabling to visualize which type of crime has increased or decreased compared to previous month. In this paper the data mining techniques were applied to crime data was based on theories in Criminology. Criminology mainly focuses on Rational Choice Theory and Routine Activity Theory. The machine learning techniques that were employed were KNN (Jha, Ahuja and Rana, 2020)and Naïve Base.

In paper (McClendon, Meghanathan, 2015) a comparative study is conducted to compare violent crime patterns from the Communities and Crime Unnormalized Dataset provided by the University of California-Irvine repository and actual crime statistical data for the state of Mississippi that has been provided by neighborhoodscout. com using WEKA an open source data mining software. Machine learning algorithms like Linear Regression, Additive Regression, and Decision Stump algorithms were used on the dataset to predict violent crime patterns. The crime statistics used from this site is data that has been provided by the FBI and had been collected for the year 2013. It is a socio-economic data from the 1990 Census, law enforcement data from 1990 Law Enforcement Management and Admin Stats survey, and crime data from the 1995 FBI UCR

In (Sathyadevan, Devan and Gangadharan, 2014), data mining techniques have been applied on crime data. The process starts off with data collection by web scraping different web sites, blogs, social media, RSS feeds which generate a lot of unstructured data which is stored in a NoSQL database, MongoDB. Once the data is collected, cleaned and preprocessed it is fed to a Naïve Bayes classifier which requires features like data related to robbery, highway robbery, snatching, armed robbery. Naïve Bayes gives an accuracy of more than 90%. This paper also integrated the concept of Named Entity Recognition (NER) which finds and classifies elements in text into pre-defined categories such as person name, organization, location, date and time. With respect to crimes like burglary, it extracts the list of weapons used while committing the crime.

PROBLEM DEFINITION

Availability of huge amount of data in digital form and development of suitable algorithms has facilitated performance of data analysis on a large scale to help us solve real-world problems. Analyzing crime related data is a key area where correct predictions will provide a meaningful impact and help to create a safer world around us. Different aspects of crime data can be analyzed to provide valuable insights as to the nature of the crime, the frequency and geographical distribution of occurrence, the likelihood of occurrence in future and so on. Detailed analysis on crime data with respect to each such aspect has been performed and classified using varied approaches where each approach is designed to provide actionable information with respect to criminal activities. The goal of the system is to predict whether a given location is crime prone or not given certain attributes, predict the type of crime given the location of a place and predict the crime rate at a location using regression.

THE FIRST APPROACH

In this approach it is to be predicted if a location is crime prone or not. The database that has been used is the Boston house prices dataset (Scikit Learn, n.d.). It has 506 rows and the attributes of the database are:

- CRIM=per capita crime rate by town
- ZN=proportion of residential land zoned for lots over 25,000 sq.ft.
- INDUS= proportion of non-retail business acres per town
- CHAS=Charles River dummy variable (equal to 1 if tract bounds river; 0 otherwise)
- NOX =nitric oxides concentration (parts per 10 million)
- RM =average number of rooms per dwelling
- AGE =proportion of owner-occupied units built prior to 1940
- DIS =weighted distances to five Boston employment centers
- RAD =index of accessibility to radial highways
- TAX =full-value property-tax rate per $10,000
- PTRATIO= pupil-teacher ratio by town
- B 1000(Bk - 0.63)^2= where Bk is the proportion of black people by town
- LSTAT % =lower status of the population
- crim_yn=1 if CRIM > mean(CRIM); CRIM: crime rate, crim_yn=0 if otherwise

This database enables crime mapping that focuses on understanding the geographic aspect of a crime prone area. In addition, crime patterns can also be found by examining situations in which victims and offenders come together in time and space (Boba, Rachel, 2005). Such situations can be examined by considering land attributes such as residential lands, presence of important landmarks such as Charles River (in this database), employment centers and highways. Other factors including property tax and pupil to teacher ratio also affects the crime rate of the place. It is observed that the crime rates are higher in those areas that are not used for residential purposes. This is because such places lack urban equipment and becomes deserted at certain hours of the day when the surveillance decreases (Aksoy, 2017). Criminals can travel around more easily with good road and transportation connections so crime rates are high near employment centers, highways and not near Charles river (Geography of crime, 2021). Also in places where pupil to teacher ratio is high those areas are considered to be have low literacy rates such places contribute to high the crime rate as unemployment rate is quite high due to low literacy rate. Land valuation attribute such as property tax also contributes to crime rate, higher the tax rate higher must be the crime rate. This approach aims to analyze the database and find if such assumptions are true. Since the database does not contain attribute that exactly tells if the place is crime prone or not a categorical column is introduced. Hence the target is a categorical data column (crim_yn) indicating that if the place is crime prone or not is added to the database. It is found by first calculating the mean of the crime rate of the database. The newly created categorical column will contain 1 if the corresponding crime rate of that row is greater than the mean and will contain 0 if otherwise (Kim, Joshi, Kalsi and Taheri, 2018). Thus, it is a binary classification problem for which Logistic regression has been used.

Logistic regression is used to predict the values of the newly created categorical column (Geron (2017)). Logistic regression is a regression algorithm that is used for classification. It is especially used for estimating the probability that an instance belongs to a specific class. If the estimated probability is greater than 50%, then the model predicts that the instance belongs to the positive class labeled as 1 else it predicts that it belongs to the negative class labeled 0. This makes it a binary classifier. The logistic also known as the logit, denoted by $\sigma(\cdot)$ is a sigmoid function (which is S-shaped) that outputs numbers between 0 and 1. The function is defined by the following (Starmer, 2018):

$$p = \sigma\left(x\right) = \frac{1}{1 + e^{-x}} \tag{1}$$

If the model is trying to predict for more than one numerical or categorical independent variable then the equation becomes (Logistic Regression(2021)):

$$p = \sigma\left(t\right) = \frac{1}{1 + e^{-\left(b_0 + b_1 x_1 + b_2 x_2 + \dots + b_n x_n\right)}} \tag{2}$$

Once the Logistic Regression model has estimated the probability p for an instance x it can make its prediction y easily, whereby predicting its class (Geron(2017)).

$$y = \begin{cases} 0, if\ p < 0.5 \\ 1, if\ p \geq 0.5 \end{cases} \tag{3}$$

From equation number 2, the log likelihood can be easily found for a given line(Logistic Regression. (2021)):

$$\ln\left(\frac{p}{1-p}\right) = b_0 + b_1 x_1 + b_2 x_2 + \ldots + b_n x_n \tag{4}$$

The log likelihood for other coefficients (by rotating the line) is calculated and is repeated until LL (Log Likelihood) does not change significantly. The model coefficients corresponding to the maximum LL (Log Likelihood) is selected as the best model. The algorithm finds the optimal fit after a few rotations. Thus the Linear Regression predicts the model coefficients $(b_0, b_1, b_2, \ldots, b_n)$ for best fit, by using the Maximum Likelihood estimation (MLE)(Logistic Regression(2021)) (Starmer(2018)).

Methodology or Algorithm

Step 1: Importing the python inbuilt Boston house price database
Step 2: Importing the necessary libraries like: preprocessing, sklearn.model_selection, matplotlib.pyplot, seaborn, pandas
Step 3: Creating a dataframe using the database
Step 4: The target is crim_yn a categorical data column and is created using the conditions:
  ◦ crim_yn=1 if CRIM > mean(CRIM); CRIM: crime rate
  ◦ crim_yn=0 if otherwises
Step 5: Storing the independent variables in x and storing the target or the dependent variable that is crim_yn in y
Step 6: Preprocessing the dataset by Standardization, fitting the data and then transforming it. Then the database is split into random train and test subsets, test size is 27% of the dataset
Step 7: The machine is trained with the train data subset using Logistic regression for binary classification
Step 8: Displaying the predicted values, the confusion matrix, and classification report along with accuracy of the model that is 99%

THE SECOND APPROACH

The crime rate of a place is dependent upon various factors. Some of the significant factors are: probability of arresting criminal, span for their prison sentence, average police number station in each station, population density of an area, weekly wage of people residing in that area, is that area a city or a metropolitan and existence of any minority in that area. There are(Xu, Fu, Kennedy, Jiang and Owusu-Agyemang(2018) that also state that street light has a significant impact on the crime rate of an area.

Dataset

That database (Cornwell and Trumbull (1994))(Baltagi (2006))has 631 rows and 25 columns consisting a panel of 90 observations from 1981 to 1987in different regions of USA.

Methodology or Algorithm

The first step is to preprocess the database so that any tuple containing any null value or missing value will be removed, then the value in year has '19' common, that part is removed only the last 2 digits are kept intact for the sake of optimization. Now the database is normalized and prepared for further execution. This type of prediction use classification or SVM algorithm, but we opted for multiple linear regression technique. Multiple linear regression technique tries to find the relationship between two or more explanatory variables and a response variable just by fitting a linear equation to observed data. Every value of the independent variable x is associated with a value of the dependent variable y. The advantage of using regression technique over other technique is that we will use the numerical results obtained through the predictions. Therefore, it is efficient to use a continuous variable throughout the work, instead of discretizing the target variable and latter recovering a numeric value at each iteration (Cavadas, Branco, Pereira(2015)). One can use multiple linear regressions to know how strong is the relationship between two or more independent variables and one dependent variable and the value of the dependent variable at a certain value of the independent variables. There are certain assumptions that need to be made while using multiple linear regressions, it is same as linear regression where the size of the error in our prediction doesn't change significantly across the values of the independent variable and the observations in the dataset were collected using statistically valid methods, and there are no hidden relationships among variables. The formula for a multiple linear regression is:

$$y = \beta_0 + \beta_1 X_1 + \ldots + \beta_n X_n + \varepsilon \tag{5}$$

y   = the predicted value of the dependent variable

    ◦ β_0 = the y-intercept (value of y when all other parameters are set to 0)

- ○ $\beta_1 X_1 =$ the regression coefficient (β_1) of the first independent variable (X_1) (a.k.a. the effect that increasing the value of the independent variable has on the predicted **y** value)
- ○ ... = do the same for however many independent variables you are testing
- ○ $\beta_n X_n =$ the regression coefficient of the last independent variable
- ○ $\varepsilon =$ model error (a.k.a. how much variation there is in our estimate of **y**)

More complex models may include higher powers of one or more predictor variables, e.g.,

$$y = \beta_0 + \beta_1 x^2 + \cdots + \varepsilon \qquad (6)$$

or interaction effects of two or more variables

$$y = \beta_0 + \beta_1 x_1 + \beta_2 x_2 + \beta_{12} x_1 x_2 + \cdots + \varepsilon \qquad (7)$$

The proposed model predicts the crime data with the help of independent variables and finds the difference between predicted and original data. In ideal cases there should not be any difference but to achieve that we need huge database of last 5-6 decades, that is impossible as most of the police department data at that time were stored non-digitally.

THE THIRD APPROACH

In this approach, we strive to predict the crime type of a place given certain attributes. The target variable under consideration is crime type. We choose to perform the analysis on the Boston Crime Dataset (Crimes in Boston (2018)). This dataset offers many different crime types such as aggravated assault, homicide, firearm violations, warrant arrests, drug violations and so on. The input features we have considered are year, month, hour, latitude and longitude. For prediction, a Naïve Bayes classifier has been used. The metadata for the dataset is shown as follows:
This dataset has 2,60,760 rows and 17 columns.

- INCIDENT_NUMBER= numerical code to identify each incident.
- OFFENSE_CODE= numerical code for each offence.
- OFFENSECODEGROUP= textual name of the offense.

- OFFENSE_DESCRIPTION=textual information about the nature of the offense committed.
- DISTRICT= district where the crime was committed.
- REPORTING_AREA= the police station or institution where the crime was reported.
- SHOOTING= specifies if there was any incidence of shooting (gun) involved.
- OCCURREDONDATE= the date of occurrence of crime.
- YEAR=the year of occurrence of crime.
- MONTH= the month of occurrence of crime.
- DAYOFWEEK= the day of the week on which crime occurred.
- HOUR=the at which the crime was committed.
- UCR_PART=Uniform Crime report.
- STREET= street name on which crime occurred.
- LATITUDE=the latitude of occurrence of crime.
- LONGITUDE= the longitude of occurrence of crime.

Next, we discuss some mathematical preliminaries with respect to Bayes Theorem. Bayes theorem of conditional probability is defined as follows

$$P\left(A \mid B\right) = \frac{P\left(B \mid A\right) * P\left(A\right)}{P\left(B\right)} \tag{8}$$

Where P(B) = P(B|A)*P(A) + $P\left(B \mid \overline{A}\right) * P\left(\overline{A}\right)$

In general, the term P(A|B) is defined as the posterior probability, P(A) is defined as the prior probability, P(B|A) is defined as likelihood and P(B) is defined as evidence. Naïve Bayes is an application of Bayes theorem where an assumption is made that the features are independent of each other. Different probability distribution functions maybe selected for performing naïve Bayes, in our case, the Gaussian probability density function was applied.

Methodology or Algorithm

The Boston crime dataset (Crimes in Boston(2018))was subjected to Naïve Bayes for crime type prediction. The number of training samples per crime type was visualized to get a better understanding of the distribution of training samples over the available types. The input features as defined are used to compute the required statistics during training. The crime types are encoded and the input features subjected to normalization. These computed values are used next for predicting to know which is the most likely crime type for a new data point. The predictions are performed for the top two, top three and top four crime categories and the results obtained are analyzed graphically.

RESULTS AND ANALYSIS

To implement the approaches described in the previous section, a system with 4GB RAM, Intel Core i3 processor and 1GB hard disk or SSD were used. The programming tool used was Python 3.x and its associated libraries like NumPy, Matplotlib, Pandas. The entire application was executed on the Windows 10 platform using Google Colaboratory.

The First Approach

Crime rate or a place being crime prone depends upon land valuation and was evident from the graph:

Figure 1. Plot of TAX vs. CRIM

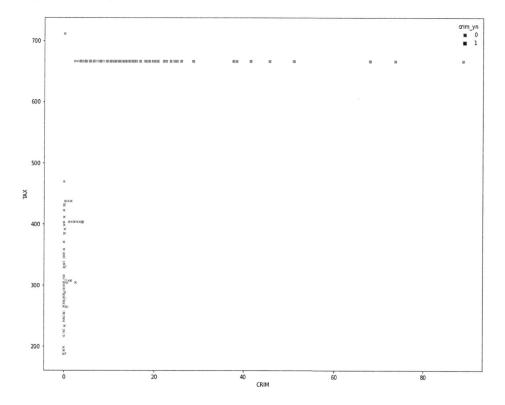

In Figure 1 it is clearly evident that when the tax is over 600, the crime rate also increases and thereby making such places crime prone.

Figure 2. Plot of ZN vs. CRIM

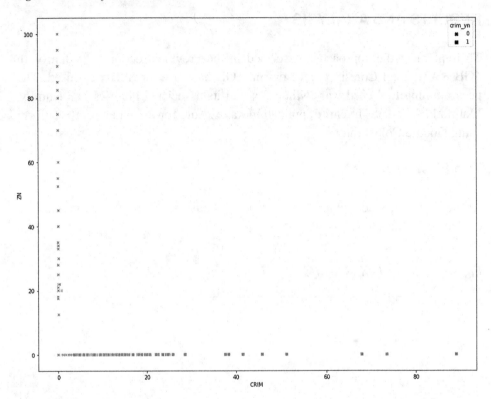

From Figure 2, it can be seen that those places that are not residential are crime prone.

Figure 3. Plot of INDUS vs. CRIM

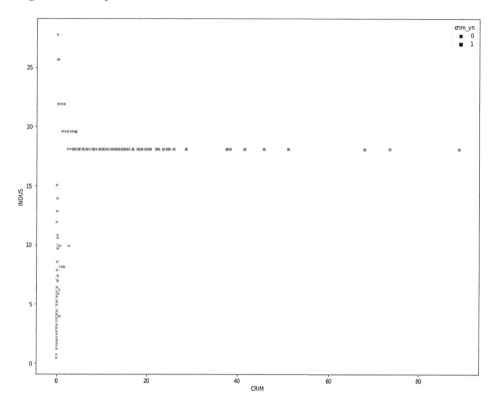

From Figure 3 it can be concluded that crime rate is high when the non-retail business aces per town is between 15 and 20.

Figure 4. Plot of CHAS vs. CRIM

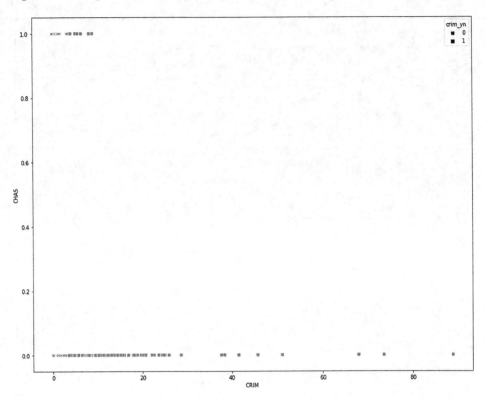

From Figure 4 it can be seen that the crime rate is high when if the tract does not bounds river.

Figure 5. Plot of NOX vs. CRIM

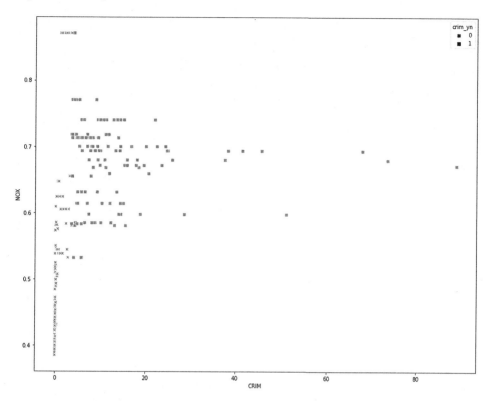

From Figure 5 it can be said that where nitric oxide concentration more than 0.5 the crime rate increases, but it may not be true for all places.

Figure 6. Plot of DIS vs. CRIM

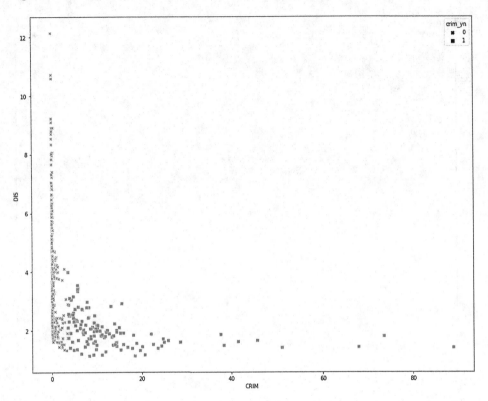

From Figure 6 it can be said that crime rate is high when the weighted distances to five Boston employment centers is less that is between 0.5 to 4 is, but it may not be true for all places.

Figure 7. Plot of RAD vs. CRIM

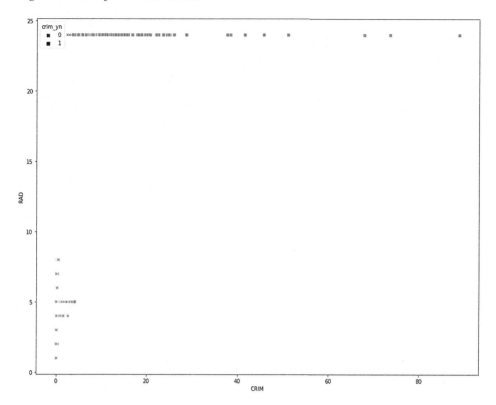

From Figure 7 it can be said that crime rate is high when index of accessibility to radial highways is 24.

Figure 8. Plot of PRATIO vs. CRIM

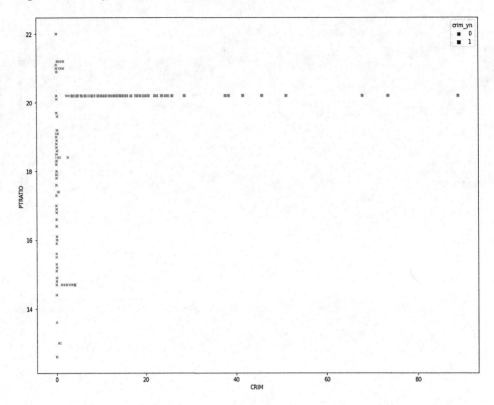

From figure 8 it can be concluded that the crime rate is high when the pupil-teacher ratio by town is 20.2, but it may not be true for all places.

Figure 9. Confusion matrix for first approach

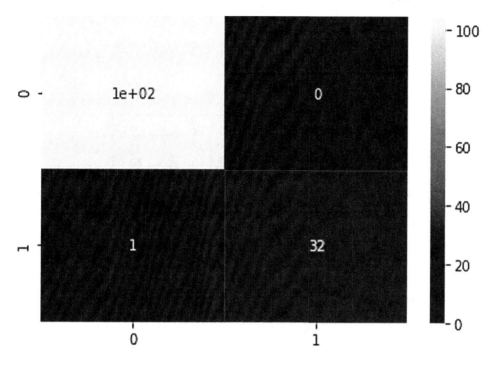

From Figure 9 it can be seen that the accuracy of the model is quite high that is 99% as the number of true negative is 32 and true positive is 102 whereas the false positive is 1 and false negative is 0.

Accuracy of the model is given by (Understanding confusion matrix (2021)):

The Second Approach

Figure 10. Graph between crime rate(y) and probability of arrest(x)

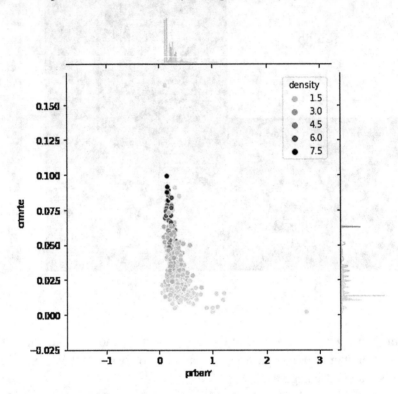

Figure 10 depicts the relation between crime rate and the probability of arresting a criminal. The crime rate tends to high where the probability of arrest is low; it encourages criminals to commit crime without being caught.

Figure 11. Graph between crime rate and population density

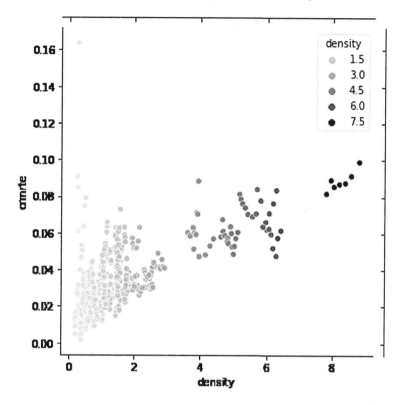

Figure 11 is the relation between crime rate and density of population; it is clear in the graph the crime rate is high in least populated and high populated areas.

According to the model the mean absolute error between predicted and original value is: 0.008811873308054585.

Mean squared error is: 0.0005775674301444617 and the root square of mean squared error is:0.02403263260952619

The Third Approach

Figure 12 depicts the number of training samples for top 4 crime categories. Figure 13 shows the number of training samples for all the crime type. Figure 14 shows the accuracies obtained for the top 2, top 3 and top 4 crime types.

Figure 12. Number of training samples for top 4 crime types

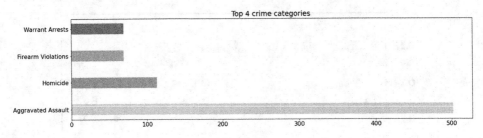

Figure 13. Number of training samples per crime type

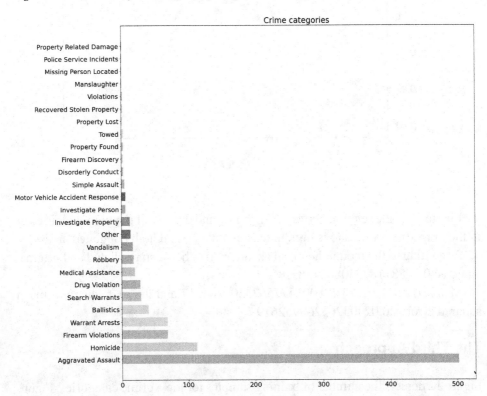

Figure 14. Accuracies obtained for the top 2, top 3 and top 4 crime types

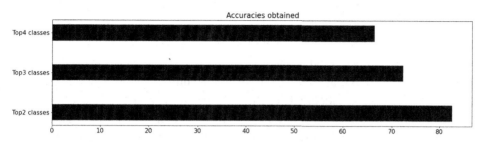

Table 1 depicts a comparative study among the three approaches explained in this paper.

Table 1. Comparative study of the approaches

	First Approach	**Second Approach**	**Third Approach**
Aim:	To predict if a location is crime prone or not.	To predict the crime rate of a place	To predict the crime type of a place given certain attributes
Database used:	The database that has been used is the Boston house prices dataset (Scikit Learn(n.d.)).	Crime data from North Carolina (Cornwell and Trumbull (1994))(Baltagi (2006))	Boston Crime Dataset(Kaggle)
Database modified?	Yes, crim_yn has been added	No	No
Machine learning algorithm used:	Logistic regression for binary classification	Multiple linear regression	Naïve Bayes classifier for multi-class classification
Accuracy of the model:	99%	NA	Top 2 classes accuracy 83%, top 3 classes accuracy 72% top 4 classes accuracy 66%
Difference between Predicted value and original value:	NA	Mean absolute error=0.008811873308054585 Mean squared error= 0.0005775674301444617 Root square of mean squared error is:0.02403263260952619	NA

FUTURE SCOPE AND CONCLUSION

In first approach it is seen that the land attributes can directly affect or contribute to the crime rate of that place and such characteristics might change over time. Hence with time, crime patterns might change. As a future scope, changes in crime pattern must be reflected dynamically as and when attribute values changes. Such ideal system must learn automatically with change in crime pattern. It might happen new attribute values are contributing to the crime patterns then such attributes must also be automatically be included in the system. Real time crime detection can also be one of the crime prevention methodologies. Such can be achieved by image processing on the instantaneous CCTV footage.

In second approach the model performs well for classifying crime types associated with aggravated assault but performance reduces when trying to predict for less commonly occurring crimes. As future scope, more data can be collected with respect to the other crime types so as to ensure a more uniform distribution of the classes.

The inherent nature of human is violence that is almost having the potential, which is different from the tendency, to be violent. Violence had molded the species and there is nothing that can be done to completely wipe off crime from the face of the earth (Gabbatiss(2017)). However mitigating violence and crime rate has been possible. With technological advancement, now crime can be detected and almost prevented before it can take place. In the proposed work, analyzing crime data has been attempted with respect to different aspects to obtain valuable information from the data that would help law enforcement officials to inhibit and mitigate crime rate.

REFERENCES

Aksoy, E. (2017). Geography of Crime and Its Relation to Location: The City of Balıkesir (Turkey). *IOP Conf. Series: Materials Science and Engineering, 245*. 10.1088/1757-899X/245/7/072012

Baltagi, B. H. (2006, May/June). Estimating an economic model of crime using panel data from North Carolina. *Journal of Applied Econometrics*, *21*(4), 543–547.

Boba, R. (2005). *Crime Analysis and Crime Mapping*. Sage Publications.

Cavadas, B., Branco, P., & Pereira, S. (2015). *Crime Prediction Using Regression and Resources Optimization*. doi:10.1007/978-3-319-23485-4_51

Cornwell, C., & Trumbull, W. N. (1994). Estimating the economic model of crime with panel data. *The Review of Economics and Statistics*, *76*, 360–366.

Crimes in Boston. (2018). *Kaggle*. https://www.kaggle.com/AnalyzeBoston/crimes-in-boston

Curtis-Ham, S., & Walton, D. (2017). Mapping crime harm and priority locations in New Zealand: A comparison of spatial analysis methods. *Applied Geography*, *86*, 245–254. https://doi.org/10.1016/j.apgeog.2017.06.008

FBI, Crime in the United States 2013. (n.d.). https://www.fbi.gov/about-us/cjis/ucr/crime-in-the-u.s/2013/crime-in-the-u.s.-2013

Gabbatiss, J. (2017, July 12). Is Violence Embedded in Our DNA? *Sapiens*. https://www.sapiens.org/biology/human-violence-evolution/

Geography of crime. (2021). *Bitesize*. https://www.bbc.co.uk/bitesize/guides/zytycdm/revision/2

Geron, A. G. (2017). Hands-On Machine Learning with Scikit-Learn and TensorFlow. O'Reilly Media, Inc.

Jha, G., & Ahuja, L., & Rana, A. (2020). Criminal Behaviour Analysis and Segmentation using K-Means Clustering. *8th International Conference on Reliability, Infocom Technologies and Optimization (Trends and Future Directions) (ICRITO)*, 1356-1360. doi: 10.1109/ICRITO48877.2020.9197791

Kawthalkar, I., Jadhav, S., Jain, D., & Nimkar, A.V. (2020). A Survey of Predictive Crime Mapping Techniques for Smart Cities. *National Conference on Emerging Trends on Sustainable Technology and Engineering Applications (NCETSTEA)*, 1-6. 10.1109/NCETSTEA48365.2020.9119948

Kim, S., Joshi, P., Kalsi, P. S., & Taheri, P. (2018). Crime Analysis Through Machine Learning. *IEEE 9th Annual Information Technology, Electronics and Mobile Communication Conference (IEMCON)*, 415-420. 10.1109/IEMCON.2018.8614828

Labor-Statistics. (n.d.). *United States Department of Labor - Bureau of Labor Statistics: Police and detectives*. https://www.bls.gov/ooh/protective-service/police-and-detectives.htmtab-1.Accessed:21-01-2015

Logistic Regression. (2021, May 5). https://www.saedsayad.com/logistic_regression.htm

McClendon, L., & Meghanathan, N. (2015, March). Using Machine Learning Algorithms to Analyze Crime Data. *Machine Learning and Applications: An International Journal*, *2*(1), 1–12. Advance online publication. doi:10.5121/mlaij.2015.2101

Sathyadevan, S., Devan, M. S., & Gangadharan, S. S. (2014). Crime analysis and prediction using data mining. *First International Conference on Networks & Soft Computing (ICNSC2014),* 406-412. 10.1109/CNSC.2014.6906719

ScikitLearn. (n.d.). *Toy Dataset.* https://scikit-learn.org/stable/datasets/toy_dataset.html

Starmer, J. (2018, June 11). *Logistic Regression Details Pt 2: Maximum Likelihood* [Video]. YouTube. https://www.youtube.com/watch?v=BfKanl1aSG0

Toppireddy, H. K. R., Saini, B., & Mahajan, G. (2018). Crime Prediction & Monitoring Framework Based on Spatial Analysis. In *Procedia Computer Science* (Vol. 132, pp. 696–705). Elsevier B.V. doi:10.1016/j.procs.2018.05.075

Understanding confusion matrix. (2021, May 5). *Towardsdatascience.* https://towardsdatascience.com/understanding-the-confusion-matrix-and-how-to-implement-it-in-python-319202e0fe4d

Xu, Y., Fu, C., Kennedy, E., Jiang, S., & Owusu-Agyemang, S. (2017). The impact of street lights on spatial-temporal patterns of crime in Detroit, Michigan. *Cities.* doi:10.1016/j.cities.2018.02.021

Yadav, S., Timbadia, M., Yadav, A., Vishwakarma, R., & Yadav, N. (2017).Crime pattern detection, analysis & prediction. *International conference of Electronics, Communication and Aerospace Technology (ICECA),* 225-230. 10.1109/ICECA.2017.8203676

Chapter 6

Design and Implementation of IoT–Based Smart System for Monitoring Soil and Parameters in the Agricultural Scenario

Parth Gautam
Uttarakhand Open University, India

Ashutosh Kumar Bhatt
Uttarakhand Open University, India

Anita Rawat
*Uttarakhand Science Education and
Research Centre, Dehradun, India*

Om Prakash Nautiyal
*Uttarakhand Science Education and
Research Centre, Dehradun, India*

Saurabh Dhanik
*Pal College of Technology and
Management, Haldwani, India*

ABSTRACT

Monitoring of soil elements is essential in characterizing the soil and, therefore, making proper decisions regarding fertilizer application and choice of crops sown. Laboratory soil testing involves the collection of soil samples from different locations and more time and cost. It should upgrade with current technologies like the internet of things (IoT), sensors, and data science. These emerging technologies are smart enough to replace lab testing in real time with minimum effort and with the most accurate results. So, in this research work with a portable IoT device that is coupled with sensors, we can test the soil from wide locations. The system tends to implementation of portable handheld device for soil testing in the Haldwani region. The system is a microcontroller-based device connected to temperature, moisture, and pH sensor. It takes readings from sensors and shows them on LCD. Finally, the data is used for further analysis and comparison. The main idea behind the system is to make it portable to identify the temperature, moisture, and pH of soil.

DOI: 10.4018/978-1-6684-2443-8.ch006

INTRODUCTION

In the agriculture field, lots of researchers are working on new equipment which can become useful for the monitoring of soil productivity and soil fertility. Here we have designed an IoT-based system through Arduino technology which helps observe soil health. For the soil health system, soil elements are very important, also known as basic minerals, organic matter, water, and air. Soil tests enclose the analysis of a soil sample to determine nutrient content, composition, and other characteristics such as temperature, moisture, and pH level. In IoT based soil testing system we are trying to place sensors on the soil sample and try to calculate the soil temperature, moisture, gas, and pH level over some time. Now in this era IoT is the main concern of any electrical equipment. So we make soil testing equipment that performs the soil test at a remote location and takes the real-time soil testing reading.

Lots of research is going in this direction. In earlier days, a support vector machine is used to estimate soil property values and soil type classification based on the physicochemical properties of soil (Lamorski et al., 2008). A comprehensive SVM (Support Vector Machine) based classification (Kovaˇceviˊc et al., 2009) was implemented for urban soil quality assessment and predicted the water quality based on chemical Parameters (Koranga et al., 2021). Different machine learning techniques were applied to analyze the soil texture in southwest china (Huang et al., 2010), Bhimtal, Uttarakhand (India) (Pant et al., 2021), also in Feature Selection towards Soil Classification in the context of Fertility classes using Machine Learning (Pant et al., 2019). This review paper (Liakos et al., 2018) elaborates on the applications of ML methods in agriculture. Use of NN (Neural Network), ANN (Artificial Neural Network), and other soft computing techniques in agriculture like the classification of fruit in the following papers (Bhatt et al., 2012, 2013, 2020). Also use in water quality (Bisht et al., 2017), soil quality, and soil fertility (Pant et al., 2020a, 2020b). In modern agriculture, we also used the Image classification technic for fruit analysis based on color and geometric features (Kumari et al., 2020a, 2020b). Various models have been used to predict soil properties over the last few years. Soil phosphorus is predicted using the statistical techniques (Yang et al., 2019) in this paper they tried to develop the best model to predict phosphorus (P) using the different statistical techniques which have intelligent methods and regression models (Hosseini et al., 2017). In the future, we can also use the Hybrid Approach. For this purpose SVM and ANN are used and finally, these techniques were compared in terms of accuracy (Liu et al., 2016). A statistical approach like Multiple Linear Regression (MLR) (Wu et al., 2019), is also used along with SVM and ANNs to train the model (Li et al., 2014), (Pant et al., 2019).

OBJECTIVES OF RESEARCH

The objectives of the study are to build a low-cost IoT Device for testing parameters of soil and to check the pH value of soil. The other objectives are to find the moisture level in the soil and to calculate the Temperature of the soil.

RESEARCH METHODOLOGY

We divide the work into two-phase first is soil collecting and the second is soil testing with the help of the IoT device.

In the first phase, we collect soil samples from various locations in Haldwani. Some key points for collecting soil from the field are Deep aiming to sample to plow depth or to 15cm in grassland and the Sampling pattern is traditional to walk across the field in the shape of a 'V' taking a sample every few paces.

Figure 1. Collecting soil for testing

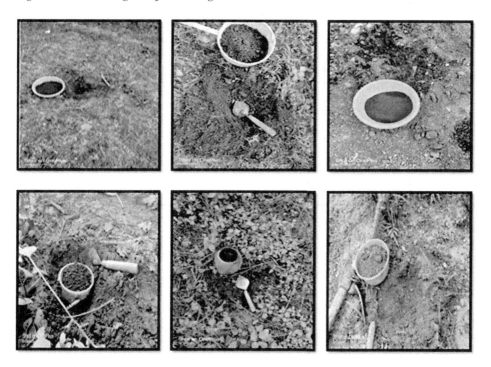

In the second phase our system is ready for soil testing with the following equipment and Sensor:

Table 1. Sensors and sensor's property

S. No.	Name of Sensor	Property
1	DS18B20 Sensor	Soil Temperature
2	MP304	Soil moisture Sensor Detector
3	SEN049 pH sensor	pH level

Figure 2. System architecture

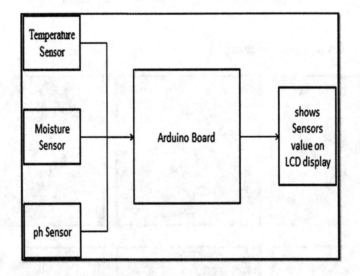

Figure 3. IOT device with sensors

In fig 2 Arduino Mega will be used as a controller that forms the core part of the IoT-enabled soil and its atmosphere quality monitoring system. Sensors are directly interfaced with the microcontroller. The power will be supplied through a Li-Po ion battery or some higher-quality power source. The sensor parameters such as pH of the soil, Humidity of Soil, Moisture of atmosphere, available Nitrates on soil, available carbon complexes on soil, and Temperature are measured by placing the sensor into different positions of soil. The measured parameters can be viewed by using LCD. The sensor data values, as well as results, will be stored in excel form for future study.

Figure 4. Soil sample reading

RESULT AND ANALYSIS

After the integration of all the hardware components and sensors, the prototype was tested with various soil samples and the statistics were recorded for analysis. The table 2 shows the recorded data of the soil test.

Table 2. Soil testing data

S. No.	Date	Soil Moisture	Soil pH	Soil Temp
1	06-07-2021	20	1.16	34.44
2	07-07-2021	17	4.53	34.13
3	08-07-2021	7	2.97	85
4	09-07-2021	34	4.05	31.06
5	10-07-2021	45	2.72	31.5
6	13-07-2021	29	1.59	29.88
7	14-07-2021	30	2.7	30.58
8	15-07-2021	21	3.71	-127
-			-	
-			-	
199	31-10-2021	67	5.79	23.63
200	31-10-2021	62	5.83	23.63

The soil sample collection and testing phase was carried out in about three months in which the devices were placed at various locations in Haldwani.

We have managed the data in excel form and the following are the analysis:

- **Soil Moisture:** After analysis of soil moisture data we can categorize the data into three categories which are no irrigation required, irrigation required, and low soil moisture. The following table shows how our tested data falls into the three categories mentioned above.

Table 3. Soil moisture analysis

Categories	Tested Data Falls into the Categories
No Irrigation is Needed (80-100)	13
Irrigation to Be Applied (60-80)	28
Low Soil Moisture (Below 60)	159

Figure 5. Soil moisture analysis

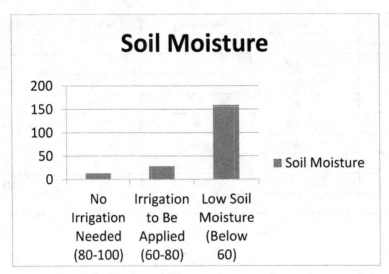

From the above graph and table, we can say that 93.5% of soil forms the sample data is low soil moisture and need irrigation. Only 6.5% of soil forms sample data is no need for irrigation.

- **Soil pH:** After analysis of soil pH data we can categorize the data into six categories which are extremely acidic, very strongly acid, strongly acid, moderately acid, slightly acid and Neutral. The following table shows how our tested data falls into the six categories mentioned above.

Table 4. Soil pH analysis

Soil PH Range	Tested Data Falls into the Categories
<4.5 Extremely acidic	87
4.5–5.0 Very strongly acid	26
5.1–5.5 Strongly acid	19
5.6–6.0 Moderately acid	24
6.1–6.5 Slightly acid	27
6.6–7.3 Neutral	17

Figure 6. Soil pH analysis

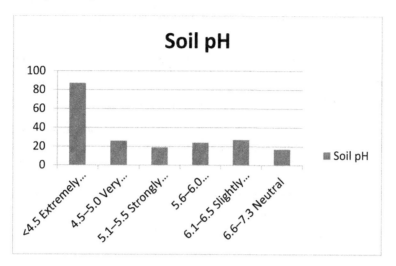

From the above chart and table, we can say that 43.5% of soil from the sample data is extremely acidic. Only 8.5% is Neutral soil from the sample data.

CONCLUSION

In this research work, the IoT Enabled Soil Testing system takes readings from soil moisture sensor and humidity sensor and displays them on an LCD screen, and analyses the variations in soil moisture, temperature, and humidity level of the soil samples. All observations and experimental setup prove that this is a mobile solution to test the soil at any time and any place with more accuracy and minimal error. Users can have access to the data and can know if there are any deviations concerning pH value and soil moisture. Implementing this system will allow users like farmers to monitor and improve the productivity of the vegetables. The coding is done by using Arduino IDE. This work can be extended by adding advanced engineering technologies that provided new approaches for soil testing cost-effectively.

REFERENCES

Bhatt, A. K., & Pant, D. (2013). Automatic Apple Grading Model Development Based On Back Propagation Neural Network & Machine Vision, and Its Performance Evaluation. AI & Society: Journal of Knowledge, Culture and Communication, 30(1).

Bhatt, A. K., Pant, D., & Singh, R. (2012). An Analysis of the Performance of Artificial Neural Network Technique for Apple Classification. *AI & Society: Journal of Knowledge, Culture and Communication, 24*(115).

Bisht, A. K., Singh, R., Bhutiani, R., & Bhatt, A. K. (2017). Water Quality Modelling of the River Ganga using ANN with reference to the various training function. *Environment Conservation Journal, 18*(1&2), 41-48.

Hosseini, M., Agereh, S. R., & Khaledian, Y. (2017). Comparison of multiple statistical techniques to predict soil phosphorus. *Appl. Soil Ecol., 114*, 123–131. doi:10.1016/j.apsoil.2017.02.011

Huang, Y., Lan, Y., Thomson, S. J., Fang, A., Hoffmann, W. C., & Lacey, R. E. (2010). Development of soft computing and applications in agricultural and biological engineering. *Comput. Electron. Agric., 71*(2), 107–127. doi:10.1016/j. compag.2010.01.001

Koranga, M., Pant, P., Pant, D., Bhatt, A. K., & Pant, R. P. (2021). SVM Model to predict the Water Quality based on Physicochemical Parameters. *International Journal of Mathematical, Engineering and Management Sciences.*

Kovaˇcevi'c., M., Bajat, B., & Gaji'c, B. (2009). Soil type classification and estimation of soil properties using support vector machines. *Geoderma, 154*, 340–347.

Kumari, N., Bhatt, A. K., Dwivedi, R. K., & Belwal, R. (2020). Automatic Grading of Mangoes based on surface defect detection using a combined approach of Image Segmentation. *Environment Conservation Journal, 21*(3), 17-23.

Kumari, N., Bhatt, A. K., Dwivedi, R. K., & Belwal, R. (2020). Hybrid Approach of Image Segmentation in classification of fruit mango using BPNN and discriminate analyzer. *Multimedia Tools and Application, 79*(37-38).

Kumari, N., Bhatt, A. K., Dwivedi, R. K., & Belwal, R. (2020). Non-destructive classification of fruit mango based on extracted color–geometric features and used sample size in training phase of machine learning. *Journal of Xidian University, 14*(4), 3066-3074.

Lamorski, K., Pachepsky, Y., Slawin'ski, C., & Walczak, R. T. (2008). Using support vector machines to develop pedotransfer functions for water retention of soils in Poland. *Soil Sci. Soc. Amer. J., 72*(5), 1243–1247. doi:10.2136ssaj2007.0280N

Li, H., Leng, W., Zhou, Y., Chen, F., Xiu, Z., & Yang, D. (2014), Evaluation Models for Soil Nutrient Based on Support Vector Machine and Artificial Neural Networks. *Sci. World J., 478569.*

Liakos, K., Busato, P., Moshou, D., Pearson, S., & Bochtis, D. (2018). Machine Learning in Agriculture: A Review. *Published in Sensors*, *18*(8), 2674. doi:10.339018082674 PMID:30110960

Liu, Y., Wang, H., Zhang, H., & Liber, K. (2016). A comprehensive support vector machine-based classification model for soil quality assessment. *Published in Soil Tillage Res.*, *155*, 19–26. doi:10.1016/j.still.2015.07.006

Pant, H., Lohani, M. C., Bhatt, A., Pant, J., & Joshi, A. (2020). Soil Quality Analysis and Fertility Assessment to Improve the Prediction Accuracy using Machine Learning Approach. *International Journal of Advanced Science and Technology, 29*(3), 10032-10043.

Pant, H., Lohani, M. C., Bhatt, A., Pant, J., & Singh, M. K. (2020). Rule Descriptions for Soil Quality and Soil Fertility Assessment using Fuzzy Control System. *International Journal of Recent Technology and Engineering, 8*(6), 1341-1346.

Pant, J., Pant, P., Bhatt, A., Pant, H., & Pandey, N. (2019). Feature Selection towards Soil Classification in the context of Fertility classes using Machine Learning. *International Journal of Innovative Technology and Exploring Engineering, 8*(12), 4000-4004.

Pant, J., Pant, P., Pant, R. P., Bhatt, A., Pant, D., & Juyal, A. (2021). Soil Quality Prediction For Determining Soil Fertility In Bhimtal Block Of Uttarakhand (India) Using Machine Learning. *International Journal of Analysis and Applications*, *19*, 91–109. doi:10.28924/2291-8639-19-2021-91

Wu, W., Li, A. D., He, X. H., Ma, R., Liu, H.-B., & Lv, J.-K. (2018). A comparison of support vector machines, artificial neural network and classification tree for identifying soil texture classes in southwest China. *Comput. Electron. Agric.*, *144*, 86–93. doi:10.1016/j.compag.2017.11.037

Yang, M. H., Xu, D. Y., Chen, S. C., Li, H., & Shi, Z. (2019). Evaluation of machine learning approaches to predict soil organic matter and pH using Vis-NIR spectra. *Sensors (Basel)*, *19*(2), 263. doi:10.339019020263 PMID:30641879

Chapter 7
Determining the Influence of Social Media Platforms on Youth Buying Intention

Vishal Srivastava
 https://orcid.org/0000-0002-8119-4550
Jain University (Deemed), India

Anni Arnav
 https://orcid.org/0000-0002-4203-5063
Presidency University, India

Neel Rai
NTPC School of Business, India

ABSTRACT

Social media has been creating a strong presence among youth in making buying decisions. The convenience and the usage perception are also leading the youth to look at different social networking sites for more information. The advertising content on various social networking sites are also witnessing radical changes as per the ever-changing necessities. The integrated marketing communication has been instrumental in taking the marketing communication strategies to a different level. The study gives an insight to the marketing teams of the companies who bank upon the various social media platforms looking at exploring the different opportunities to enhance their business opportunities with reference to youth buying intentions. The findings reveal the influence of social media platforms on youth buying intentions.

DOI: 10.4018/978-1-6684-2443-8.ch007

INTRODUCTION

We should look at the defining the social media strategies to make the customers loyal towards the products and services over a period of time. It is becoming little complicated for the companies monitoring the various social channels at the same time. The feedback section also makes the job much more challenging for brands to convince the youth on social media platforms. Sometimes one's view point may not be necessarily the representation of other customer views and definitely it leads to a chorus with the negative approach. The content plays a dominant role in creating opportunities about products as well as services. The youth have the fluctuating nature of their preferences over different brands based on the influence of the social media platforms like Facebook, Linkedin, Twitter, YouTube, Google+ & blogs. There has been a major difference in the buying patterns when we look at the various research findings with the available literature with reference to the transition from traditional marketing initiatives towards online engagement with the effective social media strategies by the brands.

REVIEW OF LITERATURE

This paper basically focuses on the major influencing factors of end user buying behaviour which usually get trendy like fashion variable after every stage of decision making process. Due to this variability it is hard to catch hold the nerves of the consumer. As we all know the consumer is the king in the market and he/she shows the Impulsive and sometime expulsive decision on situational basis which is one of the hard times of the marketer. Consumer always follows the BTPD approach while focusing on the desired product. This BTPD is abbreviated as Better/Best Targeted Precise Decision Maker. So by considering the above said statements the researcher has gone through literature review part and concluded through thoughts. Companies while promoting the product plays a vital role in social media platform by different planned marketing strategies to grab or influence the consumer while purchasing the product (Pütter, M., 2017). The fashion industries not only sell their product on offline route like shops but also on online mode via different marketing promotional social media channels to have a good grip on consumers. (Aragoncillo, L., & Orus, C.,2018).

In this unprecedented time of covid19 has created a panic consumer buying theory and it also leads to the new formation of social media (Naeem, M., 2021). The Social media platform in online mode is also regarded as Electronic Word of Mouth Communication where the person discusses not only with friends and near one (Erkan, I., & Evans, C., 2016). To get success on social media, the B2B companies are implementing various new marketing trending strategies. (Diba, H. et al, 2019). As the fashion keeps on changing as per the comfort space and luxury part of the product, the companies are working with an extensive effort to deal with the same (Godey, B. et al., 2016). The consumer behaviour decision plays a vital role in the satisfaction of a product, and it will lead to customer loyalty (Yadav, M., & Rahman, Z., 2018) (Srivastava V., Srivastava M.K., 2021). It is important to understand the taste and preference of consumer fashion trends by implementing practical approach (Evans, M., 1989) (Srivastava, V., & Tyagi, A., 2013). The Social media uses various levels to attract the consumer X and Y in fashion domain via internal or external motivations (Nash, J., 2019). The consumer motivation plays an important role not only in self but also in social empowerment (Irshad, M., 2020).

Social media is now a hub where the retailers can extend different marketing campaign for its targeted customers (Paquette, H., 2013). Consumer positive attitude towards the advertising message will lead to reach on clicking the end confirmation of product (Mir, I. A., 2012). In Social media, the consumer decision depends on two factors i.e., user generated content and marketer generated content (Goh, K. Y et al., 2013). Social media market research focuses on the understanding of market and consumer preference (Alalwan, A. A., et al., (2017). Celebrity endorsement and their advertising blogs have an impact on impulsive decision process on consumer (Zafar, A. U. et al., 2019). Strong content of a product give power to purchase a product by consumer on social platform (Kim, A. J., & Johnson, K. K., 2016). The plan positive strategy is the key of successful sales of a product (Lindsey-Mullikin, J., & Borin, N., 2017).

The Social media comprises of social media on three key customer metrics: spending, cross-buying, and customer profitability (Kumar, A. et al., 2016). For frontline sales social media plays a right catalyst to earn the profit in market (Constantinides, E. et al., 2008). The digital marketing on social media is dependent on each other on the basis of product content (Stephen, A. T., 2016). On pre- purchase stage of consumer decision process the social media plays a vital role to make an evaluated decision (Song, Sujin, and Myongjee Yoo., 2016).

It is important to build consumer communities to build a long term relation by considering different factors on social media (Akar, E., & Topçu, B., 2011). In social marketing the consumer needs and segmentation is important to be considered (Müller, J. M., 2018). There is a difference between a social and social media i.e., a cross cultural difference between online and offline purchase in decision making process (Goodrich, K., & De Mooij, M., 2014). The promotion value of customer attitudes towards the product on social media works on credibility perception (Shareef, M. A., 2019).

PROBLEM STATEMENT

The current scenario is demanding the marketers to have clarity on the youth's buying intention with their perceptions on certain social media platforms. The study looks at exploring the different aspects of analyzing the demographic and promotional strategies which marketers can incorporate in their social media strategies with reference to social media platforms to enhance the persuasiveness of youth towards the buying intentions.

OBJECTIVES

- To find out the influence of Social Media Sites on youth's buying intention
- To compare the influence of Facebook, Linkedin, Twitter, YouTube, Google+ & blogs on youths' buying intentions
- To measure the level of influence of Facebook, Linkedin, Twitter, YouTube, Google+ & blogs on youths' buying intentions.

HYPOTHESIS

- H01: social media has uniform influence on buying intention of the youth population, across the various levels of age (Age), education (Edu) & experience (Exp).
- H02: The social media platforms, under study (Facebook, Linkedin, Twitter, YouTube, Google+ & blogs) have uniform influence on youths' buying intentions.

RESEARCH METHODOLOGY

The attain the abovementioned objective, the researcher collected the data from 112 youth of Bangalore, about the overall influence they perceive from social network sites (SNS), as well as specifically from Facebook (FB), Linkedin (LKDN), Twitter (TWTR), YouTube (YT), Google+ (GP) & blogposts (BP). The randomly selected sample respondents are belonging to age from 20 to 30 years, Below PUC (less than 12th Standard education) to postgraduation, having experience 0 years to 20 years. For data analysis "R 4.1.0"is used. The chi-square descriptive analytics, chi-square test & Cramer's V are applied to study the sample characteristics, test the hypothesis, and determine the level of association.

Figure 1. Research work

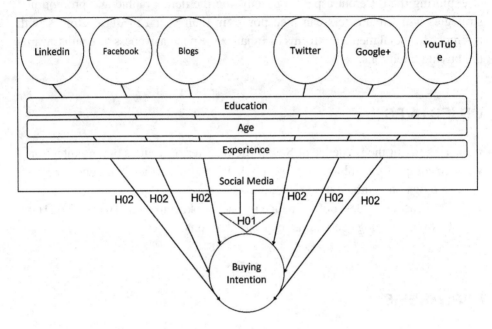

DATA ANALYSIS

Dir data analysis, research used R platform. The data file 'df' used 9 character variables, Age, Education (Edu), Experience (Exp), Facebook (FB), Linkedin (LKDN), Twitter (TWTR), YouTube (YT), Google+ (GP) & blogposts (BP). For analysis purpose the character variables are converted in to factors by using 'as. factor' code-

```
> str(df)
tibble [107 x 10] (S3: tbl_df/tbl/data.frame)
 $ Age: chr [1:107] "Below 20 Years" "Below 20 Years" "Below 20
Years" "Below 20 Years" ...
 $ Edu: chr [1:107] "Under graduation" "Under graduation"
"Under graduation" "Under graduation" ...
 $ Exp: chr [1:107] "Less years than 06 Years" "Less years than
06 Years" "Less years than 06 Years" "Less years than 06 Years"
```

```
...
 $ FB : chr [1:107] "Not so important" "Important" "Moderate"
"Important" ...
 $ LKDN: chr [1:107] "Moderate" "Moderate" "Moderate" "Very
important" ...
 $ TWTR: chr [1:107] "Important" "Important" "Very important"
"Important" ...
 $ YT : chr [1:107] "Very important" "Very important" "Very
important" "Very important" ...
 $ GP : chr [1:107] "Very important" "Important" "Very
important" "Very important" ...
 $ BP : chr [1:107] "Very important" "Very important" "Very
important" "Very important" ...
 $ SNS: chr [1:107] "Strongly agree" "Agree" "Strongly agree"
"Strongly agree" ...
view(df)
> df$Age=as.factor(df$Age)
> df$Edu=as.factor(df$Edu)
> df$Exp=as.factor(df$Exp)
> df$FB=as.factor(df$FB)
> df$LKDN=as.factor(df$LKDN)
> df$TWTR=as.factor(df$TWTR)
> df$YT=as.factor(df$YT)
> df$GP=as.factor(df$GP)
> df$BP=as.factor(df$BP)
> df$SNS=as.factor(df$SNS)
```

The summary of the revised variables are reviewed by code 'summary'.

```
Age                    Edu                         Exp
21- 30 Years:42        12th Standard and below:15` 6-10 Years: 7
Below 20 Years:65      Diploma: 4                  Less years than 06
Years:96
                       Post Graduation:24          NA's: 4
                       Under graduation:64


FB                     LKDN                        TWTR YT
Important:18           Important:23                Important:17
Important:23
Moderate:17            Moderate:16                 Moderate:9
```

```
Moderate:7
Not required:2        Not required:4        Not required:5
Not so important:1  Not so important:7  Not so important:2
Not so important:3
Very important:73   Very important:59   Very important:59
Very important:72
NA's:3               NA's:4               NA's:3 NA's:1
```

```
GP                    BP                    SNS
Important:18         Important:9          Agree:18
Moderate:8           Moderate:10          Neutral:12
Not required:3       Not required:3       Strongly agree:76
Not so important:4  Not so important:4  NA's: 1
Very important:73   Very important:79
NA's:1               NA's:2
```

To conduct Ch-square test, R requires 'MASS' Library.

```
library(MASS)
```

H01: Social media has uniform influence on buying decision of the population, across the various levels of age (Age), education (Edu) & experience (Exp).

To test the uniform influence of Social Network Site over various level of youth age, research applied chi-square test. Code used for chi-square test are given below-

```
> Age_SNS <- data.frame(df$Age, df$SNS)
> FB_SNS <- table(df$Age, df$SNS)
> chisq.test(FB_SNS)
        Pearson's Chi-squared test
data:  FB_SNS
X-squared = 0.50416, df = 2, p-value = 0.7772
```

Similarly, the test is conducted with education (Edu) & experience (Exp). The outcomes are compiled in Table 1.

```
> Edu_SNS <- data.frame(df$Edu, df$SNS)
> Edu_SNS <- table(df$Edu, df$SNS)
> chisq.test(Edu_SNS)
```

```
        Pearson's Chi-squared test
data:  Edu_SNS
X-squared = 6.7115, df = 6, p-value = 0.3484
> Exp_SNS <- data.frame(df$Exp, df$SNS)
> Exp_SNS <- table(df$Exp, df$SNS)
> chisq.test(Exp_SNS)
        Pearson's Chi-squared test
data:  Exp_SNS
X-squared = 1.2976, df = 2, p-value = 0.5227
```

Table 1. Influence of social media to make buying intention

	Chi Square Value	P Value
Age	0.50416	.7772
Education	6.7115	.3484
Experience	1.2976	.5227

The test outcomes are evident from Table 1 that social media is uniformly influencing the buying intention of youth, irrespective of their- age, education & work experiences. The test retains the null hypothesis, as in all the three cases the p values are more than 0.05.

H02: The social media platforms, under study (Facebook, Linkedin, Twitter, YouTube, Google+ & blogs) have uniform influence on youths' buying intentions.

To test the hypothesis, the research conducted chi-square test in between age, education & experience of respondent vs the social network platforms under study. The test codes & outcomes for Age vs Facebook (FB) is given below.

```
> Age_FB <- table(df$Age, df$FB)
> chisq.test(Age_FB)
        Pearson's Chi-squared test
data:  Age_FB
X-squared = 3.3469, df = 4, p-value = 0.5015
> Age_LKDN <- data.frame(df$Age, df$LKDN)
> Age_LKDN <- table(df$Age, df$LKDN)
> chisq.test(Age_LKDN)
        Pearson's Chi-squared test
```

```
data:  Age_LKDN
X-squared = 8.2588, df = 4, p-value = 0.08255
> Age_TWTR <- data.frame(df$Age, df$TWTR)
> Age_TWTR <- table(df$Age, df$TWTR)
> chisq.test(Age_TWTR)
         Pearson's Chi-squared test
data:  Age_TWTR
X-squared = 5.532, df = 4, p-value = 0.2369
> Age_YT <- data.frame(df$Age, df$YT)
> Age_YT <- table(df$Age, df$YT)
> chisq.test(Age_YT)
         Pearson's Chi-squared test
data:  Age_YT
X-squared = 3.4645, df = 3, p-value = 0.3254
> Age_GP <- data.frame(df$Age, df$GP)
> Age_GP <- table(df$Age, df$GP)
> chisq.test(Age_GP)
         Pearson's Chi-squared test
data:  Age_GP
X-squared = 10.315, df = 4, p-value = 0.03545
> Age_BP <- data.frame(df$Age, df$BP)
> Age_BP <- table(df$Age, df$BP)
> chisq.test(Age_BP)
         Pearson's Chi-squared test
data:  Age_BP
X-squared = 3.9435, df = 4, p-value = 0.4137
```

Similarly, the other tests are also conducted. The outcomes are given in Table 2.

Table 2. Influence of social media sites on buying intentions of youth

	Age		Education		Experience	
	Chi Square Value	P Value	Chi Square Value	P Value	Chi Square Value	P Value
Facebook	3.3469	0.5015	9.4200	0.6667	2.0348	0.0111
Linkedin	8.2588	0.08255	12.4870	0.4077	6.0297	0.1969
twitter	5.532	0.2369	8.6697	0.7309	4.4415	0.3495
YouTube	3.4645	0.3254	28.7430	0.000716	0.95423	0.0128
Google+	10.315	0.03545	9.5124	0.65870	4.1584	0.3850
Blogs	3.9435	0.4137	13.9310	0.30510	6.9863	0.1366

As mentioned in the Table 2, it is found that Google+ has varied influence on buying intention of different age group youths. Similarly, the YouTube has varied influences on different education level & experience, whereas the Facebook differently influences the buying intentions of different experience level of youths.

To know more about the influences of identified Facebook, YouTube & Google+, the researcher applied Cramer's V Test.

```
install.packages("rcompanion")
> library(rcompanion)
> cramerV(Age_GP)
Cramer V
   0.3119
```

Similarly, the Cramer's V Test also applied to find out association in between the education vs YouTube, experience vs Facebook & YouTube. The results are given below. To interpret the Cramer's V test research follows the below mentioned guidelines.

If, ES ≤ 0.2, association is week & not significant; 0.2 < ES ≤ 0.5, association is moderate and if ES > 0.5, association is strong & significant.

The test score and results are given in Table 3.

Table 3. Correlation of experience vs. social media influence in buying intention

Demographic Factor	Social Media	Cramer's V	Correlation
Age	Google+	0.3119	Moderately Associated
Education	YouTube	0.5462	Strong Associated
Experience	Facebook	0.4512	Moderately Associated
Experience	YouTube	0.4140	Moderately Associated

RESEARCH FINDINGS AND IMPLICATION

The research outcome suggests that undoubtedly the social media influences the buying intention of youth, across their age, education & experience. Among the social platform under study, Google+ has moderate varied influence on buying intention of different age groups of youth, whereas YouTube also influences differently the buying intention of youth as per their education. Moreover, Youth of different experience years have different influences on their buying intention from Facebook & YouTube. Nowadays, youth spend their major active life with a social media platform, to reach them effectively through these digital media, marketers need to identify- specific social media, format & associated content design. This study will assist the marketers in formulating promotional strategy, specifically in identifying social media considering youth- age-group, education-level & experience. Another challenge what digital marketers are facing is due to improper utilization of social media, unknowingly marketers are making noise and irritating the customers. This research will help these marketers to understand youth perception & preferences in optimal utilization of these platforms to get better acceptance among target audience.

CONCLUSION

Social media influencers have been contributing in the recent years with huge followers to their credit in making the brands visible in a different approach aligned with the personality attributes. One has to rethink at the creative and innovative approaches to attract the youngsters towards their products. Companies are using digital marketing to stimulate the customers towards their brands with attractive strategies to stimulate the interest in youngsters to buy their products. Social media platforms are also proving the presence of the brand in global business context. Young people are employed in analysing the social media data and formulation of social media strategies in the companies. This helps in understanding the mind-set of the youth and derives at creating or formulating the right approach to deal with them for better reach. Artificial intelligence is being considered for drafting the marketing plan for most of the e-business. Artificial intelligence techniques would enable the companies to go for strategic positioning of their goals with systematic process on social media. The study findings have given a clear understanding of the youth perception in accepting certain social media platforms for the marketers to take clue and rework on their strategies to deal with the same.

REFERENCES

Akar, E., & Topçu, B. (2011). An examination of the factors influencing consumers' attitudes toward social media marketing. *Journal of Internet Commerce*, *10*(1), 35–67. doi:10.1080/15332861.2011.558456

Alalwan, A. A., Rana, N. P., Dwivedi, Y. K., & Algharabat, R. (2017). Social media in marketing: A review and analysis of the existing literature. *Telematics and Informatics*, *34*(7), 1177–1190. doi:10.1016/j.tele.2017.05.008

Aragoncillo, L., & Orus, C. (2018). Impulse buying behaviour: an online-offline comparative and the impact of social media. Spanish Journal of Marketing-ESIC.

Constantinides, E., Romero, C. L., & Boria, M. A. G. (2008). Social media: a new frontier for retailers? In *European retail research* (pp. 1–28). Gabler Verlag., doi:10.1007/978-3-8349-8099-1

Diba, H., Vella, J. M., & Abratt, R. (2019). Social media influence on the B2B buying process. *Journal of Business and Industrial Marketing, 34*(7), 1482–1496. doi:10.1108/JBIM-12-2018-0403

Erkan, I., & Evans, C. (2016). The influence of eWOM in social media on consumers' purchase intentions: An extended approach to information adoption. *Computers in Human Behavior, 61,* 47–55. doi:10.1016/j.chb.2016.03.003

Evans, M. (1989). Consumer behaviour towards fashion. *European Journal of Marketing, 23*(7), 7–16. doi:10.1108/EUM0000000000575

Godey, B., Manthiou, A., Pederzoli, D., Rokka, J., Aiello, G., Donvito, R., & Singh, R. (2016). Social media marketing efforts of luxury brands: Influence on brand equity and consumer behavior. *Journal of Business Research, 69*(12), 5833–5841. doi:10.1016/j.jbusres.2016.04.181

Goh, K. Y., Heng, C. S., & Lin, Z. (2013). Social media brand community and consumer behavior: Quantifying the relative impact of user-and marketer-generated content. *Information Systems Research, 24*(1), 88–107. doi:10.1287/isre.1120.0469

Goodrich, K., & De Mooij, M. (2014). How 'social' are social media? A cross-cultural comparison of online and offline purchase decision influences. *Journal of Marketing Communications, 20*(1-2), 103–116. doi:10.1080/13527266.2013.797773

Irshad, M., Ahmad, M. S., & Malik, O. F. (2020). Understanding consumers' trust in social media marketing environment. *International Journal of Retail & Distribution Management, 48*(11), 1195–1212. doi:10.1108/IJRDM-07-2019-0225

Kim, A. J., & Johnson, K. K. (2016). Power of consumers using social media: Examining the influences of brand-related user-generated content on Facebook. *Computers In Human Behavior, 58,* 98–108. doi:10.1016/j.chb.2015.12.047

Kumar, A., Bezawada, R., Rishika, R., Janakiraman, R., & Kannan, P. K. (2016). From social to sale: The effects of firm-generated content in social media on customer behavior. *Journal of Marketing, 80*(1), 7–25. doi:10.1509/jm.14.0249

Lindsey-Mullikin, J., & Borin, N. (2017). Why strategy is key for successful social media sales. *Business Horizons, 60*(4), 473–482. doi:10.1016/j.bushor.2017.03.005

Mir, I. A. (2012). Consumer attitudinal insights about social media advertising: A South Asian perspective. *The Romanian Economic Journal*, *15*(45), 265–288.

Müller, J. M., Pommeranz, B., Weisser, J., & Voigt, K. I. (2018). Digital, Social Media, and Mobile Marketing in industrial buying: Still in need of customer segmentation? Empirical evidence from Poland and Germany. *Industrial Marketing Management*, *73*, 70–83. doi:10.1016/j.indmarman.2018.01.033

Naeem, M. (2021). Do social media platforms develop consumer panic buying during the fear of Covid-19 pandemic. *Journal of Retailing and Consumer Services*, *58*, 102226. doi:10.1016/j.jretconser.2020.102226

Nash, J. (2019). Exploring how social media platforms influence fashion consumer decisions in the UK retail sector. *Journal of Fashion Marketing and Management*, *23*(1), 82–103. doi:10.1108/JFMM-01-2018-0012

Paquette, H. (2013). *Social media as a marketing tool: A literature review*. Academic Press.

Pütter, M. (2017). The impact of social media on consumer buying intention. *Marketing*, *3*(1), 7–13.

Shareef, M. A., Mukerji, B., Dwivedi, Y. K., Rana, N. P., & Islam, R. (2019). Social media marketing: Comparative effect of advertisement sources. *Journal of Retailing and Consumer Services*, *46*, 58–69. doi:10.1016/j.jretconser.2017.11.001

Song, S., & Yoo, M. (2016). The role of social media during the pre-purchasing stage. *Journal of Hospitality and Tourism Technology*, *7*(1), 84–99. doi:10.1108/JHTT-11-2014-0067

Srivastava, V., & Srivastava, M. K. (2021). Modelling Enablers of Customer-Centricity in Convenience Food Retail. In P. K. Singh, Z. Polkowski, S. Tanwar, S. K. Pandey, G. Matei, & D. Pirvu (Eds.), *Innovations in Information and Communication Technologies (IICT-2020). Advances in Science, Technology & Innovation (IEREK Interdisciplinary Series for Sustainable Development)*. Springer., doi:10.1007/978-3-030-66218-921

Srivastava, V., & Tyagi, A. (2013). The study of impact of after sales services of passenger cars on customer retention. *International Journal of Current Research and Review*, *5*(1), 127.

Stephen, A. T. (2016). The role of digital and social media marketing in consumer behavior. *Current Opinion in Psychology*, *10*, 17–21. doi:10.1016/j.copsyc.2015.10.016

Yadav, M., & Rahman, Z. (2018). The influence of social media marketing activities on customer loyalty: A study of e-commerce industry. *Benchmarking*, *25*(9), 3882–3905. doi:10.1108/BIJ-05-2017-0092

Zafar, A. U., Qiu, J., Li, Y., Wang, J., & Shahzad, M. (2019). The impact of social media celebrities' posts and contextual interactions on impulse buying in social commerce. *Computers in Human Behavior*, 106178.

Chapter 8
Diagnosis of Diabetes Types–2 Mellitus Based on Machine Learning Techniques

Somendra Tripathi
Faculty of Engineering and Technology, Rama University, India

Hari Om Sharan
Rama University, India

ABSTRACT

Diabetes Type-2 is one of the significant medical problems nowadays. Diabetes Type-2 is no longer only a disease of the wealthy; its prevalence is rapidly rising everywhere, particularly in the world's middle class income for different countries. Presently it is not an illness of transcendently developed countries. The pervasiveness of diabetes is consistently expanding all over, most extraordinarily on the planet's center pay countries. The majority of these 3.7 million deaths occur before the age of 70. The number of people who die before they are 70 as a result of high blood glucose or diabetes is higher. There are several computational ways for detecting Diabetes Mellitus, but the major downside is that the patient must undergo several medical tests in order to supply input values to the computer diagnostic system, which is both costly and tedious. There are now a variety of techniques and algorithms in artificial intelligent and machine learning that can be applied to accurately predict and detect a number of diseases.

DOI: 10.4018/978-1-6684-2443-8.ch008

INTRODUCTION

Diabetes is a long-term illness that occurs when the blood glucose level grows too high. increases significantly Blood sugar level is the most significant source of nutrients. of our physical being Blood glucose is generated from the food we eat on a daily basis (World Health Organization, 2016).

All around the world, an expected 432 million grown-ups were living with diabetes in 2016, contrasted with 108 million out of 1980. Since 1980, the global prevalence of diabetes (age-standardized) has nearly doubled, rising from 4.9 percent to 9.1 percent in the adult population. This is due to an increase in risk factors linked with being overweight or obese. In 2014, 1.8 million people died as a result of diabetes type-2. By increasing the risks of cardiovascular and other respiratory failure, and kidney infections, higher-than-ideal blood glucose resulted in an additional 2.2 million deaths (Saxena et al., 2014).

Diabetes can irritate the sensitivity, kidneys, heart, blood flow, and nerves, small deformations of an object, damage, and functioning. Type 1 diabetes, termed T1D, and type 2 diabetes, termed T2D, are two primary kinds of diabetes. Type 1 diabetes impacts usually young persons under the age of 30. This category's clinical patients may experience urination and high blood sugar levels. Medication itself will not treat type 1 diabetes, so insulin therapy is essential. Type 2 diabetes primarily affects adults and the elderly. Obesity, hypertension, dyslipidemia, and other illnesses are frequent in patients with type 2 diabetes (Kavakiotis et al., 2017).

Type 1 diabetes (as well-known as insulin-dependent diabetes, juvenile diabetes, or childhood diabetes) is based on the lack of insulin generation in the body. Type 1 diabetes people undergo daily insulin injections to keep their blood glucose levels in check. They will perish if they do not have access to insulin. Type 1 diabetes has no known aetiology and is not yet preventive. Excessive urine and thirst, persistent hunger, weight loss, visual problems, and weariness are all symptoms.

Type 2 diabetes (as well-known as adult-onset diabetes or non-insulin-dependent diabetes) is caused by the body's poor usage of insulin (Polat & Günes, 2007). The large number of persons with diabetes in the globe have type 2 diabetes (1). The symptoms are generally identical than those of type 1 diabetes.

LITERATURE REVIEW

As diabetes type-2 is a haven't ever infection, we can only manage forward. To such a reason, the sooner diabetes is detected, the easier it is to treat. Machine Learning may generate early diabetes predictions identified on the basis data, and these predictions can be helpful to clinicians. Extraction of features, selection of valid features, and classification are the processes in Machine Learning modelling (Yue et al., 2008). The accurate classification and the identification of significant and accurate features for Machine Learning modelling techniques are critical issues.

Using Machine Learning algorithm, a significant effort has been done to automate the identification of diabetes. Various algorithms have been used to diagnose diabetes in recent studies, including Machine Learning approaches such as Support Vector Machine (SVM), Decision Tree, and Logistic Regression, among others. Principle component analysis (PCA) and neuro-fuzzy inference were utilized to distinguish diabetics from healthy patients (Çalişir & Doğantekin, 2011). Linear Discriminant Analysis (LDA) was formerly used to reduce dimensionality and extract features. To examine higher dimension data, prediction models based on Regression Analysis were deployed. Support vector regression (SVR) was employed to predict diabetes in order to deal with multivariate regression difficulties (Razavian et al., 2015). We employed the ensemble technique with Random Forest to improve accuracy in this project. We employed a k Nearest Neighbor, Random Forest composite strategy, which integrates multiple Machine Learning approaches.

The most widely used Machine Learning approach, Decision Tree, provides excellent categorization capabilities. Random Forest is a system that mixes many Decision Trees to provide superior outcomes in a variety of areas (Georga et al., 2013). As a result, we employed Random Forest to predict diabetes in this project.

Along with its simplicity, ease of understanding, and relatively high accuracy, the K-Nearest Neighbour (KNN) technique has been successfully employed in many data analytic applications such as information retrieval, database, pattern recognition, data mining, and machine learning (Ozcift & Gulten, 2011).

Clustering and classification are two applications of the KNN technique. A lot of study has been done in machine learning to overcome the categorization challenge (Yadav & Sharma, 2018b). Due to missing information, the Pima Indian Diabetes dataset is extremely difficult to categorise. To increase classification accuracy, a lot of research has been done on the Pima Indian Diabetes dataset.

PROPOSED METHODOLOGY OF MACHINE LEARNING

- **Data Accommodation:** Data accommodation is the first and most important stage in putting the Machine Learning model into action. To train the model, data is gathered and cleaned in this stage. Datasets in their raw form are meaningless and contain no information. It may occasionally contain inaccurate values that compromise the model's accuracy (Yadav & Sharma, 2018a). Datasets may have missing values, which should be identified and addressed before the model is trained.

Furthermore, datasets should be gathered from reliable sources; otherwise, the model's performance may suffer.

Data is categorized into two categories:

- **Qualitative Data**: Data which is defined in measurable terms like numbers, values, and quantity
- **Quantitative Data**: Data which cannot be measured in numeric terms rather it can only be described
  - **Data Collection** Data collection is a method for gathering and examining specific information in order to provide replies to requests and inspect the outcomes (Sultana & Sharma, 2018).

Figure 1. Proposed methodology

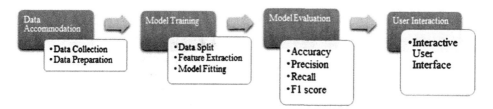

It often refers to the quality and amount of data, with the latter indicating the model's accuracy. Data representation is the result of data collecting. To use acquired data to construct Machine Learning solutions, it must be collected and stored in a form that is appropriate for the framework in question. For data professionals, there is a limit to how much data can be accommodated (Chauhan et al., 2021). Data collection allows us to see official accounts and evaluate data in order to find repeating trends.

Such patterns facilitate the creation of Machine Learning techniques that could forecast future developments. While predictive models rely on the data with which they are taught to function, they are considered to as predictive models

Figure 2. Data collection key point
(Zubchenko, 2021)

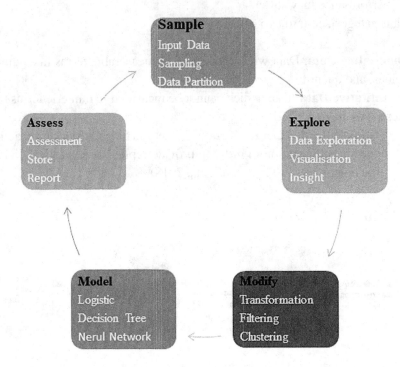

The numerous valuable to follow while gathering data are represented in Figure 1.2. The data should be error-free, with just essential points and no trash values. Keeping these considerations in mind when collecting data, a dependable model may be constructed that can assess trends and capture the subtlety of the future employing Machine Learning calculations.

- **Data Preparation:** The most demanding and time-consuming step in Machine Learning modelling is data preparation. The key explanation for this is that each dataset is unique and tailored to individual tasks. This procedure establishes a framework within which we may consider the project's data preparation responsibilities (Singh et al., 2020). This step of modelling prepares the data for training.

Figure 3. Representation of issues resolved by data preparation
(Gurumoorthy et al., 2020)

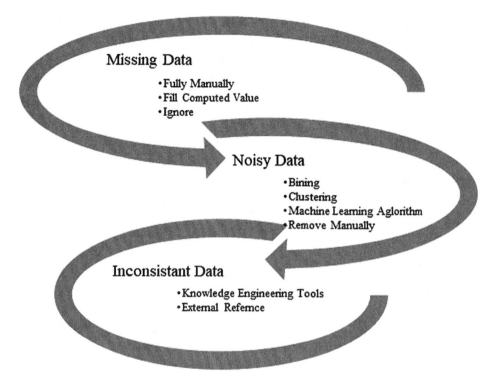

The data preparation process can be complicated by issues such as follows (Verma & Sharma, 2018):

- **Missing records:** With each record, obtaining all datasets is not possible. NULL or N/A have been used to represent missing values, but also empty cells or special characters. "?" as a character
- **Outliers:** Whenever analyzing a dataset, unexpected values may surface. This could have been due to a spelling error or an untrustworthy dataset source.
- **Incorrectly prepared data:** Data is sometimes required in a variety of formats or locations. It is recommended that domain specialists be consulted in order to resolve this issue.
- **Inconsistent values:** When data is acquired from lots of sources and then incorporated into a single dataset, the values of a given variable can change.
  - ○ **Model Training:** Data is ready for analysis once it has been acquired and packaged. The primary goal for preparing is to assure that the training is as successful as possible. The different classifiers used for training

in our proposed work are depicted in **Figure 1.4**. First and essential, we divided the dataset into two columns for training: a training set and a testing set. Often splitting is done in a 70–30 ratio. 70 percent of the data is allocated to the training set, although 30% is made available to the testing set. Although these splitting ratios are not fixed, they can be focused on meeting immediate requirements.

Figure 4. Different classifiers
(Bird et al., 2019).

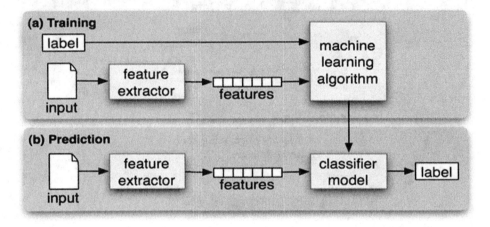

MACHINE LEARNING METHODS

K - Nearest Neighbor Algorithm

KNN is one of the most collaborative learning algorithms and one of the simplest classification methods. The supervised learning family of algorithms includes kNN. Informally, this means that we are given a labelled dataset with training observations (x, y) and would like to capture the relationship between x and y. More formally, our goal is to learn a function h: X implies to Y so that h(x) can confidently predict the corresponding output y given an unseen observation x (Singh et al., 2019).

Figure 5. KNN algorithm
(Ali, 2018)

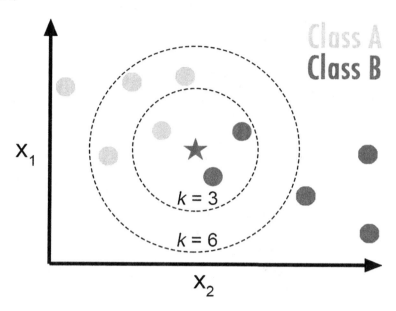

Let us both explain relatively soon in this example again using the visual. There's many 2 types according to the above figure. Which according to this diagram, Class A appeals to the yellow family, while Class B belongs to the purple family. Then train the dataset in a kNN model, with k=3 representing three nearest neighbours and k=6 representing six nearest neighbours. So, what happens when we use k=3 and what happens when we use k=6? When k=3, two people belong to the purple class and one to the yellow class, thus the purple class gets the majority vote. When k=6, four people belong to the yellow class and two to the purple class, so the purple class gets the weighted average.

The KNN approach is used to solve relapse and evaluation problems. The available state and subsequent orders of comparable measurements are frequently stored as K (K = separation work) in this KNN technology. The clear cut worth can be estimated using the Euclidean, Hamming, Murkowski, and Manhattan separations. Using the KNN demarcation estimation function, we can group information points.

How k-Nearest Neighbor Algorithm Works?

The k-Nearest neighbour approach essentially boils down to creating a majority vote between the k most comparable cases to a given 'unseen' observation in the categorization context. A distance measure between two data points is used to define similarity. A Euclidean distance is a frequent option. We utilize the Euclidean distance formula frequently, especially when calculating distance in the plane (Sultana et al., 2019). The distance between two points in the plane with coordinates (x, y) and (a, b) is determined by the Euclidean distance formula.

$$Dist\left(\left(x,y\right),\left(a,b\right)\right) = \sqrt{\left(x-a\right)^2 + \left(y-b\right)^2}$$

Given a positive integer k, an unknown observation x, and a similarity measure d, the kNN Classifier executes the two steps below.

1. It computes d between x and each training observation over the entire dataset. We'll refer to the set A as k points in the training dataset. Keep in mind that k is generally strange to avoid a predicament.
2. The conditional probability for each class is calculated as the fraction of points in A with the given class label.

Features of KNN

- The points in an n-dimensional Euclidean space correspond to all instances of the data.
- Classification is postponed until a new instance comes.
- In KNN, classification is accomplished by comparing feature vectors of various points in a space region.
- The target function could be discrete or continuous.

In KNN, n-dimensional integer descriptors are often used to describe the training samples. An n-dimensional space is used to store the training samples. When given a test sample (unknown class label), the k-nearest neighbour classifier stares longingly for the 'k' training samples that are closest to the unknown sample or test sample. The Euclidean distance has been used to define proximity. The following equation defines the Euclidean distance between any two points P and Q, i.e. P (p1,p2,.... Pn) and Q (q1, q2,.... Qn).

$$d\left(P,Q\right) = \sum_{i=1}^{n}\left(P_i - Q_i\right)^2$$

KNN Algorithm

```
• STEP 1. #Calculate D(X, Xi)
'D' - Euclidean distance between every data points.
• STEP 2. #Sort Distances "D"
In ascending order.
• STEP 3. #Figure out K points
For respective k Euclidean distances.
• STEP 4. #Calculate Ki
Data points belonging to the ith class.
• STEP 5. If Ki > Kj (where i not equal to j)
Append X in class i
```

SUPPORT VECTOR MACHINE

In comparing the positon toward other accessible categorization technique, SVM have a different methods of administration. The SVM strategy is normally praised for its incredible ability to deal with multitude of the variables. In SVM, each piece of information is viewed as a point in space. New data is first mapped to space when it comes. The classification of new system is determined by illustrating where the new data point will fall on the separating gap. The classification gap can be thought as a hyperplane in binary classification. If there are more than two classes, it can be considered as a representation of a hyperplane set in many dimensions. The Model's groping and regression are performed utilizing SVM. The feature of SVM is depicted in figure 1.6.

Figure 6. KNN algorithm
(Vidvan)

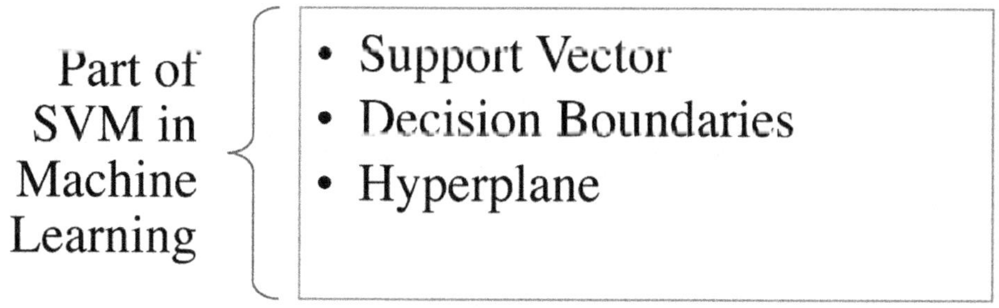

Part of SVM in Machine Learning

- Support Vector
- Decision Boundaries
- Hyperplane

SVM Algorithm

- STEP 1. #Import_packages
Import Pandas package.
- STEP 2. #Import_dataset
Dataset imported using read.csv() command.
- STEP 3. #Spliting_dataset
Differentiating dataset into training and testing using sklearn.
- STEP 4. #Import_SVM_classifier
Import SVM classifier from predefined library sklearn.
- STEP 5. #Model_fitting
Fit SVM model by utilizing svc() function.
- STEP 6. #Predict
Call predict() using SVM algorithm.

System Implementation

The objective of this study is to establish a predictor model that could still respond to user inputs such as plasma glucose concentration, blood pressure, skinfold thickness, serum insulin, BMI, and age to determine whether or not a person has diabetes. The dataset was retrieved from Open sources and furnished by the Pima Indians Diabetes Database for user evaluation.

Figure 7. System implementation
(Magudeeswaran & Suganyadevi, 2013)

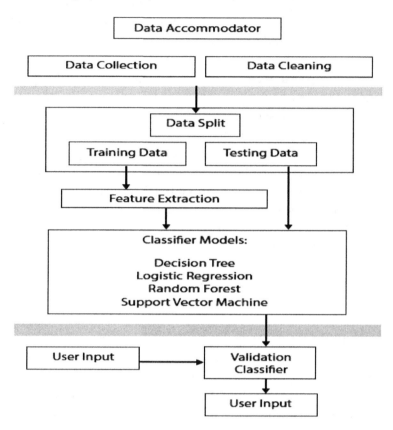

Data warehousing would be the first stage of the system. The dataset is gathered at this round. Medical predictor factors and measurement items, i.e. result, are the two main features of the dataset.

The number of pregnancies a patient has had, their BMI, their plasma concentration, their age, and some other predictor variables are illustrations.

These predictors were gathered from reliable sources. The label attribute comprises the labels that indicate whether or not a person has diabetes (Sharma et al., 2018). This label is critical in understanding if the user has diabetes or not, based on the diagnosis data in the dataset. The goal variable is designated as in this model, that both deals with training and testing.

0: Absence of Diabetes
1: Presence of Diabetes

The data preparation procedure guaranteed that neither of the attributes in the dataset had any null values. There are no null values in the dataset. Furthermore, data preparation methods are performed to increase the dataset's quality and the performance of the classifiers by presenting the dataset in a format that the classifiers can understand.

Medical predictor factors and the target variable, which is the outcome. As indicated in the diagram, the dataset comprises nine columns. The label attribute is used to store binary values, such as 0 or 1.

The dataset is ready to be delivered to the various classifiers once it has been divided into training and testing halves. For our study, we used unique classifiers such as the Random Forest classifier, SVM classifiers, and Decision Tree classifier. After all of the classifiers' models have been fitted, the confusion matrix for all of them is compared (Mahajan et al., 2020). Models are evaluated using the "Accuracy" metric. The ratio of correct record estimations to the total number of records in the dataset is known as accuracy.

CONCLUSION

Diabetes is a horrific disease that produces a signal dangerous complications in the body. As a result, it is critical to detect as soon as conceivable. How Diabetes is precisely predicted using cutting-edge Machine Learning. worthy of investigation Diabetes has a relationship with mental health since it affects the blood circulation. Nervous tissue Machine Learning techniques are discussed in this paper. The use of particular diagnostic measurements to detect diabetes is preferred. For We used Machine Learning methods in this study. The suggested The book presents an error-free, precise, and reliable prediction model for trying to assess but whether or not the citizen has diabetes.

Python is the technology used for problem formulation, and Jupyter Notebook is the tool. We apparently started our task on our prediction model with data accommodation, which includes data collecting and preparation. Model fitting followed, which included dataset segmentation and model training. Finally, we assessed three Machine Learning techniques focusing on their precision and recall and confusion matrix. The Random Forest classifier is the best fit for our dataset in our research project.

REFERENCES

Ali, A. (2018). K-Nearest Neighbor with Practical Implementation. *Medium*. Retrieved from https://medium.com/machine-learning-researcher/k-nearest-neighbors-in-machine-learning-e794014abd2a

Bird, S., Klein, E., & Loper, E. (2019). Learning to Classify Text. Natural Language Processing with Python. *NLTK*. Retrieved from https://www.nltk.org/book/ch06.html

Çalişir, D., & Doğantekin, E. (2011). An automatic diabetes diagnosis system based on LDA-wavelet support vector machine classifier. *Expert Systems with Applications*, *38*(7), 8311–8315. doi:10.1016/j.eswa.2011.01.017

Chauhan, P., Sharma, N., & Sikka, G. (2021). The emergence of social media data and sentiment analysis in election prediction. *Journal of Ambient Intelligence and Humanized Computing*, *12*(2), 1–27. doi:10.100712652-020-02423-y

Georga, E. I. I., Protopappas, V. C., Ardigo, D., Marina, M., Zavaroni, I., Polyzos, D., & Fotiadis, D. I. (2013). Multivariate prediction of subcutaneous glucose concentration in type 1 diabetes patients based on support vector regression. *IEEE Journal of Biomedical and Health Informatics*, *17*(1), 71–81. doi:10.1109/TITB.2012.2219876 PMID:23008265

Gurumoorthy, Parvezi, & Pavan. (2020). Data Preparation. *Devopedia*. Retrieved from https://devopedia.org/data-preparation

Kavakiotis, I., Tsave, O., Salifoglou, A., Maglaveras, N., Vlahavas, I., & Chouvarda, I. (2017). Machine learning and data mining methods in diabetes research. *Computational and Structural Biotechnology Journal*, *15*, 104–116. doi:10.1016/j.csbj.2016.12.005 PMID:28138367

Magudeeswaran & Suganyadevi. (2013). Forecast of Diabetes using Modified Radial basis Functional Neural Networks. *International Journal of Computer Applications*.

Mahajan, A., Rastogi, A., & Sharma, N. (2020). Annual rainfall prediction using time series forecasting. In *Soft Computing: Theories and Applications* (pp. 69–79). Springer. doi:10.1007/978-981-15-4032-5_8

Ozcift, A., & Gulten, A. (2011). Classifier ensemble construction with rotation forest to improve medical diagnosis performance of machine learning algorithms. *Computer Methods and Programs in Biomedicine*, *104*(3), 443–451. doi:10.1016/j.cmpb.2011.03.018 PMID:21531475

Polat, K., & Günes, S. (2007). An expert system approach based on principal component analysis and adaptive neuro-fuzzy inference system to diagnosis of diabetes disease. *Digital Signal Processing, 17*(4), 702–710. doi:10.1016/j.dsp.2006.09.005

Razavian, N., Blecker, S., Schmidt, A. M., Smith-McLallen, A., Nigam, S., & Sontag, D. (2015). Population-level prediction of type 2 diabetes from claims data and analysis of risk factors. *Big Data, 3*(4), 277–287. doi:10.1089/big.2015.0020 PMID:27441408

Saxena, Khan, & Singh. (2014). Classification Diagnosis of Diabetes Mellitus using K Nearest Neighbor Algorithm. *International Journal of Computer Science Trends and Technology, 2*(4).

Sharma, S., Juneja, A., & Sharma, N. (2018). Using deep convolutional neural network in computer vision for real-world scene classification. *2018 IEEE 8th International Advance Computing Conference (IACC)*, 284–289. 10.1109/IADCC.2018.8692121

Singh, B., Kumar, P., Sharma, N., & Sharma, K. P. (2020). Sales forecast for Amazon sales with time series modeling. *2020 First International Conference on Diabetes Prediction Model 155 Power, Control and Computing Technologies (ICPC2T)*, 38–43. 10.1109/ICPC2T48082.2020.9071463

Singh, N., Sharma, N., Sharma, A. K., & Juneja, A. (2019). Sentiment score analysis and topic modelling for gst implementation in India. In *Soft Computing for Problem Solving* (pp. 243–254). Springer. doi:10.1007/978-981-13-1595-4_19

Sultana, N., & Sharma, N. (2018). Statistical models for predicting swine flu incidences in India. *2018 First international conference on secure cyber computing and communication (ICSCCC)*, 134–138. 10.1109/ICSCCC.2018.8703300

SultanaN.SharmaN.SharmaK. P. (2019). Ensemble model based on NNAR and SVR for predicting influenza incidences. *Proceedings of the International Conference on Advances in Electronics, Electrical & Computational Intelligence (ICAEEC)*. https://ssrn.com/abstract=3574620

Verma, S., & Sharma, N. (2018). Statistical models for predicting chikungunya incidences in India. *2018 First International Conference on Secure Cyber Computing and Communication (ICSCCC)*, 139–142. 10.1109/ICSCCC.2018.8703218

Vidvan, T. (n.d.). *SVM in Machine Learning – An exclusive guide on SVM algorithms.* Retrieved from https://techvidvan.com/tutorials/svm-in-machine-learning/

World Health Organization. (2016). *Global report on diabetes.* Retrieved from https://apps.who.int/iris/bitstream/handle/10665/204871/9789241565257_eng.pdf;jsessionid=71FB7458A7A77906729C4A96EEC4B3F7?sequence=1

Yadav, S., & Sharma, K. P. (2018a). Statistical analysis and forecasting models for stock market. *2018 First International Conference on Secure Cyber Computing and Communication (ICSCCC)*, 117–121. 10.1109/ICSCCC.2018.8703324

Yadav, S., & Sharma, N. (2018b). Homogenous ensemble of time-series models for indian stock market. *International Conference on Big Data Analytics*, 100–114. 10.1007/978-3-030-04780-1_7

Yue, C., Xin, L., Kewen, X., & Chang, S. (2008). An intelligent diagnosis to type 2 diabetes based on QPSO algorithm and WLS-SVM. *Proceedings of the 2008 IEEE International Symposium on intelligent Information Technology Application Workshops.* 10.1109/IITA.Workshops.2008.36

Zubchenko, A. (2021). Data collection for machine learning: The complete guide. *Waverly.* https://waverleysoftware.com/blog/data-collection-for-machine-learning-guide/

Chapter 9

Digitization and Digital Preservation of the Heritage Sites of Uttarakhand Using Machine Learning and Innovative Techniques

Sunil Kumar
Kumaun University, Nainital, India

Ashutosh Kumar Bhatt
Uttarakhand Open University, Haldwani, India

Rahul Kumar Mishra
IFTM University, Moradabad, India

ABSTRACT

History should be preserved so that it can be made available for future generations. Thus arises the need for digitization of cultural heritage. The present chapter discusses digitization of cultural heritage of the temples of the state of Uttarakhand, the one which fall in the Kumaon region of North India. Preserving such heritage with the help of digital technology is a fast-emerging trend in the current century. Digital technologies support the recording, analysis, and management of cultural heritage around the world. The chapter brings forth the multiple ways in which it is done and how the same has helped in the preservation, interpretation, and appreciation of the rich cultural heritage. Undoubtedly, they facilitate accessibility and improve understanding of these sites. At the same time, there are fears too in some quarters that digital technologies undermine the need to conserve the "real thing." The chapter proposes various methods and processes to preserve temples, an important component of cultural heritage.

DOI: 10.4018/978-1-6684-2443-8.ch009

1. INTRODUCTION

Culture encompasses life values, customs, ethics, beliefs, arts, games, songs, music, dance etc. of a particular set of people living in a geographical region. Our beliefs, our talks and our behaviour all reflect our culture. Taylor (1871) has defined culture as "knowledge, belief, art, morals, law, custom and other capabilities and habits acquired by man as a member of society". Cultural Heritage is a human creation intended to inform. It is an expression of the ways of living developed by a community and passed on from generation to generation, including customs, practices, places, objects, artistic expressions and values.

Heritage, on the other hand, refers to a period of time during which comparisons of how people used to live are made. The same can also be learnt by going to museums, archives and libraries. Cultural heritage can be preserved with history becoming a witness to it. The IT revolution has made this preservation easy, interesting and long-lasting.

Visiting heritage sites have always been popular with students, researchers and travellers. Notwithstanding a physical presence in such sites does lead to feeling of historical awe, on the flip side, it entails on the part of the onlooker. Also, some of the overenthusiastic people are also not averse to defacing the sites they visit, by unsuccessfully trying to add to the history of the place.

However, now in the tech driven world of the 21st century, a transformation is being seen as with regard to our attitude towards cultural heritage. Depending on how much technology has advanced in a nation, experiencing cultural heritage can give different experiences to different people. It is the digital media in its various forms which is shaping people's experiences now. It is all the truer for today's youngsters who are more than happy to have a 'digital surrogate' experience of this world.

As the world wide web becomes lightning fast, the 'digital' is replacing the 'physical' even in the case of heritage sites. The graphical user interface of technical devices is increasingly replacing the face-to-face interaction with other visitors and staff of heritage sites. Action has definitely shifted to the digital domain with on-line discussion forums, sharing of photos, videos and opinions via social networks and even something like computer gaming. While social networking tools like blogs, podcasts, RSS feeds, Flickr, YouTube give individuals the opportunity to make their experiences public, online games with heritage themes, digital collections, and interactive kiosk applications in exhibitions, all offer new possibilities for heritage organizations to interact with their visitors.

This use of the digital platform can also be termed as an effort at democratization by heritage institutions. It allows them wider reach and also opens them for more brickbats and bouquets. However, as we initiate efforts for transcending heritage to the digital world, we also need to search for answers to many questions. But where do we stand in this two-way use of the digital medium vis-à-vis heritage sites is a moot point? What are the features of this new way of communication? What is the profile of these virtual visitors? Who should control and moderate this communication, if at all they happen to take place? Should there be curators in this free and democratic exchange of information?

The rich cultural heritage of India is the consequence of India being one of the most ancient cultural civilizations. The heritage resources exits are both tangible and intangible forms. If one talks about manuscripts, it turns out that India is the largest repository of manuscripts ranging from religion to astrology, astronomy, mathematics and ancient medicines. Over 4,00,000 Indian ancient manuscripts have been digitized and stored in DVDs/File Savers by Indira Gandhi National Centre for Arts and National Mission for Manuscripts (NMM) nmm.gov.in. However, lack of a comprehensive digital preservation policy coupled with not much thought given to dissemination of information on digitization measures, accessibility to these is not as widespread as it should have been. Preservation of valuable ancient resources needs to be given top priority, otherwise the large amount available in various archives and museums in India is likely to be endangered. Moreover, the very concept of digital preservation has seen an inordinate entry, coming into force in the year 2008 with the launch of National Digital Preservation Programme (NDPP), but the programme has been implemented in fits and starts. These are some issues and challenges which must be overcome. A collaborative approach is the need of the hour.

Uttarakhand- 'Land of the Gods'-: The state of Uttarakhand happens to be a place where it is said that temples meet travellers in every 500 km distance. It is the land of sages and saints. The landscape is dotted with temples devoted to various Gods and Goddesses, but at the same time there are also some famous shrines like Narayankoti temple, Chota Char Dham, Panch Kedar, Panch Prayag, Panch Badri, Shakti Peeth and Siddha Peeth which greatly contribute to religious/pilgrimage tourism of the state.

There are temples devoted to Maa Durga, the (fire) form of Lord Shiva. Chandika, representing Kali in her most dreadful forms has nine temples in Garhwal and two in Kumaon. Sitala, the 'Goddess of Small Pox' has temples dedicated to her in Almora, Srinagar, Jageshwar and other places.

The top 8 historical temples with amazing architecture are Kedarnath, Tungnath, Baleshwar (Gi. 2), Katarmal(Fig. 5), Mahasu Devta Temple, Lakhamandal, Triyuginarayan and Baijnath (Fig. 1). (https://www.euttaranchal.com/tourism/temples-with-best-architecture-in-uttarakhand.php). Thus, the place has always generated a lot of interest among historians and archaeologists.

The research article examines 'applications' included under the term 'Digital Heritage.' It is the current digital heritage practices which the research article seeks to explore. The term 'applications' encompass all types of digital technology applied to the cultural heritage field, while 'apps' refer to programs designed to run on a smartphone or tablet.

The important feature of digital technologies is its are cost effectivity. The "Quebec Declaration" passed in the 17th ICOMOS General Assembly also recommends their use with constant up-dation of documentation leading to the preserving the spirit of those places where such heritage sites are located. The Declaration also mentions the need for research and training to understand the use of the technology better.

Digitisation and digital preservation are different processes that require diverse methods to be followed for the preservation.

Figure 1. Baijnath Temple

Figure 2. Baleshwar Mahadev, Champawat

Figure 3. Jageshwar Dham, Almora

Figure 4. Kot Bhramari Temple, Kausani

Figure 5. Katarmal Sun Temple, Almora

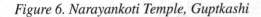

Figure 6. Narayankoti Temple, Guptkashi

2. BACKGROUND

Digitization and application technology of cultural heritage assets are discussed as follows,

2.1 Virtual and Augmented Reality

Virtual Reality (VR) has been used in the cultural heritage field to describe a variety of applications usually related with highly visual, immersive, 3D environments. The use of VR applications in cultural heritage leads to creation of experiences, trying to give the users the feeling of being there.

At the same time some critics also think that virtual reality with human-computer interaction lets users browse the information needed than promote the preservation of cultural assets.

According to (Burdea & Coiffet, 2003) there are four elements which are required to compose VR. First and foremost, they have to have an immersive experience and they call it the Immersion component. The feedback of human-computer interaction comes next, which makes it (Interaction) the second component. Solving specific problems with developer's ideas results in the third component termed as Imagination. Finally, the versability of V R fulfils the requirements of everyone, whether the student community or researchers, giving the users Insight, the fourth component.

In the case of Augmented Reality (AR), rather than immersing the user in a whole simulated world (as is usually the case with virtual reality), it superimposes and adds simulated elements to existing aspects of the physical world. These digital supplementary elements can take various forms such as sound, video, graphics, or data related to geographical positioning, often combined to enhance users' perception of their surrounding reality. AR, as the name suggests, gives a closer feel of the real and hence can be called an extension of the VR. The latest technology processes and equipment used bring the virtual world closer to the real. The theory of "Reality–Virtuality Continuum", propounded by Paul Milgram and Fumio Kishino, talks about the mixed reality of the real and virtual environments. AR Technology, proposed by Vassilios in 2001, restores the health of damaged heritage. The role played by AR enables the tourists to see the original appearance of the Temple of Hera through the mobile devices.

2.2 Mobile Applications

The ability of cell/mobile phones to be used in conditions and in an environment of the users' choice opens up new possibilities for the communication as well as learning of cultural content of heritage sites. Also, it brings the heritage organizations and their users closer, leading to a win-win situation for both.

2.3 Geographic Information Systems and 3D Modelling

To record and store information about heritage sites, countries are increasingly restoring to Geographic Information Systems (GISs) and 3D modelling. Even the complex socio-economic data becomes easy to interpret as its location gets recorded in GISs. GIS also facilitates the preservation of these sites against the vagaries of climate change. GIS is also used to identify areas of archaeological interest.

To get a clear and better representation of heritage sites 3D modelling is used. It is 3D technology which brings alive these heritage sites- some of which may become decrepit, if not suitably cared for, with the passage of time. Thus, 3D visualization also indirectly helps in conservation and restoration of such monuments. 3D modelling is used to create both 'real representations' of existing objects as well as 'reconstructed versions' leading to better understanding of the site being examined. Moreover, data otherwise bland becomes palatable with 3D models used as intuitive graphical interface.

2.4 Photogrammetry

It helps in determining mathematical measurements and 3D geometric data from overlapping images.

2.5 LiDAR (Light Detection and Ranging)

In space archaeology remote sensing technology, the target is illuminated with laser to measure the distance. The reflected light is analysed to draw conclusions.

2.6 Unmanned Aerial Vehicles

Drones are also being used to document monuments and sites. Their cost effectiveness makes them the ideal aerial vehicles to cover large areas.

2.7 Machine Learning

With technology invading every sphere of our life, it follows that machine learning techniques are now at the centre of not only the preservation and enhancement of cultural heritage but also its presentation.

It is a given that machines can easily capture, analyze, interpret, and preserve the complex cultural heritage data. Damage prediction with the help of machines can forestall consequent repair work by taking timely action. Not only this, valuable cultural artifacts whether books, statues or paintings get a lease of life with the help of machines. Languages and dialects, important components of culture, get digitized, translated, accessible and promoted with the use of machine learning techniques.

Machine learning algorithm is used to recognize patterns as well as hand-written and spoken words. Moreover, machine learning gives a boost to user experience because the visitor is able to create a personal narrative trail when on a virtual tour of culture sites. Facial expressions can be decodified to reveal hidden responses of visitors.

2.8 Artificial Intelligence (AI)

The use of AI has given a whole new dimension to creativity, making music composition, novel writing and painting effortlessly easy.

2.8.1 *Virtual Visits*

The use of the virtual has obliterated the need for physical tours especially for those unable to go out. The attractive pictures of the historical sites, till now marvelled from afar by those who do not suffer from wanderlust, have been brought closer to people by Microsoft AI. Then there are teams from the French company Iconem, creating 3-D digital models of cultural landmarks from Cambodia to Syria.

The virtual makes an unforgettable immersive experience, coalescing AI with reality, like the one that pays homage to the French cultural icon Mont-Saint-Michel, off the coast of Normandy. All this is leading to a near-real interaction between the sites and the travellers.

2.8.2 *Open Access*

The Open Access Initiative launched by the Metropolitan Museum of Art in 2017 has made its vast collection open to everyone on-line. It has recently collaborated with Microsoft and the Massachusetts Institute of Technology to help take this initiative to the next level. It is using AI to explore, enrich and enable interactions of art collections with its aficionados.

2.8.3 *Language Preservation*

As urbanisation spreads, there is genuine fear of losing art and culture spanning several tribes and centuries.

With language being an important component of culture, there are efforts worldwide to preserve languages which are on the verge of becoming extinct with the speakers either shrinking in size or abandoning these while coming into contact with the modern world. Microsoft is working in this field to protect endangered languages like Yucatec Maya and Queretaro Otomi.

2.8.4 *Interpreting Expressions*

Machine learning tools are being used to unravel enigmatic expressions like the Mona Lisa smile. Thus, the importance of machines cannot be understated.

3. REVIEW OF WORK ALREADY DONE

Institutions like Indira Gandhi National Centre for the Arts (IGNCA), the National Archives of India and the National Mission for Manuscripts aim to digitise cultural heritage to widen its reach. Among these, the IGNCA perhaps has the largest collection in formats like manuscripts, microfilms, micro-fiches, negatives, photographs, audio-visuals, etc. The IGNCA, following the guidelines of UNESCO, IFLA, UNC, has made nearly 50% of its resources digitally available which has over 5,50,000 in the form of books, periodicals, manuscripts, microfilms, images, audio, and video recordings [Khan et. al., 2017; Bakshi *et. al.*, 2016]

Then there is the 'National Mission for Manuscripts (NAMAMI),' tasked with discovering and collecting the manuscripts scattered all over the country and digitise the same. It has "Manuscript Resource Centre" (MRCs) and manuscript collections across four regions of India. The digitisation of manuscripts has been undertaken to maintain several documents and total pages along with a zone-wise list of Manuscript Resource Centres (MRCs) [Sahoo *et. al.*, 2015].

The author recommends Galleries, libraires, archives and museums (GLAMs) need to explore the crowdsourcing potential in the process of digitisation especially converting contents from one form to another such as handwritten documents, transcribing text, or notation of audio and artifacts description [Singh A., 2012].

There are many other centres and institutions which are working in the field of digitization of past records. Some of these are National Library of India, Kolkata, National Archives of India, Nehru Memorial Museum and Library (NMML), Rampur Raza Library and Khuda Bakhsh Oriental Public Library, the latter on its way to becoming the country's first library to computerise its handwritten collection for universal dissemination through the Internet.

These institutions have also started the digitisation process of manuscripts and other rare collections to preserve and provide access to their users or clients. Some regional institutions started digitisation to preserve records from damage, larceny, and decay of manuscript such as Panjab University, Chandigarh has started a digitisation project to digitise manuscripts and rare literature at the Punjab level [Harpreet Kaur, 2015].

The Indian Digital Heritage (IDH) Project of the Department of Science & Technology (DST), Government of India, is another unique initiative supporting collaborative projects among researchers working in this field. Technologies employed have ranged from laser scanning, modelling and gesture based interactive displays, haptic explorations, experiential multimedia renditions and ontological explorations.

There are many institutions working in the field of preservation of culture and cultural artifacts, progressing from 2-D to 3-D images bringing out the finer intricacies which remain latent in 2-D. Some of these institutions are like the Bhubaneswar-based Centurion University. Mitra and his team, while working closely with the tribals, uses Unity Technologies' 2D-3D software. Similarly, Gram Tarang is making efforts to preserve art and culture in 3D using VR, AR and UAVs to protect art and monuments which face the risk of getting lost over time.

In India, Iconem is involved in digitisation in 3D format of the 16th-century necropolises at the Qutb Shahi Heritage Park in Hyderabad.

3.1 Need for the Study

The different heritage organisations may be adopting different strategies to recover and preserve the heritage resources, but their ends converge on eventual digitisation. The challenge for the government in power is to make new policies and take new measures not only integrating different technological programs, but also remaining in sync with rapidly changing technology of digital preservation, which means continuous up-dation of manpower, application of uniform codes for all and above all uninterrupted funding.

Therefore, uniformity in standards and protocols become an essential component of the aim of digitisation. The technical specifications need to be spelled out and made mandatory for all the players on the digital field. This will automatically ensure quality control. [Rieger, 202]. Moreover, there are round 45000 temples digital across India. Digital preservation of temples has been executed very less so far.

Imbued with religious mythology, legends and legacy, Uttarakhand is home to a number of venerated temples, holy rivers and spiritual sites. Devotees flock here for pilgrimages to Char Dham (four religious centres namely Kedarnath, Badrinath, Yamunotri and Gangotri) and to Panch Prayag, the confluence of rivers in five sites/ locations that ultimately form River Ganga, one of India's most sacred rivers and worshipped as a goddess, along with visits to several other destinations of religious importance (like Bageshwar, Joshimath, Baijnath to name a few) in the state that is also referred to as the land of pilgrims.

Most of the case studies that have been conducted related to digitization of heritage resources are institution-specific. No comparative study of the digitization process and practices followed among the heritage organizations have not been found so far. A casual investigation has revealed that in Uttarakhand, no digitization work has been done so far to preserve the cultural heritage. Therefore, it is felt that applications of standards for digitization, metadata preservation, and discovery of heritage resources need to be undertaken institutionally and collectively.

4. OBJECTIVES OF THE STUDY

1.   To review the state of the art in digitization of cultural heritage technologies and to understand the current practices of the digitization of heritage resources in India with existing available knowledge.
2.   To develop techniques for digital preservation for cultural heritage sites.

4.1 Digital Preservation

It is not only digitized, but also born digital contents which come under this preservation process so that the same can be accessed any time in future. However, technology getting outdated, impermanency of current storage media, information surplus and internet revolution have made the preservation of digital information not an easy task and this despite the fact that digital preservation involves systematic guidelines, processes, strategies, technology and approaches.

The importance of digital preservation cannot be overstated. After all materials whether in print form or non-print form have a limited life. Here digital preservation comes into the picture. There are options like microfilm and digitization, but it is generally seen that libraries are going for complete digitization, so that they have a wider reach. Simultaneous sharing among multiple users and remote access to digitized resources are some of the advantages which are the driving force behind digitization.

4.2 Digital Preservation Methods

Digital data can be preserved in three principal ways. The method most commonly used is migration which is the transfer of digital data from one storage to another. Then comes emulation which is preserving data in its present form and state in which a computer environment is created. Different computer systems act in similar pattern and digital information resources are originated by emulation. Thirdly, the markup languages method in which the mark up languages tags like text, graphics, audios and videos to define elements within digital documents.

5. PROCEDURE/METHODOLOGY

The cultural heritage should be digitally preserved in this era of technology. The following are necessary in the process of digitization.

1. Capturing the image of temples using drone camera for 360^0 views.
2. Record narration of chief priest's traditional knowledge and their beliefs of temples about glory of legacy to encourage cultural heritage.
3. Shooting videos and capturing photographs of temples.
4. Digitization of literature about the temples provided by the temple's authorities.
5. 3D laser scanning to perform the digitalized archives for the interior and exterior body work of the temple which contains integration of 3D scanner technology.

6. These 3D models can then be used as an aid to physical reconstruction. Visual inspections are carried out on screen to look for defects, wear and tear and for structural analysis. This technology called Augmented technology will be also be used to present the object to the public for educational purposes.
7. Development of digital content in videos laboratory will be done.
8. Development of portal, YouTube videos, uploading, cloud management etc.
9. Development of virtual tour guides using machine leaning technique.
10. Development of images depicting the rear and the front view of the temples using classification and clustering techniques.
11. Prediction of the functional service life of heritage buildings like temples using machine learning techniques.
12. Restoration of Ancient Text inscribed on temples building using deep learning.
13. Development of heritage site tour recommender system using machine learning technique.
    xiv Completion of missing or broken object image like statue, monument using machine learning.

6. CONCLUSION AND FUTURE SCOPE

Protecting cultural heritage is of prime concern and can pass on customs, practices, places, objects, artistic expressions and values from generation to generation. By digital preservation of temples of the Kumaun region of Uttarakhand, we can make possible darshan/virtual tour/virtual guide of temples. This is fruitful for the tourism industry. Revenue can be generated by getting advertisements on website. Social traditions/festivals/melas associated with temples information/knowledge shall spread among the society. YouTube channels viewership can be increased. This can be extended to the Garhwal region of Uttarakhand Temples after successful implementation of these digital techniques. Finally, this will help to save our environment, because organizing virtual tour will surely reduce the crowd in the precious heritage sites.

REFERENCES

Bakhshi, S. I. (2016). Digitization and digital preservation of cultural heritage in India with special reference to IGNCA, New Delhi. *Asian J. Inf. Sci. Technol, 6*(2), 1–7.

Borghoff, U. M., Rödig, P., Schmitz, L., & Scheffczyk, J. (2006). *Long-term preservation of digital documents: Principles and practices.* Springer.

Burdea, G. C., & Coiffet, P. (2003). *Virtual reality technology* (2nd ed.). John Wiley & Sons, Inc. doi:10.1162/105474603322955950

Gaur, R., & Chakraborty, M. (2009). Preservation and access to Indian manuscripts: A knowledge base of Indian cultural heritage resources for academic libraries. ICAL 2009 – Vision and Roles of the Future Academic Libraries, 90-98.

Kaur, H. (2015). Digital preservation of manuscripts: An Indian perspective with special reference to Punjab. *Proc. 4th International Symposium on Emerging Trends and Technologies in Libraries and Information Services (ETTLIS)*, 271-274. 10.1109/ETTLIS.2015.7048210

Khan & Ali. (2017, Jan.). Digital preservation of manuscripts: Initiative in India. *J. Indian Libr. Assoc.*, 25-30.

Khuda Bakhsh Oriental Public Library. (n.d.). http://kblibrary. bih.nic.in/

Quebec Declaration. (2015). https://www.international.icomos.org/quebec2008/quebec_declaration/pdf/GA16_Quebec_Declaration_Final_EN.pdf

Rieger, O. Y. (n.d.). *Preservation in the age of large-scale digitization: A white paper*. https://www.clir.org/pubs/ reports/pub141/

Sahoo, J., & Mohanty, B. (2015). Digitization of Indian manuscripts heritage: Role of the National Mission for Manuscripts. *Int. Fed. Libr. Assoc. Inst.*, *41*(3), 237–250. doi:10.1177/0340035215601447

Singh, A. (2012). Digital preservation of cultural heritage resources and manuscripts: An Indian Government initiative. *Int Fed. Libr. Assoc. Inst.*, *38*(4), 289–296. doi:10.1177/0340035212463139

Taylor, E. B. (1871). *Primitive Culture*. John Murray.

Chapter 10

Machine Learning Techniques to Diagnose and Treat Cancer Disease

Mercedes Barrachina

https://orcid.org/0000-0003-4718-4495
Universidad Politécnica de Madrid, Spain

Laura Valenzuela
Universidad Politécnica de Madrid, Spain

ABSTRACT

Cancer is one of the most common diseases nowadays, and it is a very heterogeneous disease that consists of several different subtypes. According to data from the World Health Organization (WHO), this disease caused death to approximately 10 million people during 2020, and in the same period, 19.3 million new cases were identified. Breast cancer is the most common cancer diagnosed for women, and lung cancer is the most detected cancer in men. Artificial intelligence has many different applications, and specifically, machine learning techniques are used for detecting and treating cancer. The methods associated with machine learning are computer algorithms that are considering different types of logic, and therefore, those types can be classified into supervised, unsupervised, reinforcement learning, self-supervised learning, active learning, etc. The main purpose of this work is to review and evaluate the different techniques associated to machine learning used by medical professionals but also by researchers with the main objectives of detecting and treating cancer.

DOI: 10.4018/978-1-6684-2443-8.ch010

1. INTRODUCTION

Several fields suffered from dramatic changes in the last years, but for Medicine and Healthcare, the evolution of the technology has been completely revolutionary. In the last 40 years, many innovative research were performed, the reason for several diseases were unveiled, different innovative diagnostic methods were designed or new drugs and medicines were created.

Cancer is one the leading death causes in the developed world and there are still a lot of shades in the origin of the disease, the factor that influence in the tumor creation and the different treatments. The ideal situation would be to use technology to beat cancer and avoid its appearance, but meanwhile this is achieved, there are different techniques applied to try to diagnose cancer as soon as possible and to characterize it, to achieve a better reaction to drugs, medicines and treatments.

Machine learning is already applied in several different fields such as the banking sector to predict the evolution of the interest rates, in the supply chain sector, to try to discover patterns based on real-time and historic delivery records with the purpose of optimizing the logistics in a company or in the creation of Smart Cities, by trying to create the most efficient route to drive by avoiding traffic jams.

This chapter will review the utilization of machine learning techniques for diagnosing and treating cancer. The most known algorithms will be detailed and the best results found in the literature will be shown to identify the most novel techniques to fight cancer disease.

Overall, the work has been organized as follows. First, literature review supporting the research provided. Then, the research methodology and data collection have been highlighted along with the main results of this study, together with the discussion. Finally, conclusions, as well as limitations and future lines of research have been proposed.

2. BACKGROUND

Cancer is a very heterogeneous disease and consists of several different subtypes and is one of the most challenging barrier to increase life expectancy (Bray et al. 2021). Cancer is a disease that starts with a transformation from normal cells to tumor cells and those continue growing to a pre-cancerous lesion and potentially into a malignant tumor. That critical transformation can be caused by 2 different categories of agents: genetic factors and external agents. Those external agents can be classified are physical carcinogens (for example, ionizing or ultraviolet radiation), chemical carcinogens (for example, tobacco smoke, food contaminants or drinking water contaminant) and biological carcinogens (for example, baterias, viruses or parasites) (WHO, 2021).

In the last 20 years, the cancer research has been in constant evolution and the scientific interest in the disease has increased exponentially (Hanahan & Weinberg, 2011).

According to information from the World Health Organization (WHO, 2021), cancer was the leading cause of death in 2020, causing around 10 million deaths in the mentioned year. In 2020, occurred a around 19.3 million in terms of new cases of cancer. The most common types are: breast, lung, colon and rectum, prostate, skin and stomach.

Cancer's early detection is critical for decreasing mortality and this activity has two important approaches:

1. Early diagnosis: It is key to diagnose cancer in an early phase to facilitate the treatment response and therefore, having a greater probability of survival. This includes also applying a less expensive treatment. The early diagnosis has 3 different components:
    a. Being concerned about the symptoms of the different cancer types so the individual can identify if a visit to the specialist is needed.
    b. Having access good clinical services that could diagnose the disease
    c. Treatment referral when it is needed.
2. Screening: The screening activity is crucial to identify different cancer types in an early phase. The screening programs are mainly based on the age and the risk factors, and aim to identify individuals with findings that could be indicating a potential tumor in a cheap and easy way, even before the patient develop symptoms. Once those individuals have been identified, then, more tests and exams are developed to confirm or reject the cancer diagnosis.

It is important to highlight that up to 50% of the detected cancers (WHO, 2021) can be prevented by performing some activities, but mainly by avoiding the main risk factors and developing strategies with prevention purposes.

Machine Learning techniques are the key tool to identify patterns in the data, to analyze the relationship between the different variables and to be able to predict the outcome of the cancer type. One of the most interesting activity for doctors is having the possibility of predicting with accuracy if patient is having cancer or if he/she is going to suffer it in the future.

The input for the machine learning techniques to diagnose or treat cancer are based on biosignals and biomedical images. The most utilized biosignals in medical applications are the polysomnogram (PSG), electrocardiogram (ECG), the electroencephalography (EEG), the photoplethysmogram (PPG), the electromyogram

(EMG), the electro-oculogram (EOG), the electrodermal signal (EDA), the Heart rate Variability (HRV), and the blood pressure (BP). In relation to the biomedical images, the most utilized images are the magnetic Resonance Imaging (MRI), radiography image (RX) and the Positron emission tomography (PET) scans.

There are several applications utilizing machine learning techniques for understanding genomics (mainly based on DNA classification), social networking analysis, speech recognitions, computational finance, traffic forecasting (Das et al, 2015). Related to medical purposes, machine learning applications are already being used for dealing different diseases, such with Parkinson disease (Barrachina-Fernández et al. 2021), for diagnosing Alzheimer (Tanveer et al. 2020) or breast cancer (Houfani et al. 2020).

The main objective of the study is to review and evaluate the different machine learning techniques utilized by researchers and medical professionals to diagnose and treat cancer. Those techniques could be using different input elements, such as image, biosignals…etc. This chapter will be focused on trying to provide an answer to the following questions: Which are the most common and reliable machine learning techniques to diagnose cancer? Which are the most common challenges for doctors when using these machine learning techniques? Is there a specific cancer type that is already been treated massively using machine learning techniques?

3. MAIN FOCUS OF THE CHAPTER

3.1 Relation Between Telemedicine and Cancer Disease Detection

The telemedicine industry is growing exponentially and the growth prevision was around 53$ billion by 2026, before the pandemic lockdown (Smith, 2020). With the coronavirus lockdown, the situation change dramatically and the adoption of the telemedicine was developed in many countries to avoid the direct contact between the doctors and the patients and, except in mandatory cases, prevent the COVID-19 expansion. This event showed the great power of telemedicine for detecting and treating diseases, especially in developed countries.

Telemedicine can be seen as a resource to enhance the services offered to the patients, with the main purpose of improving their life's quality. Telemedicine can provide access to medical care, give access to personalized treatments and also enrich the service and the experience offered to the patient. Telemedicine relies on technology and there are many elements participating in this service: such as sensor designing and implementation, workflow implementation, protocols configuration, interaction between the doctor and the patient using different resources, protection of the personal data to comply with the existing regulations....etc.

Different medical areas have already implemented different services using telemedicine. To name a few, sleep disorders are already diagnosed and treated using telemedicine services (Barrachina & Valenzuela, 2021), as well as Alzheimer patients (Costanzo et al. 2020), or dementia affected individuals (Yi et al. 2021)

Oncology is a medical area in which telemedicine can support in many different ways. Some specific examples of successful telemedicine applications related to cancer are cancer telegenetics, palliative care provided to patients with special medical conditions, symptom management, management and evaluation to access to clinical trials, cancer-related tele applications, remote supervision of the chemotherapy (Sirintrapun & Lopez, 2018).

In general, there are different benefits when applying telemedicine applications to a specific disease, considering different perspective. Figure 1 details the perspective for the 3 main agents in the medical system: the patient, the provide and the health system.

Figure 1. General benefits telehealth.
Source: own elaboration based on (Singh and Keer, 2020)

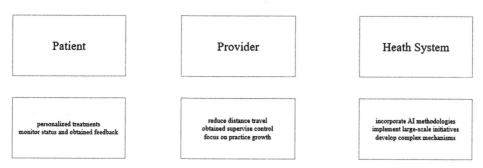

Patient Approach

The usage of telemedicine provides to the patient the possibility of arranging the visits depending on his/her availability. Telemedicine also will lower the barriers to access to care and will offer monitoring services when needed. Personalized treatments will also offered as having data about the patient and powerful technology behind are great resources to be able to create patient-oriented treatments.

Provider Approach

The usage of telehealth will provide different benefits to the provider of the service, like for example minimize the distance travel, customize the applications to adapt them to the practice needs, increment the capacity to review the results of the patients and the status of the critical ones. Moreover, the technology linked to telehealth also provides great opportunity to develop a more mature practice and support its growth.

Health Care System Approach

The utilization of services related to the health to the different medical areas usually apply different technologies advances such as Artificial Intelligence and provides resources to implement large-scale initiatives with also complex mechanisms.

3.2 Machine Learning Advantages in Cancer Disease Management

Machine learning (ML) is a discipline of artificial intelligence that is capable of making predictions about data sets through the search for patterns in them.

Among its main advantages are the flexibility and scalability it provides compared to traditional biostatistical methods. Also the ability to analyze many different types of data, such as medical images, electrophysiological measurements, demographic data, etc. (Ngiam and Khor 2019).

This makes its use possible and very useful in the field of medicine, especially in the diagnosis of diseases, prognosis, treatments, etc.

Within the area of cancer, ML makes it possible to predict the state and evolution of the disease, in many cases before it appears. In addition, exhaustive analysis of different data sets through ML techniques can also provide information on more aspects of vital importance in this disease that help to know the prognosis and the survival rate.

In cancer research, ML is very important as it contributes to a better understanding of cancer progression. This would lead to the development of better patient survival models allowing, for example, to modify the treatment and find the most appropriate for each of the patients (Kourou et al. 2015; El Naqa and Murphy 2015).

In addition to the data commonly used in the prediction of diseases, in the case of cancer, microarray technologies have recently been used to collect thousands of data on the level of gene expression of cancer cells, which can also be analyzed by ML techniques. Using genomic data with ML techniques can allow a more accurate knowledge of the survival prediction, provide appropriate and individualized treatments to patients, and improve the prognosis of cancers (Bashiri et al. 2017).

For example, thanks to ML techniques, it is possible to detect molecular alterations that make it possible to distinguish malignant tumors from benign tumors in women with suspected premenopausal breast cancer. These women have much higher survival rates after cancer is detected, so early detection is key to its evolution (Fröhlich et al. 2018).

In addition, it can help in the prediction of results, which would allow modifying the treatment and finding the most appropriate for each patient.

In the specific case of cancer treatments with radiotherapy, the use of ML is able to help in the control of radiation physics quality, contouring and personalized treatment planning, and can also help in image-guided radiotherapy (El Naqa and Murphy 2015).

3.3 Cancer Types

There are different types of cancer and the most common information for each type is detailed below (Stanford, 2021):

- Carcinoma: this is related to the cancer initiated in the organs, glands or even in the body structures. The carcinomas are linked to 80-905 of all the cancer cases detected. Some of those carcinoma's types includes the melanoma, the Merkel cell carcinoma or the basal cell carcinoma.
- Sarcoma: this is a malignant tumor that grows in the connective tissues (for example, cartilage, fat, muscle, bones or even the tendons). The most typical sarcoma is related to the bones (osteosarcoma) that usually appears in young people or the cartilage (chondrosarcoma).
- Lymphoma: this is related to a malignant tumor that appears in the nodes or in the glands of the lymphatic system. It is interesting to highlight that the lymphatic system manage the production of white blood cells and clean body fluids. The lymphomas are categorized into two different types: Hodgkin's lymphoma and non-Hodgkin's lymphoma.
- Leukemia: this type of cancer is also known as "blood cancer" and stop the normal production of the blood elements, such as the red and white cells and also the platelets. Some examples of this types are the acute myelogenous leukemia, chronic myelogenous leukemia or the chronic lymphocytic leukemia.
- Myeloma: this type of cancer grows in the plasma cells of the bone marrow. There are two types of myeloma, depending on the tumors created. If the myeloma cells compose a single tumor, then it is called plasmacytoma, and if those cells form several tumor, then it is called multiple myeloma.

3.4 Evaluation of the Methods to Detect Cancer

The application of algorithms to detect cancer has been in use for nearly 35 years (Simes 1985; Ciccheti, 1992). When evaluating the methods that can be applied to fight cancer, there are two different strategies. First of all, the proactive approach, which is focused on diagnosis and detection and the detective approach, which is based on prediction (cancer susceptibility or cancer recurrence). Below it is possible to find more information about them:

- Proactive approach: the methods applied are focused on identifying and detecting the existing disease before it is in an advance stage and can be less aggressively treated and obtained a better long-term prognosis.
- Detective approach: the techniques are employed with the purpose of identifying the disease in any of its forms and stages. Usually, the detected patterns are related to a cancer evolution in a higher stage.

There are many techniques utilized nowadays to detect and diagnose cancer. Some of the most knows techniques are: mammography, digital mammography, ultrasound, computed tomography, magnetic resonance imaging, the magnetic resonance spectroscopy or the positron emission tomography (Kumar & Pawaiya, 2010). There are other more novel techniques such as the hybridization, the flow cytometry or the microarray technology, for example.

Cancer is diagnosed based on different parameters, mainly based on clinical symptoms, imaging, cytologic and histopathological techniques, tumor markers, serological methods or immunohistochemistry (Kumar & Pawaiva, 2010). Below is it possible to find a diagram (figure 2) of the most relevant diagnosis methods:

Figure 2. Diagnosis methods for cancer.
Source: own elaboration

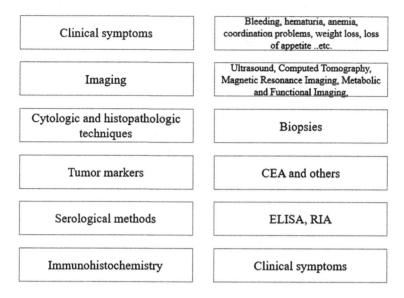

There are different clinical symptoms for the cancer disease. Depending on the type of cancer, the symptoms can be very different. Some of them are: hematuria, bleeding, anemia, coordination problems...etc. Most of those symptoms needs specific tests to evaluate the diagnosis. Some of the tests are laboratory screening tests, CT scan, X.rays..etc.

Related to the imaging, this is one of the most common technique to suspect about the malignancy of a tumor. There are different types of images:

- Ultrasound: this technique is focused on utilizing high frequency sound waves. Those waves are mainly reflected by the different tissues and then, an image is produced. It is very popular when evaluating lesions in the heart, muscles, tendons, abdominal organs...etc.
- Computed Tomography: this is a technique to composed images from the internal organs of the body, combining X-ray images from different angles.
- Magnetic Resonance Imaging: this technique utilizes mainly magnetic fields and also radio waves with the purpose of producing images of the body with high details.
- Metabolic and Functional Imaging: those techniques includes the Positron Emission Tomography (PET) and the magnetic resonance spectroscopy. More details are given below:

- ◦ **PET**: it utilizes a trace (mainly a radioactive drug) with the purpose of showing the metabolic activity of the body. Therefore, this scan can identify the abnormal metabolism as a proof of a disease.
- ◦ **Magnetic resonance spectroscopy**: this technique helps to identify the location of a tumor as it usually compares the chemical composition of the normal tissues with the tumor tissue.

Another set of methods that are usually employed when diagnosing cancer are based on the cytologic and histopathologic techniques. The biopsy is one of the most common methods to diagnose cancer is relation with those methods.

The markers that are produced by the tumors are a very significant patterns when trying to diagnose cancer. The tumors produce biochemical substances, that today are quantified in hundreds of different substances. The most common one utilized is the carcino-embryonic-antigen (CEA) and there are a lot more under investigation.

The carcinogenesis process includes inherited but also specific acquired factors and the serum or plasma can contain specific markets for the carcinogenesis process. Identify those markers would be ideal as this would permit to identify cancer in its early stages. Some of the most known markers are ELISA or RIA (Kumar & Pawaiva, 2010).

Finally the immunohistochemistry method is based on the detection of antigenic presence on the tissues' cells using monoclonal or polyclonal antibodies. It is utilized for example in breast cancer to identify the response to progesterone or to estrogen, predicting the therapy's response.

3.4.1 *Databases*

There are different public databases on cancer. The largest are those created in large-scale collaborative oncology projects, such as the International Cancer Genome Consortium (ICGC), the Cancer Genome Atlas (TCGA), and The National Cancer Database (NCDB) (Pavlopoulou et al. 2015). On the other hand, the World Health Organization (WHO) is also immersed in different projects to collect cancer data from around the world, as collected in the CI5 databases, the IARC cancer mortality database, the database created in collaboration with the Association for Nordic Cancer Registries (NORDCAN) and the Automated Childhood Cancer Information System (ACCIS) (Global Cancer Observatory n.d.).

Another interesting database is the only from the University of Wisconsin and named "Wisconsin Breast Cancer Database". This database contains information about the cell nucleus of potential tumors. The features extracted from each potential tumor are the following: radius, texture, perimeter, area, smoothness, compactness, concavity, concave points, symmetry and fractal dimension (Street et al. 1993).

A very utilized database in the research is the Mammographic Image Analysis Society database (MIAS), created by different UK research groups. This database contains 322 digitized images from mammographic images.

Another similar database is the Digital Database for Screening Mammography (DDSM), containing mammographic images from 2620 different patients and it is fully available online.

There is a public database named "LC25000 dataset" which contains information about histopathological images from lung and colon cancer patients (Kaggle, 2020). It contains around 25.000 images and were collected in the Haley Veterans' Hospital, located in Tampa, Florida, in United States.

The ICGC database collects especially genomic data, such as simple somatic mutations (SSM) and genes with SSM. But it also consists of other type of data which could be interesting for other types of studies, such as the primary site of the tumor at the diagnosis, gender of the patient, tumor stage at diagnosis, etc. (Pavlopoulou et al. 2015).

Cancer Genome Atlas (TCGA), a collaborative project between the National Cancer Institute (NCI) and the National Human Genome Research Institute (NHGRI), managed to characterize more than 20,000 primary cancers molecularly and matched normal samples spanning 33 types of cancer. It contains clinical information about the patients, but especially it contains genomic data, such as gene expression, copy number, somatic mutations, single nucleotide polymorphisms (SNP), etc. (Pavlopoulou et al. 2015; The Cancer Genome Atlas Program - National Cancer Institute n.d.).

CI5 databases are a group of three different databases (CI5 I-X, CI5plus and CI5 XI) that collect detailed information on the incidence of cancer recorded by cancer registries (regional or national) worldwide for 5 years (CI5 - Home n.d.).

There is another database that contains cancer mortality statistics by country, which is called IARC. This database gives information about the mortality rate of each type of cancer (e.g., colon, breast, lung, etc.) and in each country per year (IARC: Home n.d.).

NORDCAN database contains data organized by country with different type of information: cancer incidence, mortality, prevalence, survival, year or period related to survival, cancer entity, patient gender, and age (Nordcan 2.0 n.d.).

Also, there is a database with only information on the incidence of cancer in children and adolescents. ACCIS contains information on 19 European countries, collected by gender, age, date of birth, date of cancer diagnosis, tumor sequence number, primary site, morphology, behavior, etc. (ACCIS: The Automated Cancer Information System n.d.).

All these databases contain information that can be of great use in multiple studies analyzing it with ML techniques. For example, ACCIS is currently used to analyze temporal trends and geographic patterns in the child population. On the other hand, NORDCAN could be used to create better survival predictions, and for example to be able to choose a more appropriate treatment according to the patient's condition. And for example, CI5 could be used to analyze why the prevalence of a specific type of cancer is higher in one country than in another, and see if there are any external factors that are conditioning it and could be avoided. So, having this large amount of information, and used with artificial intelligence techniques, could allow many great discoveries about cancer.

3.4.2 Machine Learning Techniques Utilized

In cancer research, different machine learning techniques are used to develop predictive models that help early detection, better knowledge of the progression of the disease, and in decision-making. Specifically, it is frequently used in cancer detection, but also for the prediction of cancer survival, prediction of cancer recurrence, and prediction of cancer susceptibility.

This section will identify the most relevant machine learning techniques to diagnose cancer for the most prevalent cancer types.

Breast Cancer

The most typical algorithms for breast cancer detection are the following: Artificial Neural Networks (ANN), Support Vector Machines (SVM), Decision Trees (DT), k-nearest neighbor (KNN) and naïve Bayesian (Alkhathlan & Khader Jilani, 2020).

The ANN algorithm is one of the most utilized when working in the medical field and it is highly utilized in several fields for analyze and predict data. This algorithm works trying to simulate the functionality of the human brain and therefore, tried to learn to execute complex tasks. In the literature it is possible to find cases using data from the Wisconsin Breast Cancer Database and applying ANN algorithms to classify between a benign or malignant tumor, with very good results (accuracy up to 99%).

The utilization of SVM algorithm is focused on using N-1 hyperplanes to distinguish between two different classes. The research from Akay (2009) utilized the SVM method to diagnose breast cancer and reach an accuracy of 99.51% using several features from the Wisconsin Breast Cancer Database. Other studies suggested the potential utilization of digital mammograms with SVM, reaching accuracy's values near to 87% (Dheeba & Selvi, 2011).

The third most utilized algorithm in the literature for detecting cancer is the DT. This method applies decision rules from the input data. Basically, this method is utilized for classifying the potential tumor into benign or malign. A complex version of the decision tree, (fuzzy decision tree) was utilized in xx to classify the tumor, obtaining an accuracy of 98.4%.

The KNN algorithm utilizes information to determine the group to which a point belongs to. This technique is applied in the literature to classify the type of tumor (xx), obtaining an accuracy of 98.48% (Medjahed et al. 2013). In more recent studies, the KNN method obtained an accuracy of 99.28% (Kumary & Singh, 2018), by using intermediate techniques to choose the best attribute to include in the classifier.

Finally, Näives Bayes algorithm utilizes the Bayes theorem along with the naïve assumption with the conditional feature between the features utilized as input. In the literature, this algorithm has been used to predict the severity of the breast cancer, reaching an accuracy of 91.83% (Sakr et al. 2017). 25 also utilized the näives Bayes algorithm to classifier between 2 types of tumor and reached an accuracy of 93% (Kharya et al. 2014).

Lung Cancer

The number of hospitals using supporting applications to identify malignant nodules in one of the most dangerous cancer is increasing exponentially. Normally, machine learning techniques are applied to classify indeterminate pulmonary nodules. This technology should improve decision making and also reduce the number of benign nodules that are marked to be followed-up.

In the literature, there are different machine learning techniques evaluated for fighting the lung cancer disease.

CNNs are used for recognizing lung cancer from Computed Tomograpy images in many studies (Sun et al. 2016; Yu et al, 2020).

Another recent and novel method to early diagnose cancer is to identify a biomarker (plasma metabolites) in the blood using machine learning techniques (Xie et al. 2021). This study obtained the best accuracy results using a Näive Bayes algorithm, so it can be concluded that a potential tool utilizing a Näive Bayes method would be beneficial when trying to early diagnosed the lung cancer using biomarkers.

Colon Cancer

Related to colon cancer, there are evidence in the literature of histological images to evaluate the colon cancer prognosis. Tsai & Tao (2021), reviewed the utilization of deep learning techniques with the purpose of classifying the colorecta cancer tissue, based on some characteristics, such as the texture, cell composition, size…etc. There are different convolutional neural networks models applied to classify the type of tumor. Some of those models are AlexNet, SqueezeNet, VGGNet, GoogLeNet, ResNet…etc. Most of the models provide accuracy values higher than 90%, which a very good reference to continue validating those models to identify cancer tumors.

Using gene expression, Hu et al. (xx) performed a research study to evaluate the results of different algorithms, such as Back-propagation, SVM and S-Kohonen neural network. The best results were obtained with the S-Kohonen neural networks as the accuracy of the classification reached 91%.

Masud et al. (2021) utilized a CNN algorithm to classify cancer tumor from tissues, obtaining an accuracy classification of 96.33%.

In general, there is a lack of studies to identify the prognosis stage for the tumors. Jiang et al (2020) evaluated the utilization of a convolutional neural network with a machine learning classifier with the purpose of predicting the prognosis of colon cancer in stage III from stained tissue slides. In general, the results obtained reach an average predictive accuracy of 75.5% for the complete test group.

Gupta et al. (2019) utilized the most influential parameters from histopathology information with the purpose of predicting the survival period using machine learning techniques, and more specifically, the tumor, the node and the metastasis information. The best performance in this study was obtained with the Random Forest algorithm with an accuracy of 84% for predicting the five years disease-free survival period.

DISCUSSION

Technology applied to medicine and health is a field that is growing exponentially and the prediction is that it will be one of the most innovative sectors in the following years. Cancer disease is a leading cause of death in the world, specially in the developed world, and academia, industry and governments are investing multiple resources and budget in trying to find a solution, at least from a detection point of view. Technology is already applied to identify cancer in its early phases to save lives and also to cut the costs of very long treatments.

In this chapter, the most relevant machine learning techniques have been introduced and the most innovative applications associated with the cancer diagnosis and treatment have been identified. It has been shown that, at present, in addition to being used for cancer detection, three main types of investigations are carried out using machine learning techniques: prediction of cancer survival, prediction of cancer recurrence, and prediction of cancer susceptibility.

Deep learning is a subfield of machine learning that is using algorithms, trying to imitate the processing method of the human brain to solve problems. Deep learning algorithms, such as the neural networks, have been utilized in the literature to diagnose cancer with very good results. Apart from that, other algorithms such as the Näive Bayes algorithm, the SVM or the Random Forest are widely used to identify different types of cancer.

LIMITATIONS, FUTURE RESEARCH DIRECTIONS AND CONCLUSIONS

The main purpose of this work is to review and evaluate the different machine learning techniques and used when diagnosing and treating cancer disease. This study could be used as a reference for practitioners or researchers that could be interested in learning about the different techniques related to technology applied when fighting cancer. It also gives information that could be useful to understand the technology employed and its characteristics.

A potential future research direction for this work could be related to the utilization of wearable devices to monitor cancer patients to try to understand their status and evolution. Now, there are plenty of studies using this kind of devices to understand what is happening in the heart, brain or skin and it could be very interesting to extend the knowledge to patients suffering from cancer disease.

ACKNOWLEDGMENT

This research received no specific grant from any funding agency in the public, commercial, or not-for-profit sectors.

REFERENCES

ACCIS. (2021). *The Automated Cancer Information System*. Available at: https://accis.iarc.fr/

Akay, M. F. (2009). Support vector machines combined with feature selection for breast cancer diagnosis. *Expert Systems with Applications*, *36*(2), 3240–3247. doi:10.1016/j.eswa.2008.01.009

Alkhathlan, L., & Khader Jilani, A. (2020). Machine Learning Techniques for Breast Cancer Analysis: A Systematic Literature Review. *International Journal of Computer Science and Network Security*, *20*(6), 83–90.

Barrachina, M., & López, V. L. (2021). Machine Learning Techniques to Identify and Characterize Sleep Disorders Using Biosignals. In Advancing the Investigation and Treatment of Sleep Disorders Using AI. IGI Global.

Barrachina-Fernández, M., Maitín, A. M., Sánchez-Ávila, C., & Romero, J. P. (2021). Wearable Technology to Detect Motor Fluctuations in Parkinson's Disease Patients: Current State and Challenges. *Sensors (Basel)*, *21*(12), 4188. doi:10.339021124188 PMID:34207198

Bashiri, A., Ghazisaeedi, M., Safdari, R., Shahmoradi, L., & Ehtesham, H. (2017). Improving the prediction of survival in cancer patients by using machine learning techniques: experience of gene expression data: a narrative review. *Iranian Journal of Public Health*, *46*(2), 165. PMID:28451550

Bray, F., Laversanne, M., Weiderpass, E., & Soerjomataram, I. (2021). The ever-increasing importance of cancer as a leading cause of premature death worldwide. *Cancer*, *127*(16), 3029–3030. doi:10.1002/cncr.33587 PMID:34086348

CI5 – Home. (2021). Available at: https://ci5.iarc.fr/Default.aspx

Costanzo, M. C., Arcidiacono, C., Rodolico, A., Panebianco, M., Aguglia, E., & Signorelli, M. S. (2020). Diagnostic and interventional implications of telemedicine in Alzheimer's disease and mild cognitive impairment: A literature review. *International Journal of Geriatric Psychiatry*, *35*(1), 12–28. doi:10.1002/gps.5219 PMID:31617247

Dheeba, J., & Selvi, S. T. (2011). Classification of malignant and benign microcalcification using SVM classifier. In *2011 International Conference on Emerging Trends in Electrical and Computer Technology* (pp. 686-690). IEEE. 10.1109/ICETECT.2011.5760205

El Naqa & Murphy. (2015). What Is Machine Learning? *Machine Learning in Radiation Oncology*, 3–11.

Fan, C. Y., Chang, P. C., Lin, J. J., & Hsieh, J. C. (2011). A hybrid model combining case-based reasoning and fuzzy decision tree for medical data classification. *Applied Soft Computing*, *11*(1), 632–644. doi:10.1016/j.asoc.2009.12.023

Fröhlich, H. (2018). Premenopausal Breast Cancer: Potential Clinical Utility of a Multi-Omics Based Machine Learning Approach for Patient Stratification. *EPMA Journal, 9*(2), 175–86.

Global Cancer Observatory. (2021). Available at: https://gco.iarc.fr/

Gupta, P., Chiang, S.-F., Sahoo, P., Mohapatra, S., You, J.-F., Onthoni, D., Hung, H.-Y., Chiang, J.-M., Huang, Y., & Tsai, W.-S. (2019). Prediction of Colon Cancer Stages and Survival Period with Machine Learning Approach. *Cancers (Basel), 11*(12), 2007. Advance online publication. doi:10.3390/cancers11122007 PMID:31842486

Hanahan, D., & Weinberg, R. A. (2011). Hallmarks of cancer: The next generation. *Cell, 144*(5), 646–674. doi:10.1016/j.cell.2011.02.013 PMID:21376230

Houfani, D., Slatnia, S., Kazar, O., Zerhouni, N., Merizig, A., & Saouli, H. (2020). Machine Learning Techniques for Breast Cancer Diagnosis: Literature Review. In M. Ezziyyani (Ed.), *Advanced Intelligent Systems for Sustainable Development (AI2SD'2019). AI2SD 2019. Advances in Intelligent Systems and Computing* (Vol. 1103). Springer. doi:10.1007/978-3-030-36664-3_28

Hu, H., Niu, Z., Bai, Y., & Tan, X. (2015). Cancer classification based on gene expression using neural networks. *Genetics and Molecular Research, 14*(4), 17605–17611. doi:10.4238/2015.December.21.33 PMID:26782405

IARC Home. (2021). Available at: https://www.iarc.fr/

Jiang, D., Liao, J., Duan, H., Wu, Q., Owen, G., Shu, C., Chen, L., He, Y., Wu, Z., He, D., Zhang, W., & Wang, Z. (2020). A machine learning-based prognostic predictor for stage III colon cancer. *Scientific Reports, Vol., 10*(1), 10333. doi:10.103841598-020-67178-0 PMID:32587295

Kaggle. (2020). *Lung and Colon Cancer Histopathological Images*. Kaggle. Available online: https://www.kaggle.com/andrewmvd/lung-and-colon-cancer-histopathological-images

Karabatak, M., & Ince, M. C. (2009). An expert system for detection of breast cancer based on association rules and neural network. *Expert Systems with Applications, 36*(2), 3465–3469. doi:10.1016/j.eswa.2008.02.064

Kharya, S., Agrawal, S., & Soni, S. (2014). Naive Bayes classifiers: A probabilistic detection model for breast cancer. *International Journal of Computer Applications, 92*(10).

Kourou, K., Exarchos, T. P., Exarchos, K. P., Karamouzis, M. V., & Fotiadis, D. I. (2015). Machine Learning Applications in Cancer Prognosis and Prediction. *Computational and Structural Biotechnology Journal, 13*, 8–17. doi:10.1016/j.csbj.2014.11.005 PMID:25750696

Kumar, P., & Pawaiya, R. (2010). Advances in Cancer Diagnostics. *Brazilian Journal of Veterinary Pathology, 3*, 141–152.

Kumari, M., & Singh, V. (2018). Breast Cancer Prediction system. *Procedia Computer Science, 132*, 371–376. doi:10.1016/j.procs.2018.05.197

Marcano-Cedeño, A., Quintanilla-Domínguez, J., & Andina, D. (2011). WBCD breast cancer database classification applying artificial metaplasticity neural network. *Expert Systems with Applications, 38*(8), 9573–9579. doi:10.1016/j.eswa.2011.01.167

Masud, M., Sikder, N., Nahid, A. A., Bairagi, A. K., & AlZain, M. A. (2021). A Machine Learning Approach to Diagnosing Lung and Colon Cancer Using a Deep Learning-Based Classification Framework. *Sensors (Basel), 21*(3), 748. doi:10.339021030748 PMID:33499364

Medjahed, S. A., Saadi, T. A., & Benyettou, A. (2013). Breast cancer diagnosis by using k-nearest neighbor with different distances and classification rules. *International Journal of Computers and Applications, 62*(1).

Nordcan 2.0. (2021). Available at: https://nordcan.iarc.fr/en/database

Pavlopoulou, A., Spandidos, D. A., & Michalopoulos, I. (2015). Human cancer databases. *Oncology Reports, 33*(1), 3–18. doi:10.3892/or.2014.3579 PMID:25369839

Sakr, S., Elshawi, R., Ahmed, A. M., Qureshi, W. T., Brawner, C. A., Keteyian, S. J., & Al-Mallah, M. H. (2017). *Comparison of machine learning techniques to predict all-cause mortality using fitness data: the Henry ford exercIse testing (FIT) project. In BMC medical informatics and decision making* (Vol. 17). BMC.

Singh, J., & Keer, N. (2020). Overview of Telemedicine and Sleep Disorders. *Sleep Medicine Clinics, 15*(3), 341–346. doi:10.1016/j.jsmc.2020.05.005 PMID:32762967

Sirintrapun, S. J., & Lopez, A. M. (2018). Telemedicine in Cancer Care. American Society of Clinical Oncology Educational Book, 38(1), 540-545. doi:10.1200/EDBK_200141

Smith, R. (2020). *Telehealth market to hit $53.1 billion by 2026.* Insurance Business America. https://www.insurancebusinessmag.com/us/news/breaking-news/telehealth-market-to-hit-53-1-billion-by-2026--report-213866.aspx

Stanford. (2021). *Cancer types.* Available at: https://stanfordhealthcare.org/medical-conditions/cancer/cancer/cancer-types.html

Street, W. H., Wolberg, W. H., & Mangasarian, O. L. (1993). Nuclear feature extraction for breast tumor diagnosis. *IS&T/SPIE 1993 International Symposium on Electronic Imaging: Science and Technology, 1905*, 861-870.

Sun, W., Zheng, B., & Qian, W. (2016). Computer aided lung cancer diagnosis with deep learning algorithms. In Medical imaging 2016: computer-aided diagnosis. International Society for Optics and Photonics.

Tanveer, M., Richhariya, B., Khan, R. U., Rashid, A. H., Khanna, P., Prasad, M., & Lin, C. T. (2020). Machine Learning Techniques for the Diagnosis of Alzheimer's Disease: A Review. *ACM Transactions on Multimedia Computing Communications and Applications, 16*(1), 1–35. doi:10.1145/3344998

The Cancer Genome Atlas Program - National Cancer Institute. (2021). Available at: https://www.cancer.gov/about-nci/organization/ccg/research/structural-genomics/tcga

Tsai, M.-J., & Tao, Y.-H. (2021). Deep Learning Techniques for the Classification of Colorectal Cancer Tissue. *Electronics (Basel), 10*(14), 1662. doi:10.3390/electronics10141662

WHO. (2021). *Cancer*. Available at: https://www.who.int/news-room/fact-sheets/detail/cancer

Xie, Y., Meng, W. Y., Li, R. Z., Wang, Y.W., Qian, X., Chan, C., Yu, Z.F., & Fan, X.X. (2021). Early lung cancer diagnostic biomarker discovery by machine learning methods. *Translational Oncology, 14*(1). doi:10.1016/j.tranon.2020.100907

Yi, S. J., Pittman, C. A., Price, C. L., Nieman, C. L., & Oh, E. S. (2021). Telemedicine and Dementia Care: A Systematic Review of Barriers and Facilitators. *Journal of the American Medical Directors Association, 22*(7), 1396–1402. doi:10.1016/j.jamda.2021.03.015 PMID:33887231

Yu, K. H., Lee, T. M., Yen, M. H., Kou, S. C., Rosen, B., Chiang, J. H., & Kohane, I. S. (2020). Reproducible Machine Learning Methods for Lung Cancer Detection Using Computed Tomography Images: Algorithm Development and Validation. *Journal of Medical Internet Research, 22*(8), e16709. doi:10.2196/16709 PMID:32755895

ADDITIONAL READING

Bashiri, A. (2017). Improving the Prediction of Survival in Cancer Patients by Using Machine Learning Techniques: Experience of Gene Expression Data: A Narrative Review. *Iranian Journal of Public Health, 16*(2), 165. PMID:28451550

Cruz, J. A., & Wishart, D. S. (2006). Applications of Machine Learning in Cancer Prediction and Prognosis. *Cancer Informatics, 6*, 59–77. doi:10.1177/117693510600200030 PMID:19458758

Gupta, S., Tran, T., Luo, W., Phung, D., Kennedy, R. L., Broad, A., Campbell, D., Kipp, D., Singh, M., Khasraw, M., Matheson, L., Ashley, D. M., & Venkatesh, S. (2014). Machine-learning prediction of cancer survival: A retrospective study using electronic administrative records and a cancer registry. *BMJ Open*, *4*(3), 1–7. doi:10.1136/bmjopen-2013-004007 PMID:24643167

Kourou, K., Exarchos, T. P., Exarchos, K. P., Karamouzis, M. V., & Fotiadis, D. I. (2015). Machine Learning Applications in Cancer Prognosis and Prediction. *Computational and Structural Biotechnology Journal*, *13*, 8–17. doi:10.1016/j.csbj.2014.11.005 PMID:25750696

Li, J., Zhou, Z., Dong, J., Fu, Y., Li, Y., Luan, Z., & Peng, X. (2021). Predicting breast cancer 5-year survival using machine learning: A systematic review. *PLoS One*, *16*(4), e0250370. doi:10.1371/journal.pone.0250370 PMID:33861809

Murali, N., Kucukkaya, A., Petukhova, A., Onofrey, J., & Chapiro, J. (2020). Supervised Machine Learning in Oncology: A Clinician's Guide. *Digestive Disease Interventions*, *4*(1), 73–81. doi:10.1055-0040-1705097 PMID:32869010

Nagy, M., Radakovich, N., & Nazha, A. (2020). Machine learning in Oncology: What should Clinicians Know? *Clinical Cancer Informatics*, (4), 799–810. doi:10.1200/CCI.20.00049 PMID:32926637

KEY TERMS AND DEFINITIONS

Cancer: It is a group of diseases characterize by the abnormal growing process of cells in an uncontrollable manner.

Carcinoma: This is related to the cancer initiated in the organs, glands or even in the body structures. The carcinomas are linked to 80-905 of all the cancer cases detected. Some of those carcinoma's types includes the melanoma, the Merkel cell carcinoma or the basal cell carcinoma.

CNN: Convolutional Neural Networks. It is a specific class of neural networks that are normally used to evaluate images.

Diagnose: To identify or recognize the patterns that describe a specific disease.

Machine Learning: It is defined as group of techniques that combine mathematics with computational processing to learn patterns in a set of data with different purposes: classification, prediction, etc.

SVM: Support Vector Machines. It is a specific supervised learning model, that is usually applied in regression problems or in classification analysis.

Chapter 11

Neural Network Model Based on Feature Extraction and Empirical Thresholding for Mango Fruit Quality Grading

Praveen Tripathi

https://orcid.org/0000-0002-0535-5092
SGRR University, India

Sanjay Sharma
SGRR University, India

ABSTRACT

This work supports a new feature extraction image pre-processing system followed by back propagation-artificial neural networks-based system for class categorization of mango fruit images. For back propagation, scale conjugate gradient (SCG) algorithm is used. The methodology comprises of three parts. First, various external image-based attributes of mango were taken and processed in MATLAB. Size and weight features were also considered as important parameters as only color is not sufficient to judge the quality. Second, features extraction was done at image pre-processing for making the algorithm lighter by focusing only key features. Finally, a single hidden layer BP-ANN (back propagation-artificial neural network) was used with sigmoid activation functions. The result came in terms of a suitable output variable, which is the quality class of the mango, which is chosen A, B, C, and D, respectively. It will also reduce the cost of classification or sorting of the fruits.

DOI: 10.4018/978-1-6684-2443-8.ch011

INTRODUCTION

Sorting the fruits using naked eyes is a tedious task these days. Automated sorting has been a demand for fruit suppliers who are sorting the fruits at root level. Human intervention in classification tasks seems to be minimum these days as we have various successful implementation of sorting algorithms since the advent of programming languages.(Dara & Devolli, 2016) Since from the time when fruits based on their external quality may be easily sorted automatically but in a large scale, there is an urgent need to perform the same automatic classification for small scale mango producers. The Mango images are first preprocessed to remove the unwanted noise from the image. Dataset preparation of the mango must be real time based using good quality camera to achieve the true results.(Kumari, Kr. Bhatt, et al., 2021) It has been also observed from various sources that due to various reasons the quality of fruits has fall. Improper cultivation systems and afterwards maintenance of the fruit was one of the key reasons for such fall in the quality production and supply of the fruits. Non-speedy manual fruit classification, faulty inspection due to non-comprehensive knowledge is also one of major parts of lesser quality production. As a solution, various automatic classifiers were developed. This advanced way of classification may reduce the costs by promoting production efficiency. A complex supervised machine learning based fruit grading and sorting is required for implementing such smart classifiers.(Puspita et al., 2016) Computer vision systems. This empirically driven model provides an expert model to perform such operation which may be further made available on smart phones and other handheld small devices for automated sorting of fruits. A fruit may be classified by its patterns on outside surface such as color, damage, defects and using its size which is a best part.(Unay & Gosselin, 2005) These parameters are useful in categorizing the fruits. Kesar mango preprocessed images by focusing on fruit segmentation and abnormality segmentation using active contour and enhanced fuzzy-based K-means clustering approach, respectively. (Kumari, Dwivedi, et al., 2021) In the recent work, The experimental results show that the proposed model KNN? SA-CSO-FCNN is excellent in terms of accuracy of mango grading.(Kumari, Kr. Bhatt, et al., 2021) Among various computational approaches ANN is considered as the remarkable alternate for study similar things such as weather forecasting as it provides the way to minimize errors by learning back and forward.(Koklu et al., 2021) This work depicts that the root mean square error (RMSE) helped in generalizing the classification in case when small errors are encountered.(Matsumura et al., 2019) Such sorting systems are already available, but are out of the budget of the fruit framers due to their mismatched financial status. This promotes the use of ANN and SVM in assisting them in their financial need as these systems are comparatively fast, automated and in budget. Various tools and techniques including MATLAB Neural Network Toolbox provide various technical approached to develop classifier as discussed above. Literature study depicts various powerful supervised classifiers which are reliably tested for developing the sorter systems and classifier. Few such systems includes linear discriminant classifier, k-NN, fuzzy k-NN, adapting boosting and SVM.(Kumari, Kr. Bhatt, et al., 2021) The study also shows that sensors devices are helpful in achieving the classification results.(Dara & Devolli, 2016) In the work, systematic efforts have been put into continuous practice to reach objectives of this work.

In a nut shell, machine based classification is based on the features of the sample may not be used for accurate results therefore only. key features are used with the help of clustering using k-means method and is used for feature selection.

TRAINING TYPES AND MATLAB

First, this work utilizes SCG algorithm using MATLAB neural network toolbox. There are several training algorithms which have a variety of different computation and storage statistics.(Dara & Devolli, 2016) (Kumari, Dwivedi, et al., 2021) However, no algorithm found as the best suited to all application. Efforts were made to prepare a system by utilizing the SGC algorithm which is most suitable in numerical optimization techniques.(Datt et al., 2015) Detailed literature review shown that SVM based models perform much better with the accuracy from 70.006% to 71.5% when feature selection is used. SVM technique based models widely used for solving classification problems these days.(Bhatt & Pant, 2015)

Neural Network Toolbox

MATLAB neural network toolbox is utilized for supervised learning. It is powerful because back propagation algorithms are solves many classification problems especially by adjusting neurons in-between. It uses the concept of multilayer perceptron (MLP) training to converge the result. The functioning of BP-ANN has two parts. Signal transmission is the first part. The second part deals with the misclassification and to remove such errors weights were readjusted depend on the supervised expected output variables, which was in the core of BP-ANN for better learning.(Kumari, Dwivedi, et al., 2021) It has a drawback that it may fall at local minima and give erroneous results. Continuous efforts have been put by researchers. But there are many solutions proposed by many neural network researchers to overcome the slow converge rate problem.(Unay & Gosselin, 2005) The following diagram show how neural network helps in classification problem in reverse propagation if synaptic weight needs to update according to the errors in the results.

Figure 1. Basic functions of supervised back propagation neural network classification

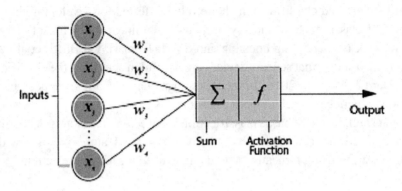

Therefore, various powerful optimization algorithms have been devised, most of which have been based on simple gradient descent algorithm as explained by Bishop such as, scaled conjugate gradient descent. In this study the training of the network is done through using SCG algorithm. The model created in this paper is a back propagation neural network with two-layer network as in Figure1 where, the input of 7 neuron and 18 hidden neuron and an output having 4 category.

SCG is a second order conjugate gradient algorithm which helps minimize goal functions of several variables. As a characteristics of SCG, it needs more looping for reaching the convergence as per compared with other similar algorithms, the number of computation in each looping has been reduced which is appreciable task in model preparation.

OBJECTIVE OF THE WORK

The objective is to develop a better classification model to sort the classes of the mango fruit. This sorting should be negligibly intervened by human, but machine. Back propagation techniques are very useful to accomplish these objectives. Here, SCG algorithm is considered for classification. Before processing the task of classification, image feature extraction techniques are also used in MATLAB which used captured images of mango. Control measures are also used before capturing the images to avoid any misclassification.

RESEARCH METHODOLOGY USED

This work utilizes digital camera to collect mango surface level external features such as pattern, color, size, damaged area etc. Weight attribute of mango is also of importance as small sized but small mango must not belong

to class A, and for this a weighing machine is used for calculating weight of each sample. Further, thresholding in MABLAB of grayscale of sample images is used. Threshold value available which has 1, 4, 6, 8, 18 or 26-connected components and this work used 8-connected components. Intensity value for all the effective values was set to 1 if its RGB value is 105 and 0 if not. This constraint helps in processing towards right feature extraction, which is important for classification in further stages. Also, to avoid small regions in image, connected pixels of binary image were removed that have fewer than 5 pixels in processed binary image. To implement this, 5-connected components is used in awareopne method which helped in segmenting unnecessary rice grains given by the thresholding function.

Figure 2. Methodology of the proposed work

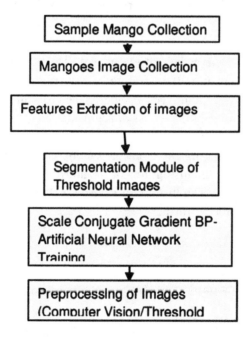

Finally after pre-processing of samples is done, SCG which is a back propagation-ANN system is used to train the neural networks. As a standard procedure validation

Figure 3. Original samples and their grayscale equivalent

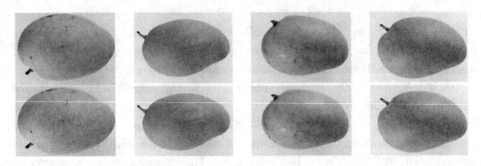

and testing is processed for all samples in the dataset. Following diagram is the flow of above research methodology.

The sample is segregated into three parts. First part which is training is kept as 70% of the sample, 15% of the dataset is kept for validation finally 15% o the sample is kept for the testing purpose.

Sample Features- Color, Size and Shape of Mangoes

The colour images of mango were captured using Nikon DSLR camera. Its size is evaluated using the RGB values of the images. This feature was considered as important as size is very important feature of any fruit classification. Grayscale and other operations with the images was performed to achieve feature extraction process which also involved the process of segmentation.

The histogram is drawn from the resulting grayscale images which is used further for segmentation and filtering the connected components for feature extraction. The following figure 4 is the histograms of the above first mango image which is already converted to gray. The histogram is also created in MATLAB and it will help in segmentation process further.

Figure 4. Histogram of one random Sample

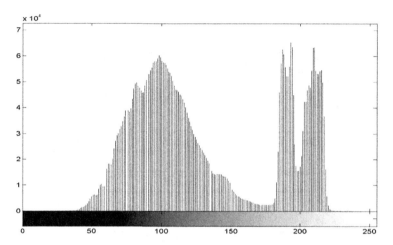

Size of the mango is equally important to consider before color features are given to the classifiers. The size of mango is also considered in this work. Further, the image is segmented by thresholding with 5 connected components. The basic size features of the sample image comprises of its area and parameters. Further, two key parameters which are major axis length and minor axis length respectively are calculated in MATLAB. To generalize the above features, mean for each parameter which are $\mu area$, $\mu perimeter$, $\mu major$ and $\mu minor$ axis length are calculated and used for further computation. The following table has few sample data:

Table 1. Feature Extracted using MATLAB for few samples

Samples	μArea	μPeri	μMajorAxis	μMinorAxis
1	61867.92	151.69	31.02	25.94
2	20525.71	79.23	15.18	11.47
3	79431.31	209.96	38.97	33.65
4	21243.34	78.12	15.13	11.15
5	39746.33	87.35	20.66	16.34
6	37695.00	78.84	19.78	15.56
7	24430.91	99.08	18.43	13.08
8	29790.21	107.99	19.96	15.28
9	28059.25	100.23	19.34	14.68
10	26142.19	97.19	18.28	13.79
11	38743.34	119.77	23.50	18.61
12	19978.01	63.72	14.03	10.47
13	8051.90	58.54	11.36	7.22
14	71514.98	193.58	35.94	30.74
15	71514.98	193.58	35.94	30.74

To show the data processing of the work, few samples were shown in this paper and grayscale images and histogram of one sample are depicted.

TRAINING DATA

Training in MATLAB

In this study, scale conjugate gradient algorithm of Matlab Neural Network Toolbox was used to develop the classifier. Initially, the desired features during image feature extraction which then normalized are stored in an input file. That input file is loaded into the SCG algorithm into Matlab. It is also a challenge to strongly select any one classifier that is suitable for all situations. In this work, endeavor to implement our system by using a SGC are made because this algorithm is good for computing numerical optimization technique for neural network.[9] Studies also says that support vector machines based models with and without considering feature selection gave accuracy 71.5% and 70.006% respectively.[3]

RESULTS

Scale Conjugate Gradient function is mostly used to achieve the classification results. The most prominent reason to use this is that it is cost effective computation for work in this area. The study guaranteed the fast fitting of the model where the work uses one hidden layer and eighteen neurons. Mean Square Error (MSE) was measured and the performance achieved was good. Five validations with 37 iterations were made for measuring the performance of the work. Training error of MSE was 6.20028e-3 while error percentage was 1.88679. On the other hand, testing error for MSE was 4.91436e-2 while error percentage was 11.36363e-0.

Above results shown the classification of the mango using SCG has produced best results with minimal errors as shown in the table below:

Table 2. Result of Training and Testing of Data

	Error(Training)	Error(Testing)
MSE	6.20028e-3	4.91436e-2
Error (in)%	1.88679	11.36363e-0

Validation performance was at 0.0074109 at epoch value 41. MSE was slightly higher but at epoch value 41 the MSE was lowest. The outcome of the work shows that the performance of the network increases as we increase the training of the network which may be summarized from the figure 5 below. As we increase the training size the error minimizes.

Figure 5. Validation Performance using trainscg (Scale conjugate gradient)

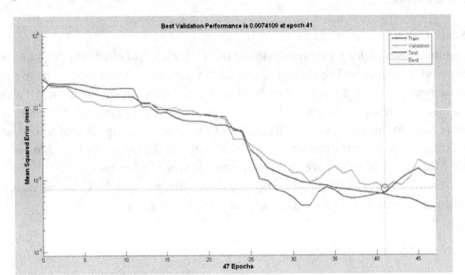

The figure below depicts the results after the processing of the scale conjugate gradient algorithm. The training stops at epochs value 41 as the training, testing and validation error gets steady because after 41 training epochs a very low training error which is 6.20028e-3 here. The task was success as the quality assessment was achieved as it reflects the perfect match between actual input and the expected output.

Figure 6. Gradient and validation checks at epoch 47

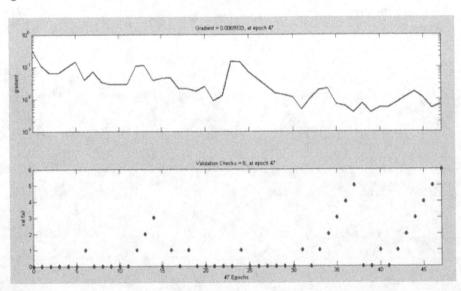

As the assumed epochs are exceeded with iterations, the training stops if the result of the function does not reach to the expected goal. The minimum gradient value generated is 0.0069933. The work focuses that either the magnitude of this value is either smaller than the mingrad value or the training time is more than seconds of max_fail the training will stop. In this work, the min gradient value is 0.0069933 and as its value starts increasing above this and the training stops at epoch 47.

Table 3. Confusion matrix of the best multi-category mango grading result by SCG algorithm

Grades	Assumed Output (4 Mango Classes)			
	A	B	C	D
A	10	2	0	0
B	0	7	0	0
C	0	2	10	0
D	0	0	1	11
Mangos	10	11	11	11
Accuracy	100%	64%	90%	100%
Overall Accuracy	88.5%			

43 mango fruit images are considered for testing which was processed after training and validation. Table 3 shows the confusion matrix based on results of SCG back propagation artificial neural network. The tested classifier was successful in its performance for expected output in terms of mango class categories as it recognizes 100%, 64%, 90% and 100% for A, B C and D categories respectively. Grade B depicts little lower accuracy in classification with approximately 64%. To convergence the result for making standard, based on closer values grade B is assigned either to A or C category. The overall performance of the work seems to approximately 88.5% with error of 11.5. The work shown the classification work is good and error is lower as compared with the existing models. It may be more minimized in the future work by more improvement during training the model and working towards better feature extraction before classification.

CONCLUSION AND FUTURE WORK

This work promotes the use of SCG neural network technique for classification tasks as it gave good results. It also showed the time saving approach as compared to its peer techniques specially for classification. It gave minimum MSE as well as RMSE. This is the reason for the promotion of ANN and SVM based techniques for supervised learning and is becoming the choice for many researchers. This work has achieved some level of feature extraction and results in good classification model preparation. If pre-classification task is refined in terms of features extraction, then models based on ANN and SVM may results in more perfection. Errors for A, B and D category mangos were found negligible and only B category mangos needs to be converged either with category A or category C which are near to category B. In a nut shell, the present model may be acceptable for mango fruit grading as the results are prone to classification process.

There are various other factors based on which the classification algorithm may also be updated using effective AI based algorithms such as deep learning. The researchers may take this work for improving the system and thereafter update this work by applying new strategies to develop robust model.

REFERENCES

Bhatt, A. K., & Pant, D. (2015). Automatic apple grading model development based on back propagation neural network and machine vision, and its performance evaluation. *AI & Society*, *30*(1), 45–56. doi:10.100700146-013-0516-5

Dara, F., & Devolli, A. (2016). Applying artificial neural networks (ANN) techniques to automated visual apple sorting. *Journal of Hygienic Engineering and Design*, *17*, 55–63.

Datt, G., Bhatt, A. K., & Kumar, S. (2015). Disaster Management Information System Framework using Feed Forward Back Propagation. *Neural Networks*, *4*(3), 510–514. doi:10.17148/IJARCCE.2015.43122

Dickson, M. A., Bausch, W. C., & Howarth, M. S. (1994). Classification of a broadleaf weed, a grassy weed, and corn using image processing techniques. *SPIE*, *2345*, 297–305.

Guyer, D. E., Miles, G. E., Gaultney, L. D., & Schereiber, M. M. (1993). Application of machine vision to shape analysis in leaf and plant identification. *TASAE*, *36*(1), 163–171.

Koklu, M., Kursun, R., Taspinar, Y. S., & Cinar, I. (2021). Classification of Date Fruits into Genetic Varieties Using Image Analysis. *Mathematical Problems in Engineering*, *2021*, 1–13. Advance online publication. doi:10.1155/2021/4793293

Kumari, N., Dwivedi, R. K., Bhatt, A. K., & Belwal, R. (2021). Automated fruit grading using optimal feature selection and hybrid classification by self-adaptive chicken swarm optimization: Grading of mango. *Neural Computing & Applications.* Advance online publication. doi:10.100700521-021-06473-x

Kumari, N., Kr. Bhatt, A., Kr. Dwivedi, R., & Belwal, R. (2021). Hybridized approach of image segmentation in classification of fruit mango using BPNN and discriminant analyzer. *Multimedia Tools and Applications, 80*(4), 4943–4973. doi:10.100711042-020-09747-z

Matsumura, R., Harada, K., Domae, Y., & Wan, W. (2019). Learning based industrial bin-picking trained with approximate physics simulator. *Advances in Intelligent Systems and Computing, 867,* 786–798. doi:10.1007/978-3-030-01370-7_61

Puspita, M. N., Kusuma, W. A., Kustiyo, A., & Heryanto, R. (2016). A classification system for jamu efficacy based on formula using support vector machine and k-means algorithm as a feature selection. *ICACSIS 2015 - 2015 International Conference on Advanced Computer Science and Information Systems, Proceedings,* 215–220. 10.1109/ICACSIS.2015.7415176

Ruiz, L. A., Moltó, E., Juste, F., & Aleixos, N. (1995). *Aplicación de métodos ópticos para la inspección automática de productos hortofrutícolas.* VI Congreso de la Sociedad Española de Ciencias Hortícolas, Barcelona, Spain.

Suen, J. P., & Eheart, J. W. (2003). Evaluation of neural networks for modelling nitrate concentration in rivers. *Journal of Water Resources Planning and Management, 129*(6), 505–510. doi:10.1061/(ASCE)0733-9496(2003)129:6(505)

Tao, Y., Morrow, C. T., Heinemann, P. H., & Sommer, J. H. (1990). Automated machine vision inspection of potatoes. ASAE Paper No. 90-3531.

Unay, D., & Gosselin, B. (2005). Artificial neural network-based segmentation and apple grading by machine vision. *Proceedings - International Conference on Image Processing, ICIP, 2*(January), 630–633. 10.1109/ICIP.2005.1530134

Varghese, Z. Y., Morrow, C.T., Heinemann, P.H., Sommer III, J.H., Tao, Y., & Crassweller, R.M. (1991). *Automated inspection of golden delicious mangos using color computer vision.* ASAE Paper No. 91-7002.

Chapter 12
Paradigm Shift in the Functioning of the Tourism and Hotel Industry Using NLP, Digital Assistant, and AI Models

Praveen Tripathi

iD https://orcid.org/0000-0002-0535-5092
IHMS Kotdwar, India

Sunil Kumar
IHMS Kotdwar, India

Pradeep Rawat
IHMS Kotdwar, India

ABSTRACT

Hotels should collaborate with the right technology partner in order to identify gaps in their processes such as customer support, concierge bookings, and in-room technology that can be closed with the help of integrating artificial intelligence and machine learning. AI is doing great for big and established hotel industry brands while, due to the cost barriers, smaller brands in this industry receive less attention from AI. Whether it is the on-season, investing in cloud computing services to facilitate the functioning of the hospitality industry seems unfeasible for smaller organizations. If a hotel provides facilities of automation using AI and ML, then the hotel staff can invest time to focus the quality of service, furnishing full range of hotel facilities to their intended guests, which in-turn results in increased operational efficiency, which may help in remarkable growth by increasing the annual revenue of the organization. It is a good choice to add the latest trends in the processes used in the tourism and hotel industries.

DOI: 10.4018/978-1-6684-2443-8.ch012

INTRODUCTION

Hotels should collaborate with the right technology partner in order to identify gaps in their processes such as customer support, concierge bookings to in-room technology that can be closed with the help of integrating Artificial Intelligence and Machine Learning. AI is doing great for big and established hotel industry brands while due to the cost barriers, smaller brands in this industry receives relatively less attention from AI (Buhalis & Licata, 2002). Whether it is the on-season, but investing on cloud computing services to facilitate the functioning of the hospitality industry seems unfeasible for smaller organizations. If hotel provides facilities of automation using AI and ML, then the hotel staff can invest his time to focus the quality of service, furnishing full range of hotel facilities to their intended guests and in-turn results in increased operational efficiency which may help in remarkable growth by increasing the annual revenue of the organization (Bonn et al., 1998).

ACTIVATING ARTIFICIAL INTELLIGENCE (AI), NATURAL LANGUAGE PROCESSING(NLP), ONLINE TRAVEL AGENTS (OTAS) AND DIGITAL ASSISTANTS FOR TOURISM AND HOSPITALITY INDUSTRY

Since a decade back, It has been promptly observed that all the domain of the societies are getting effected by the technologies. Whether it is about booking hotel rooms, booking flight, train, bus, taxi and movie tickets, the role of computational devices seems to be of prime concern. It is to be noted that not only the digitization is involved in the processed involved above but a high technology enabled system with the support of the big data is involved too. Few such areas are natural language processing and digital assistants which are being supported by artificial intelligence, the emerging technology.

Natural language processing (NLP) refers to the branch of computer science— and more specifically, the branch of artificial intelligence or AI—concerned with giving computers the ability to understand text and spoken words in much the same way human beings can.

Machine learning is giving full support to create the knowledge corpus to promptly produce customized results. Just to name the technology giant IBM, there is an artificial intelligence enabled system named IBM Watson which is serving the various domains. Few areas where IBM Watson is involved are:

- IBM Waston as oncologist
- IBM Watson as financial manager

- IBM Watson as Chef
- IBM Watson as Event Manager

There are other similar technologies which are serving the society and are providing the cutting edge technology based solutions. NLP is helping to overcome from the barrier of language translation specially when the tourist visits as place where the language used is completely non-understandable mutually between the tourist and the hospitality agents at their sites. AI is helping in various areas where a model is trained and the training is continuous till the model is not accepted at public platform.(Bonn et al., 1998) Once the model is prepared, it will replace the humans for various tasks because the model is developed in such a way that it may reply most of the queries from its data.

NLP for Next Level Tourism Industry

To understand the NLP in somewhat technical way is necessary for hoteliers as well as tourism industry employees. It will open up their knowledge of utilizing the services provided by the latest trend of AI-enabled services. NLP combines computational linguistics—rule-based modeling of human language—with statistical, machine learning, and deep learning models. Together, these technologies enable computers to process human language in the form of text or voice data and to 'understand' its full meaning, complete with the speaker or writer's intent and sentiment.

NLP drives computer programs that translate text from one language to another, respond to spoken commands, and summarize large volumes of text rapidly—even in real time. There's a good chance you've interacted with NLP in the form of voice-operated GPS systems, digital assistants, speech-to-text dictation software, customer service chatbots, and other consumer conveniences. But NLP also plays a growing role in enterprise solutions that help streamline business operations, increase employee productivity, and simplify mission-critical business processes.

Figure 1. Natural language processing

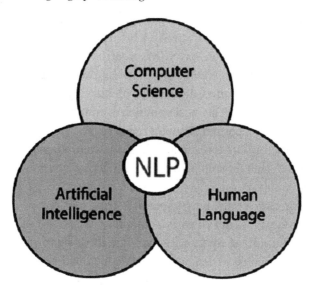

Human language is filled with ambiguities that make it incredibly difficult to write software that accurately determines the intended meaning of text or voice data. Homonyms, homophones, sarcasm, idioms, metaphors, grammar and usage exceptions, variations in sentence structure—these just a few of the irregularities of human language that take humans years to learn, but that programmers must teach natural language-driven applications to recognize and understand accurately from the start, if those applications are going to be useful.

Several NLP tasks break down human text and voice data in ways that help the computer make sense of what it's ingesting. Some of these tasks include the following:

- **Speech recognition**, also called speech-to-text, is the task of reliably converting voice data into text data. Speech recognition is required for any application that follows voice commands or answers spoken questions. What makes speech recognition especially challenging is the way people talk— quickly, slurring words together, with varying emphasis and intonation, in different accents, and often using incorrect grammar.
- **Part of speech tagging**, also called grammatical tagging, is the process of determining the part of speech of a particular word or piece of text based on its use and context. Part of speech identifies 'make' as a verb in 'I can make a paper plane,' and as a noun in 'What make of car do you own?'
- **Word sense disambiguation** is the selection of the meaning of a word with multiple meanings through a process of semantic analysis that determine the

word that makes the most sense in the given context. For example, word sense disambiguation helps distinguish the meaning of the verb 'make' in 'make the grade' (achieve) vs. 'make a bet' (place).

- **Named entity recognition,** or NEM, identifies words or phrases as useful entities. NEM identifies 'Kentucky' as a location or 'Fred' as a man's name.
- **Co-reference resolution** is the task of identifying if and when two words refer to the same entity. The most common example is determining the person or object to which a certain pronoun refers (e.g., 'she' = 'Mary'), but it can also involve identifying a metaphor or an idiom in the text (e.g., an instance in which 'bear' isn't an animal but a large hairy person).
- **Sentiment analysis** attempts to extract subjective qualities—attitudes, emotions, sarcasm, confusion, suspicion—from text.
- **Natural language generation** is sometimes described as the opposite of speech recognition or speech-to-text; it's the task of putting structured information into human language. Above detailed information is equally important for both the customers as well as service providers in the area of hospitality industry.

Steps Involved in NLP

There are general five steps involved in the NLP process that we must understand. These steps are:

1. **Lexical Analysis** – It involves identifying and analyzing the structure of words. Lexicon of a language means the collection of words and phrases in a language. Lexical analysis is dividing the whole chunk of txt into paragraphs, sentences, and words.
2. **Syntactic Analysis (Parsing)** – It involves analysis of words in the sentence for grammar and arranging words in a manner that shows the relationship among the words. The sentence such as "The school goes to boy" is rejected by English syntactic analyzer.
3. **Semantic Analysis** – It draws the exact meaning or the dictionary meaning from the text. The text is checked for meaningfulness. It is done by mapping syntactic structures and objects in the task domain. The semantic analyzer disregards sentence such as "hot ice-cream".
4. **Discourse Integration** – The meaning of any sentence depends upon the meaning of the sentence just before it. In addition, it also brings about the meaning of immediately succeeding sentence.

5.   **Pragmatic Analysis** – During this, what was said is re-interpreted on what it actually meant. It involves deriving those aspects of language which require real world knowledge.

Figure 2. Steps involved in NLP

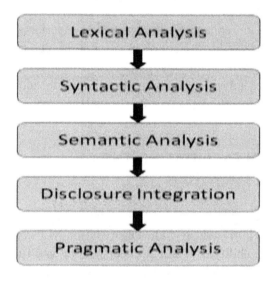

FOSTER THE BUSINESS USING NLP

Virtual assistants may increase the hit count of travelers, vacationers, business guests etc who expect the consummate customer experience. Companies in the hotel field relies on natural language processing (NLP) by the IT giants such as Apple's SIRI, Amazon's ALEXA, Cortana from Microsoft. Even to facilitate the customers and employees, to converse effortlessly with hotel guests from any part of the world, use of AR (Augmented Reality) headsets for real-time translation may be used easily. To quote for an example, the UK's largest hotel chain named Premier Inn uses AI based interactive wall map containing local visiting spots.(Li et al., 2018) Similarly, to support the domain of serving the customers using AI enabled virtual assistants, Edwardian Hotels London stands at the first position. AI-chatbots are also used to fulfill the requirements of the valued customers by assisting in the service areas such as spa, restaurant etc. Chatbots with the help of AI will transform room services completely by 2025 through the process of creating personalized experiences that will incorporate individual preferences. It will obviously make increase in their revenue.

It will evident the paradigm shift in the way the service is being given earlier and today due to the IoT implementation in the electronic gadgets used in the hotel rooms, conference halls, party halls etc. In other words, integration of IoT and AI in gadgets used in the hotels may curve down the mainly used deices such as;

- Wi-Fi access point
- Bluetooth points etc.
- It is the key to enhancing the customer experience, increasing brand recognition and loyalty along with substantial revenue gains.

To tune the hotel industry operations with today's technology, the brands are continuously looking for affordable as well as scalable guest room assistant technology.

ROLE OF NLP IN FACILITATING THE BUSINESS ALL TOGETHER

The term NLP is emerging at very high speed into all the sectors especially in the field of tourism and hotel industry. The beauty of the NLP can be considered as it provides system the ability of reading, understanding and finally converging the authentic meaning of human used languages that helps in driving the business to new heights.(Huang et al., 2018) Data science is marvelously providing the better then the ever computational power that results in lucrative benefits in travel and tourism industries.

There are various direct as well as indirect benefits involved in the business that is running using NLP and AI enabled services. Focusing the view from the perspective of both the customers and the hospitality service providers, following points must be considered to create intuition on how the things are going these days:

Remarkably Better Booking Experience

Whether it is about choosing airlines, arrangements of local transport, booking of hotel rooms, all process are from the foremost stage of travel plan by customers. Finding the perfectly suitable airlines to the customers, cheapest flights, cheapest accommodation prices are really irksome for the customers. Even there are customer support executive for all areas of tourism such as flights customer care, hotel customer care. But they are also not able to process the irritating and frequently customized queries of the customers every time.

As a solution, the NLP based chatbots may help in resolving such issues of booking process into various areas including mentioned above. Chatbots can help in replying to the customers into more satisfiable way as they are fully supported by huge data that helps chatbot to make wise decision for all. For example you may ask any query such as "Does the hotel have three conference halls?", "What is the discount for pre-booking?", "Does WiFi is accessible to all area of the hotel?" etc. You may think that NLP is so smart that it may reply any of your query related to the domain you are involved in. NLP resolves the problem of language translation from any language to the language of our choice. Even, chatbots work in 24X7 manner unlike human.

Better Personalized Tours

After the travel booking process over, spending the vacation into beautiful manner is the next target for the happy customers. It may include choosing the place to stay, duration of stay, categories of hotels, nearby places to be visited etc. Again, NLP tools helps you in analyzing the searches in hassle-free manner too. NLP is backed-up by the AI enabled big data that helps in choosing the plan which suits your budget, time and other customizable things. Really, the role of AI and NLP has given a paradigm shift in the way business processes are taking place today.

Better Maintenance and Their Procedures

The beauty of the NLP in the tourism and hotel industry is that it is not only supporting the customers but it equally also simplify the business procedures. It results in improving the financial reputation status of the business enterprise. NLP tools helps in remarkably improving the processes and procedures both by utilizing the AI. The tools can help maintenance and repair technicians easily understand the suggested information from complex manuals. Thus, a lot of time, money, and human resources can be saved by providing the employees with information in a quick and easily understandable manner i.e. NLP tools. Interestingly, NLP tools can help identify handwritten notes that are usually difficult for other individuals to understand because of typical handwritings.

Reinventing the Way Hotel Process Works

Paradigm shift can be noticed in the tourism and hotel industry due to the use of NLP and AI-enabled smart computing. From the naïve user's perspective, NLP tools are available in the form of voice assistants which are used in the hotel to make the process more smooth as well as hassle-free. For example, in present days, controlling the temperature of air conditioned installed, turning the lights on or off, playing movies or web series of your choice etc, NLP tools are available assisting you round the day. Popular voice assistants such as SIRI, Alexa and other such similar assistants are customized to provide personal voice assistance to all the guests at the hotel. However, investing the budget in this process is not easy going for developing brands, but giants and established brands in the tourism and hotel industry are using these facilities on regular basis. The customized robots are utilized smartly to deliver food items or take the customer's clothes for washing or can be also used for cleaning the rooms according to the instructions provided. These tools are so smart to recognize the customers by their voice and facial gesture and features. These technologies can help in identifying the guests that are entering, staying or visiting for a less time or leaving the hotel premises. Needless to say that in case of any robbery, voice and facial recognition technologies can help identify the criminal very easily.

Thanks to the NLP and AI that not only provides the fantastic experience to both the customers and service providers but make the whole process panic-free all the time.

Redefining the Experiences

Using NLP tools in tourism operation provides an effective instrument for customers who are facing language barriers especially to some new places. These tools helps in automatically translation of texts written on entry area and help tourists easily get directions to the required location. Simultaneously, these tools can help with ticketing at tourist's sightseeing places by upgrading the conversations between employees & the tourists, help easily understand timings & other instructions provided by informatory boards and even suggest other nearby attractions depending upon the customer's location in an easy to understand manner. This new model has totally redefined the experiences of both customers as well as the employees providing the facility to their customers.

TRANSFORMING THE FURTHER PROCESSES USING NLP AND AI

After the booking process is done, the question arises that "how to spend that beautiful vacation?", which includes deciding the place to stay, the number of days to stay, the kind of hotels to choose from and the places that need to be visited on a priority basis. NPL tools can help in suggesting & curate tailor-made travel packages for individuals.(Buhalis & Licata, 2002) What the NLP tools do is basically analyze the kind of searches an individual does regarding their holiday preferences. This includes data regarding the holiday destination, the vacation duration and the budget preferences of the individual. All this data can be combined to form big data which is further implemented by artificial intelligence algorithms and NLP tools to create custom tour packages that fits one's pockets easily simultaneously providing him the experience he's looking for.

In the present era of AI-enabled smart processes, hotel industry has started transforming the way it provides facilities to both its intended customers as well as employees. When a mega program is organized the aviation sector, the hospitality industry and the government together form the travel and tourism industry to provide the service.(Li et al., 2018) All these industries are interdependent on each other, contributing to the growth of each other. Each sector has its own set of challenges wherein

Table 1. Online travel agents in trends the shortcomings and defects of one sector can result in a loss for the other partners as well.

OTAs	Detail
booking.com	• one of the oldest online travel agents, having been originally founded in 1996 • headquarters in Amsterdam, Netherlands • offers users the ability to book hotels, motels, holiday homes and other similar accommodation types • cover close to 200 different countries around the world
Expedia.com	• operated by the Expedia Group • based in Bellevue, Washington, in the United States and was founded in 2001 • one of the highest grossing travel companies in the world and has localised sites in 40 countries • Customers can book hotels, holiday homes, B&Bs, flights, rental cars, activities and other travel services • it places an emphasis on cheap and affordable accommodation.
Agoda.com	• based in Singapore • provides users with a choice of over one million hotels or holiday homes, with a strong focus on the Asian market
Laterooms.com	• based in Manchester, in the United Kingdom • founded in 1999, but did not offer online hotel bookings until 2002 • emphasis on attracting customers looking for last minute deals on overnight stays, including bookings for the very same day • a solid option for hotels that are prone to having spare rooms that they need to fill.
Tripadvisor.com	• primarily focused on reviews and other user-generated content • it also has a built-in hotel booking service • headquarters in Needham, Massachusetts, in the United States, and was founded in 2000 • works with third-party connectivity partners, displaying live hotel prices and availability listings • also has an advertising partnership with Expedia and its Priceline.com subsidiary

Above table lists some popular OTAs with their short description that allows the booking of hotel rooms.

Take an example, if an individual wants a flight ticket of some airline service, but due to some problem the ticket is not booking, then using NLP the customer might may redirect to another available airline ticket booking platform with broader facilities. It will also suggest the hotels or lodge for staying of the ticket booker automatically. Moreover, using NLP it may also provide other tentative facilities such as local transportation, local site seeing options, information on any local events etc. Also, the government will also get some income by means of collecting tourist passes to various spots into different modes. Thus, NLP gives benefit of tranquil experience to intended tourists and likely helps the business enterprises in simplifying the operations. These AI based operations make the process helpful to all the players involved in the process of hotel industry.

USING ONLINE TRAVEL AGENTS (OTAS) TO INCREASE HOTEL BOOKING

The role of OTA is emerging these days in hotel industry to make increase the booking count. It not only increases the booking but also is a very convenient way for intended users for various analytical tasks such as price compare. OTAs are important for the hotel industry as they provides marketing of the business along with a distribution channel. These days, this mode of booking is in trends due to the benefits including easiness in hotel searching, reading and writing reviews, comparing prices etc.

Commission Charges Claimed by OTAs on Booking

OTAs are now-a-days a vital part of the marketing of hotel rooms availability by doing good amount of factual analysis. They are also involved in the major distribution channel for the service based on the commission already set with tourism and hotel industry business enterprises.

Usually, OTA make bookings on behalf of their users, and they make money by charging a commission fee to suppliers which may subject to vary from the type of service offered. It is generally settled on the pre-decided percentage amount also. Ultimately, the only motive of using OTA is to sell room as much as possible. Few popular OTAs that helps in making more visibility of the hotels to the customers and thereby increasing booking count are:

CHALLENGES FOR HOTELS FOR ACCEPTANCE OF AI

Just creating the perception of paradigm shift from orthodox paper based process to paper less processes to AI-enabled processes is not as simple as it resembles. There are some challenges involved in the process before investing on this. Few challenges are:

- Inadequate or incomplete understanding of AI.
- Lack of understanding of actual capabilities of the smart AI-enabled system.
- Lack of enthusiasm to expand the prospect of innovative business opportunities
- Insufficient adaptation to innovations and experimental approach
- Limited awareness on how to leverage technology to improve the relationship with customers
- Phobic attitude of old age customers who are less involved in the cutting edge technologies.
- Budget deficiencies for small groups or small business enterprises.
- Cost involved in alternative arrangement of the services when technology fails.
- Power cut problems due to routine shutdowns and disturbances created from natural disasters

Other barriers are also involved such as lack of knowledge, digital-divide and many other conditional barriers.

FACILITIES OFFERED BY HOTELS BACKED BY INTELLIGENT SYSTEMS

The tourism and hotel industry is backed up by various IT giants to provide the hassle-free services to its customers. It also helps in increased profit by saving time and money by avoiding unnecessary expenses. Use of smart computing systems by utilizing NLP, Digital Assistants and other AI-enabled services to retrieve the maximum benefit is essential for the growing tourism and hospitality industry. It provides the various facilities including:

- Voice-activated Virtual assistants to facilitate the customers
- Room amenities controls such as lighting, TV, temperature, music etc.
- Personalized activity suggestions for improved system ahead
- AI-enabled housekeeping services for automation and uniformity in results
- IoT interconnected devices for monitoring and maintenance purpose

Similar other benefits are also incurred by implementing the latest technology enabled devices to the tourism and hospitality industry for getting more benefits.

OTHER APPLICATIONS OF NLP

NLP lie in a number of disciplines like computer and information sciences, linguistics, mathematics, electrical and electronic engineering, artificial intelligence and robotics, psychology etc. Applications of NLP include a number of fields of studies such as machine translation, natural language text processing, summarization, user interfaces multilingual and Gross language information retrieval (CLIR), speech recognition, artificial intelligence and expert system.(Li et al., 2018) Research on NLP is regularly published in a number of conferences such as the annual proceedings of ACL (Association of Computational Linguistics) and its European counter part EACL, biennial proceedings of the Message Understanding Conferences (MUCS),Text Retrieval Conferences (TRECS) and ACM-SIGIR (Association of Computing Machinery-Special Interest Group on Information Retrieval) conferences. As natural language processing technology matures, it is increasingly being used to support other computer applications. Such use naturally falls into two areas, one in which linguistic analysis merely serves as an interface to the primary program and the second one in which natural language considerations are central to the application. Natural language interfaces into a request in a formal database query language, and the program then proceeds as it would without the use of natural language processing techniques.(Marrese-Taylor et al., 2013) The design of question answering systems is similar to that for interfaces to database management systems. One difference however, is that the knowledge base supporting the question answering system does not have the structure of a database. Similarly in message understanding systems, a fairly complete linguistic analysis may be required but the messages are relatively short and the domain is often limited. Also some more application areas include information and text categorization.(Malone et al., 1987) In both applications, natural language processing imposes a linguistic representation on each document being considered. In text categorization a collection of documents is inspected and all documents are grouped into several categories based on the characteristics of the linguistic representations of the documents. In information filtering documents satisfying some criterion are singled out from a collection.

CONCLUSION

It has been observed after studying various publications and articles that established brands in the field of tourism and hotel industry are utilizing the convenience provided by the latest technologies. On the other hand, the growing and small brands are probably getting less advantage from the technology giants due to limited budget. It is also observed that there are possible alternates that helps in providing the equivalent services to low budget hotels by compromising up to some extent due to budget. As per the usage of NLP, digital assistants, OTAs and other artificial intelligent based agents the convenience is given to both stakeholders i.e. the customer as well as the employees who are welcoming the customers at the receiving end. No doubt in the coming decades there will be paradigm shift in a way the tourism and hotel industry is functioning today. The industry have to accept these changes at any cost otherwise it will be tough to survive in the coming cutting-edge era.

REFERENCES

Anckar, B. (2003). Consumer Intentions in Terms of Electronic Travel Distribution. *e-Service Journal*, 2(2), 68–86. doi:10.2979/esj.2003.2.2.68

Bennett, M., & Lai, K. (2005). The impact of the Internet on travel agencies in Taiwan. *Tourism and Hospitality Research*, 6(1), 8–23. doi:10.1057/palgrave.thr.6040041

Bonn, M. A., Furr, H. L., & Susskind, A. M. (1998). Using the internet as a pleasure travel planning tool: An examination of the sociodemographic and behavioral characteristics among internet users and nonusers. *Journal of Hospitality & Tourism Research (Washington, D.C.)*, 22(3), 303–317. doi:10.1177/109634809802200307

Buhalis, D., & Licata, M. C. (2002). The future eTourism intermediaries. *Tourism Management*, 23(3), 207–220. doi:10.1016/S0261-5177(01)00085-1

Buhalis, D., & Licata, M. C. (2002). The future of e-tourism intermediaries. *Tourism Management*, 23(3), 207–220. doi:10.1016/S0261-5177(01)00085-1

Huang, C., Wang, Q., Yang, D., & Xu, F. (2018). Topic mining of tourist attractions based on a seasonal context aware LDA model. *Intelligent Data Analysis*, 22(2), 383–405. doi:10.3233/IDA-173364

Li, Q., Li, S., Hu, J., Zhang, S., & Hu, J. (2018). Tourism review sentiment classification using a bidirectional recurrent neural network with an attention mechanism and topic-enriched word vectors. *Sustainability (Switzerland)*, 10(9), 3313. Advance online publication. doi:10.3390u10093313

Malone, T. W., Yates, J., & Benjamin, R. I. (1987). Electronic markets and electronic hierarchies. *Communications of the ACM*, *30*(6), 484–497. doi:10.1145/214762.214766

Marrese-Taylor, E., Velásquez, J. D., Bravo-Marquez, F., & Matsuo, Y. (2013). Identifying customer preferences about tourism products using an aspect-based opinion mining approach. *Procedia Computer Science*, *22*, 182–191. doi:10.1016/j.procs.2013.09.094

Ye, Q., Law, R., Gu, B., & Chen, W. (2011). The influence of user-generated content on traveler behavior: An empirical investigation on the effects of e-word-of-mouth to hotel online bookings. *Computers in Human Behavior*, *27*(2), 634–639. doi:10.1016/j.chb.2010.04.014

Chapter 13

Smart Farming:
Industry 4.0 in Agriculture Using Artificial Intelligence

Umesh Kumar Gera
Rama University, India

Dhirendra Siddarth
Rama University, India

Preeti Singh
Rama University, India

ABSTRACT

Global population growth and urbanization are ongoing at the same time. Consumption patterns are changing as discretionary money rises. Farmers are under pressure to meet rising demand, so they're looking for new methods to boost productivity. There will be more people to feed in 30 years. Because there is a finite amount of rich soil, it will be necessary to go beyond traditional farming. We need to figure out ways to assist farmers in reducing or at the very least managing their risks. On a global basis, artificial intelligence in agriculture is one of the most fascinating prospects. Artificial intelligence has the potential to change the way we think about agriculture by assisting farmers in achieving greater results with less effort while also bringing a plethora of other benefits. Artificial intelligence, on the other hand, is not a stand-alone technology. As the next step in the transition from traditional to creative farming, AI may improve existing technology.

DOI: 10.4018/978-1-6684-2443-8.ch013

INTRODUCTION

Agriculture is the mainstay of the Indian economy. Immense commercialization of an agriculture has creates a very negative effect on our environment. The use of chemical pesticides has led to enormous levels of chemical buildup in our environment, in soil, water, air, in animals and even in our own bodies. Artificial fertilizers gives on a short-term effect on productivity but a longer-term negative effect on the environment, where they remain for years after leaching and running off, contaminating ground water. Another negative effect of this trend has been on the fortunes of the farming communities worldwide. Despite this so-called increased productivity, farmers in practically every country around the world have seen a downturn in their fortunes. This is where organic farming comes in. Organic farming has the capability to take care of each of these problems. The central activity of organic farming relies on fertilization, pest and disease control. Plant disease detection through naked eye observation of the symptoms on plant leaves, incorporate rapidly increasing of complexity. Due to this complexity and to the large number of cultivated Crops and their existing psychopathological problems, even experienced agricultural experts and plant pathologists may often fail to successfully diagnose specific diseases, and are consequently led to mistaken conclusions and concern solutions. An automated system designed to help identify plant diseases by the plant's appearance and visual symptoms could be of great help to amateurs in the agricultural process. This will be prove as useful technique for farmers and will alert them at the right time before spreading of the disease over large area. Deep learning constitutes a recent, modern technique for image processing and data analysis, with accurate results and large potential. As deep learning has been successfully applied in various domains, it has recently entered also the domain of agriculture. So we will apply deep learning to create an algorithm for automated detection and classification of plant leaf diseases. Nowadays, Convolutional Neural Networks are considered as the leading method for object detection. In this paper, we considered detectors namely Faster Region-Based Convolutional Neural Network (Faster R-CNN), Region-based Fully Convolutional Networks (R-FCN) and Single Shot Multibox Detector (SSD). Each of the architecture should be able to be merged with any feature extractor depending on the application or need. We consider some of the commercial/cash crops, cereal crops, and vegetable crops and fruit plants such as sugarcane, cotton, potato, carrot, chilly, brinjal, rice, wheat, banana and guava, these leaves images are selected for our purpose. Fig. 1 shows images of the diseased affected leaves on various crops. The early detection of plant leaf diseases could be a valuable source of information for executing proper diseases detection, plant growth management strategies and disease control measures to prevent the development and the spread of diseases.

RELATED WORK

Here, we take some of the papers related to Plant leaf diseases detection using various advanced techniques and some of them shown below, In paper(Lu et al., 2017), author described as an in-field automatic wheat disease diagnosis system based on a weekly supervised deep learning framework, i.e. deep multiple instance learning, which achieves an integration of identification for wheat diseases and localization for disease areas with only image-level annotation for training images in wild conditions. Furthermore, a new infield image dataset for wheat disease, Wheat Disease Database 2017 (WDD2017), is collected to verify the effectiveness of our system. Under two different architectures, i.e. VGG-FCNVD16 and VGG-FCN-S, our system achieves the mean recognition accuracies of 97.95% and 95.12% respectively over 5-fold cross validation on WDD2017, exceeding the results of 93.27% and 73.00% by two conventional CNN frameworks, i.e. VGG-CNN-VD16 and VGG-CNN-S. Experimental results demonstrate that the proposed system outperforms conventional CNN architectures on recognition accuracy under the same amount of parameters, meanwhile maintaining accurate localization for corresponding disease areas. Moreover, the proposed system has been packed into a realtime mobile app to provide support for agricultural disease diagnosis. In paper (Kamilaris & Francesc, 2018), author discussed and to perform a survey of 40 research efforts that employ deep learning techniques, applied to various agricultural and food production challenges. Examine the particular agricultural problems under study, the specific models and frameworks employed the sources, nature and pre-processing of data used, and the overall performance achieved according to the metrics used at each work under study. Moreover, study comparisons of deep learning with other existing popular techniques, in respect to differences in classification or regression performance. Findings indicate that deep learning provides high accuracy, outperforming existing commonly used image processing techniques. In paper (Konstantinos, 2018), author discussed about convolutional neural network models were developed to perform plant disease detection and diagnosis using simple leaves images of healthy and diseased plants, through deep learning methodologies. Training of the models was performed with the use of an open database of 87,848 images, containing 25 different plants in a set of 58 distinct classes of [plant, disease] combinations, including healthy plants. Several model architectures were trained, with the best performance reaching a 99.53% success rate in identifying the corresponding [plant, disease] combination (or healthy plant). The significantly high success rate makes the model a very useful advisory or early warning tool, and an approach that could be further expanded to support an integrated plant disease identification system to operate in real cultivation conditions. In paper (Kulkarni Anand & Ashwin Patil, 2012) author describes a methodology for early and accurately plant diseases detection, using artificial neural network (ANN) and diverse image processing techniques. As the proposed approach is based on ANN classifier for classification and Gabor filter for feature extraction, it gives better results with a recognition rate of up to 91%. An ANN based classifier classifies different plant diseases and uses the combination of textures, color and features to recognize those diseases. In paper (Sabah & Navdeep, 2012) authors presented disease detection in Malus domestica through an effective method like K-mean clustering, texture and color analysis. To classify and recognize different agriculture, it uses the texture and color features those generally appear in normal and affected areas. In paper (Kaundal & Amar, 2006) authors compared the performance of conventional multiple regression, artificial neural network (back propagation neural network, generalized regression neural network) and support vector machine (SVM). It was concluded that SVM based regression approach has led to a better description of the relationship between the environmental conditions and disease level which could be useful for disease management.

PROPOSED METHODOLOGY

Plants are susceptible to several disorders and attacks caused by diseases. There are several reasons that can be characterizable to the effects on the plants, disorders due to the environmental conditions, such as temperature, humidity, nutritional excess or losses, light and the most common diseases that include bacterial, virus, and fungal diseases. Those diseases along with the plants may shows different physical characteristics on the leaves, such as a changes in shapes, colors etc. Due to similar patterns, those above changes are difficult to be distinguished, which makes their recognition a challenge, and an earlier detection and treatment can avoid several losses in the whole plant. In this paper, we are discussed to use recent detectors such as Faster Region-Based Convolutional Neural Network (Faster R-CNN), Region-based Fully Convolutional Networks (R-FCN) and Single Shot Multibox Detector (SSD) to detection and classification of plant leaf diseases that affect in various plants. The challenging part of our approach is not only deal with disease detection, and also known the infection status of the disease in leaves and tries to give solution (i.e., name of the suitable organic fertilizers) for those concern diseases.

Faster Region-Based Convolutional Neural Network (Faster R-Cnn)

Faster R-CNN is one of the Object detection systems, which is composed of two modules. The first module is a deep fully convolutional network that proposes regions. For training the RPNs, the system considers anchors containing an object or not, based on the Intersection-over-Union (IoU) between the object proposals and the ground-truth. Then the second module is the Fast R-CNN detector (Fuentes et al., 2017), (Ren et al., 2016) that uses the proposed regions. Box proposals are used to crop features from the same intermediate feature map which are subsequently fed to the remainder of the feature extractor in order to predict a class and class-specific box refinement for each proposal. Fig. 2 shows the basic architecture of Faster R-CNN. The entire process happens on a single unified network, which allows the system to share full-image convolutional features with the detection network, thus enabling nearly cost-free region proposals.

Region-Based Fully Convolutional Network (R-FCN)

We develop a framework called Region-based Fully Convolutional Network (R-FCN) for object detection. While Faster R-CNN is an order of magnitude faster than Fast RCNN, the fact that the region-specific component must be applied several hundred times per image led (Huang et al., 2017), (Fuentes et al., 2017), (Dai et al., 2016), (Dai et al., 2015) to propose the R-FCN (Region-based Fully Convolutional Networks) method which is like Faster R-CNN, but instead of cropping features from the same layer where region proposals are predicted, crops are taken from the last layer of features prior to prediction. R-FCN object detection strategy consists of: (i) region proposal, and (ii) region classification. This approach of pushing cropping to the last layer minimizes the amount of per-region computation that must be done. The object detection task needs localization representations that respect translation variance and thus propose a position-sensitive cropping mechanism that is used instead of the more standard ROI pooling operations used in object detection (Fuentes et al., 2017), (Girshick, 2015). They show that the R FCN model could achieve comparable accuracy to Faster R-CNN often at faster running times.

Single Shot Detector (SSD)

The SSD approach is based on a feed-forward convolutional network that produces a fixed-size collection of bounding boxes and scores for the presence of object class instances in those boxes, followed by a non-maximum suppression step to produce the final detections. This network is able to deal with objects of various sizes by combining predictions from multiple feature maps with different resolutions (Fuentes et al., 2017), (Liu et al., 2016). Furthermore, SSD encapsulates the process into a single network, avoiding proposal generation and thus saving computational time.

EXPERIMENTAL RESULT

In our system processing starts with Data collection, through some the pre-processing, feature extractor steps to be allowed and then finally detect the diseases from image.

Data Collection

Dataset contains images with several diseases in many different plants. In this System we consider some of the commercial/cash crops, cereal crops, and vegetable crops and fruit plants such as sugarcane, cotton, potato, carrot, chilly, brinjal, rice, wheat, banana and guava. Diseased leaves, healthy leaves all of them were collected for those above crops from different sources like images download from Internet, or simply taking pictures using any camera devices or any else.

Figure 1. Disease detection and controlling using AI

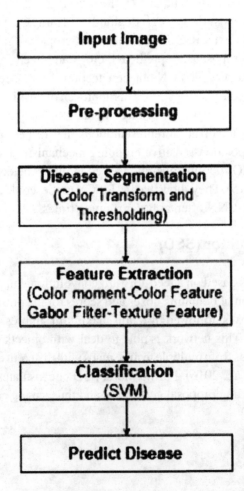

Image Pre-Processing

Image annotation and augmentation Image annotation, the task of automatically generating description words for a picture, is a key component in various image search and retrieval applications. But in this system, we manually annotate the areas of every image containing the disease with a bounding box and class. Some diseases might look similar depending on its infection status.

Annotation process might able to label the class and location of the infected areas in the leaf image. The outputs of this step are the coordinates of the bounding boxes of different sizes with their corresponding class of disease, which consequently will be evaluated as the Intersection over-Union (IoU) with the predicted results during testing.

Images are collected from various sources were in various formats along with different resolutions and quality. In order to get better feature extraction, images are intended to be used as dataset for deep neural network were pre-processed in order to gain consistency. Images used for the dataset were image resized to 256×256 to reduce the time of training, which was automatically computed by written script in Python, using the OpenCV framework (Sladojevic et al., 2016), (Howse, 2013). In machine learning, as well as in statistics, over fitting appears when a statistical model describes random noise or error rather than underlying relationship (Hawkins, 2004). The image augmentation contained one of several transformation techniques including affine transformation, perspective transformation, image rotations (Stearns & Kannappan, 1995) and intensity transformations (contrast and brightness enhancement, color, noise).

Figure 2. Image analysis

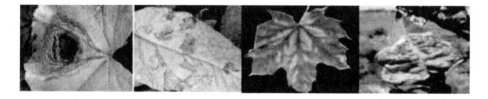

Image Analysis

Our system main goal is to detect and recognize the class disease in the image. We need to accurately detect the object, as well as identify the class to which it belongs. We extend the idea of object detection framework to adapt it with different feature extractors that detect diseases in the image. Faster R-CNN Faster R-CNN (Fuentes et al., 2017), (Ren et al., 2016) for object recognition and its Region Proposal Network (RPN) to estimate the class and location of object that may contain a target candidate. The RPN is used to generate the object a proposal, including their class and box coordinates. R-FCN Similar to Faster R-CNN,(Fuentes et al., 2017), (Dai et al., 2016), (Girshick, 2015) R-FCN uses a Region Proposal Network to generate object proposals, but instead of cropping features using the RoI pooling layer it crops them from the last layer prior to prediction. SSD SSD generates anchors that select the top most convolutional feature maps and a higher resolution feature map at a lower resolution. Then, a sequence of the convolutional layer containing each of the detection per class is added with spatial resolution used for prediction (Fuentes et al., 2017), (Liu et al., 2016). Thus, SSD is able to deal with objects of various sizes contained in the images. A Non-Maximum Suppression method is used to compare the estimated results with the ground-truth. G. Feature Extraction There are some conditions that should be taken into consideration when choosing a Feature Extractor, such as the type of layers, as a higher number of parameters increases the complexity of the system and directly influences the speed, and results of the system. Although each network has been designed with specific characteristics, all share the same goal, which is to increase accuracy while reducing computational complexity. In this system each object detector to be merged with some of the feature extractor. (Fuentes et al., 2017)The system performance is evaluated first of all in terms of the Intersection-over-Union (IoU), and the Average Precision (AP) that is introduced in the Pascal VOC Challenge (Everingham et al., 2010) .

$$IoU(A, B) = | A \cap B / A \cup B | \tag{1}$$

where A represents the ground-truth box collected in the annotation, and B represents the predicted result of the network. If the estimated IoU outperforms a threshold value, the predicted result is considered as a true positive, TP, or if not as a false positive, FP. TP is the number of true positives generated by the network, and FP corresponds to the number of false positives. Ideally, the number of FP should be small and determines how accurate the network to deal with each case is. The IoU is a widely used method for evaluating the accuracy of an object detector. (Fuentes et al., 2017)[17]The Average Precision is the area under the Precision-Recall curve for the detection task. As in the Pascal VOC Challenge, the AP is computed by averaging the precision over a set of spaced recall levels (Lu et al., 2017), and the mAP is the AP computed over all classes in our task.

$$AP = \frac{1}{11} \sum_{r \in \{0,0.1,...,1\}} p_{inter\,p}(r) \tag{2}$$

$$p_{inter\,p}(r) = \max_{\tilde{r}:\tilde{r}\geq r} p(\tilde{r})$$ (3)

Where p($\tilde{r}$) is the measure precision at recall $\tilde{r}$.

Faster R-CNN for each object proposal, (Ren et al., 2016)we extract the features with a RoI Pooling layer and perform object classification and bounding-box regression to obtain the estimated targets. We used batch normalization for each feature extractor, and train end-to-end using an Image Net Pre trained Network. To perform the experiments, our dataset has been divided into training set, validation set and testing set. Evaluation is performed on the Validation set after that training is process is performed on the training set and then final evaluation done in testing phase. As in the Pascal Visual Object Classes (VOC) Challenge (Everingham et al., 2010), the validation set is a technique used for minimizing over fitting and is a typical way to stop the network from learning. We use the training and validation sets to perform the training process and parameter selection, respectively, and the testing set for evaluating the results on unknown data.

CONCLUSION

Crop protection in organic agriculture is not a simple matter. It depends on a thorough knowledge of the crops grown and their likely pests, pathogens and weeds. In our system specialized deep learning models were developed, based on specific convolutional neural networks architectures, for the detection of plant diseases through leaves images of healthy or diseased plants. Our detector applied images captured in-place by various camera devices and also collected from various resources. Our experimental results and comparisons between various deep-architectures with feature extractors demonstrated how our deep-learning-based detector is able to successfully recognize different categories of diseases in various plants and also give solution for concern diseases. Pests/diseases are generally not a significant problem in organic systems, since healthy plants living in good soil with balanced nutrition are better able to resist pest/disease attack. We hope our proposed system will make a suggestive contribution to the agriculture research.

REFERENCES

Dai, J., He, K., & Sun, J. (2015). *Instance-aware semantic segmentation via multi-task network cascades.* arXiv preprint arXiv:1512.04412.

Dai, J., Li, Y., He, K., & Sun, J. R.-F. C. N. (2016). *Object Detection via Region based Fully Convolutional Networks.* arXiv:1605.06409v2.

Everingham, M., Van Gool, L., Williams, C., Winn, J., & Zisserman, A. (2010). The Pascal Visual Object Classes (VOC) Challenge. *Int. Comput. Vis., 88*(2), 303–338. doi:10.100711263-009-0275-4

Fuentes, A., Yoon, S., Kim, S., & Park, D. (2017). A Robust Deep Learning-Based Detector for Real-Time Tomato Plant Diseases and Pests Recognition. *Sensors (Basel), 17*(9), 2022. doi:10.339017092022

Girshick, R. (2015). Fast r-cnn. *Proceedings of the IEEE International Conference on Computer Vision*, 1440–1448.

Hawkins, D. M. (2004). The problem of over-fitting. *Journal of Chemical Information and Computer Sciences, 44*(1), 1–12. doi:10.1021/ci0342472 PMID:14741005

Howse, J. (2013). *OpenCV ComputerVision with Python.* Packt Publishing.

Huang, J., Rathod, V., Sun, C., Zhu, M., Korattikara, A., Fathi, A., Fischer, I., Wojna, Z., Song, Y., & Guadarrama, S. (2017). Speed/accuracy trade-offs for modern convolutional object detectors. *Proceedings of the IEEE Computer Society Conference on Computer Vision and Pattern Recognition.* 10.1109/CVPR.2017.351

Kamilaris, A., & Francesc, X. (2018). Deep learning in agriculture: A survey. *Computers and Electronics in Agriculture, 147*, 70–90. doi:10.1016/j.compag.2018.02.016

Kaundal, R., & Amar, S. (2006). Machine learning technique in disease forecasting: A case study on rice blast prediction. *BMC Bioinformatics.* Advance online publication. doi:10.1186/1471-2105-7-485

Konstantinos, P. (2018). Deep learning models for plant disease detection and diagnosis. *Computers and Electronics in Agriculture, 145*, 311–318. doi:10.1016/j.compag.2018.01.009

Kulkarni Anand, H., & Ashwin Patil, R. K. (2012). Applying image processing technique to detect plant diseases. *Int J Mod Eng Res, 2*(5), 3661–3664.

Liu, W., Anguelov, D., Erhan, D., Szegedy, C., Reed, S., Fu, C., & Berg, A. C. (2016). SSD: Single Shot MultiBox Detector. *Proceedings of the European Conference on Computer Vision ECCV*, 21–37.

Lu, J., Hu, J., Zhao, G., Mei, F., & Zhang, C. (2017). An in-field automatic wheat disease diagnosis system. *Computers and Electronics in Agriculture, 142,* 369–379. doi:10.1016/j.compag.2017.09.012

Ren, S., He, K., Girshick, R., & Sun, J. (2016). Faster R-CNN: Towards Real-Time Object Detection with Region Proposal Networks. *IEEE Transactions on Pattern Analysis and Machine Intelligence, 39*(6), 1137–1149. doi:10.1109/TPAMI.2016.2577031 PMID:27295650

Sabah, B., & Navdeep, S. (2012). Remote area plant disease detection using image processing. *IOSR J Electron Commun Eng, 2*(6), 31–4.

Sankaran, S., Mishra, A., Ehsani, R., & Davis, C. (2010). A review of advanced techniques for detecting plant diseases. *Computers and Electronics in Agriculture, 72*(1), 1–13. doi:10.1016/j.compag.2010.02.007

Sladojevic, S., Arsenovic, M., Anderla, A., Culibrk, D., & Stefanovic, D. (2016). Deep Neural Networks Based Recognition of Plant Diseases by Leaf Image Classification. Computational Intelligence and Neuroscience. doi:10.1155/2016/3289801

Stearns, C. C., & Kannappan, K. (1995). *Method for 2-D affine transformation of images.* US Patent No. 5,475,803.

Chapter 14
Spatio–Temporal Analysis of the Glacial Lakes of the Western Himalayas in Chamoli and Pithoragarh Districts of Uttarakhand Using Remote Sensing and GIS

Bulu Basak
International Institute of Geospatial Science and Technology (IIGST), India

Thahira Umar
Bharathidasan University, India

Shahid Gulzar
International Institute of Geospatial Science and Technology (IIGST), India

Rajeev Kumar
https://orcid.org/0000-0002-4141-1282
Chandigarh University, India

Biswajit Roy Chowdhury
Vidyasagar College, Kolkata, India

DOI: 10.4018/978-1-6684-2443-8.ch014

ABSTRACT

Remote sensing technology provides a spatial-temporal database to track the dynamics of water bodies. Global climatic change has a substantial impact on the dynamic activities of glaciers and glacial lakes and in turn affects the surrounding ecosystem. Thus, monitoring and maintaining an updated database about glacial activity is essential for disaster preparedness. In this study, spatiotemporal analysis of glacial lakes of the Western Himalayas in Chamoli and Pithoragarh District of Uttarakhand during 1994, 2000, 2010, and 2020 were done. These glacial lakes showed significant spatiotemporal changes and an increase in their aerial extent, nearly doubled from 1994 to 2020. GL_A had a sudden tremendous growth in the interim period may tend to many disasters like GLOF (glacial lake outburst floods). The study area holds many tourist pilgrimage attractions, and it needs sufficient monitoring of several factors over the entire fragile region for the construction of any infrastructures, disaster mitigation, and urban development processes.

INTRODUCTION

Glacial lakes are the outcome of the increasing rate of global temperature and climatic change and are formed in the depressions or voids created by the melting of glaciers. The surrounding regions of these voids and depressions are often unstable and weak. These break out when the water is filled in glacial lakes beyond their holding capacity. The contained amount of water rushes downward along with the stream channel with a large amount of dust, rocks, boulders, etc that may turn into disastrous Glacial lake outburst floods (GLOF) (Bhambri et al., 2015). This has a disastrous effect on human and animal lives, especially in mountainous regions (Raj&Kumar,2016). Additionally, climatic variability has a paramount influence on increasing the spatial areas of these glacier lakes and increasing or decreasing the number of glacial lakes (Ahmed et al., 2021). The expansion rate of these glacial lakes is a threatening factor to the countries near the Himalayan Region since it can result in the frequency of GLOF occurrences (Bajracharya, 2007). For the mitigation of the GLOF, monitoring the glacial lake is undoubtedly the first and the most important step to predict the chances of GLOF in the future. Remote Sensing plays a major role in monitoring and gathering information from inaccessible areas. Using remote sensing tools, we can at a minimum predict the most vulnerable zones, and thereby, enhances the mitigation process in the advent of disaster (Richardson & Reynolds, 2000). Here we propose a study on the Spatio-temporal analysis of Glacial Lakes present in the Himalayan state of Uttarkhand which is prone to many disasters like landslides, flash floods, etc. The state holds many tourist pilgrimages attractions having 35.60 million domestic tourist inflow and foreign tourist visits across

0.15 million in 2019 and has a fragile environment. Therefore, it needs sufficient monitoring of several factors over the entire fragile region for the construction of any infrastructures, disaster mitigation, urban development process, etc.

BACKGROUND

The Himalayan glaciers are the most essential source of fresh water for human living and other developmental purposes They are also the most vulnerable features to increasing global warming and sudden climatic changes. The majority of the glaciers are melting at a high rate driving the formation and extension of glacial lakes which may even lead to dangerous hazards like GLOF,ice-rock avalanche, etc, Glacial lake inventories play a major role in further investigation of the existence of glacial lakes in the area(Kulkarni et al., 2011), (Watanabe et al., 2009) . These inventories of the Uttarakhand region helped in the identification and examining the glacial lakes (Bhambri et al., 2015),(Raj&Kumar,2016). It aided in recognizing the location, its corresponding basins, and the type of the glacial lakes. Most of the glacial lakes didn't have a well renowned common or local name. The well-known lakes like Kedar Tal, Hemkund, Satopanth Tal, etc didn't have significant Spatio-temporal changes. Even though, Kedar Tal has been categorized as a very high dangerous, potentially critical lake and a high-risk lake by Worni et.al (2012), and Mal et.al(2021). Global climatic change has a paramount impact on the melting of glaciers and the origin, evolution of Glacial Lakes in the Himalayan territory (Dou et al., 2021). The corresponding impact of these is a threatening factor to the living beings that rely upon the Himalayan region for basic sources.

STUDY AREA

This study area focuses on the Chamoli and Pithoragarh districts of the Himalayan state Uttarakhand. Chamoli is the second largest district of Uttarakhand hosting varied famous pilgrim destinations and tourist attractions. The Alaknandariver originates in this district, one of the major tributaries of the river Ganga. Pithoragarh district has its northern and eastern parts with international borders, comes under the Kumaon division. Milam is one of the largest glaciers present in the district. The state has 13 districts that fall under two primary administrative units as Garhwal(Northwest part of Uttarakhand) and Kumaon (Southeast part of Uttarakhand). It has approximately 968 glaciers as one of its sources of water. The study area is depicted in the following location map (Figure 1).

DATASETS

In this study, we have used Landsat 4-5, Landsat 7, and Landsat 8(Path/Row-145/39) data for outlining and mappingglacial lakes in the area of interest (Table 1). We chose all the cloud-free data. We gathered Landsat data from Advanced Spaceborne Thermal Emission & Reflection Radiometer- ASTER DEM (Digital Elevation Model) of 30m resolution were downloaded from the portal of the Global Land Survey(GLS) data system of the United States Geological Survey(USGS). It aided in understanding the topography of the study area by creating hillside, slope, aspect maps from the gathered data. We were able to monitor the glacial lakes from 1994, 2000,2010, to 2020 for spatiotemporal changes. We used Google Earth Pro to cross-check the existing features of the lakes.

Table 1. Datasets

Date	Data and Sensor	Bands	Spatial Resolution (m)	Temporal Resolution
Oct 09, 1994	Landsat 5 -TM	7	30	16
Oct 01, 2000	LANDSAT 7-ETM	9	30	16
Oct 13, 2010	LANDSAT 7-ETM	9	30	16
Oct 16,2020	LANDSAT 8 -OLI_ TIRS	11	30	16

METHODOLOGY

In order to conduct a detailed spatial-temporal analysis of the glacial lakes, we approached a methodical series of steps in the following flowchart (Figure 2). Landsat data was chosen in 1994,2000,2010,2020 and after further process study area was chosen.

For the detection of glacial lakes from the remote sensing multispectral imagery, one needs to differentiate the water bodies from other land surface types. That can be achieved by understanding the spectral reflectance differences. Water strongly absorbs at Near-infrared wavelength regions whereas snow, soil, vegetation strongly reflects in this region. Using these wavelengths NDWI can enhance the contrast between water and the surrounding environments. NDWI was applied to check the presence and growth of the glacial lakes accurately.

The glacial lakes have been mapped and extracted effectively from satellite imagery with the help of the NDWI (Normalized Difference Water Index) first proposed by Mcfeeters in 1996. It is defined as,

NDWI = GREEN - NIR/ GREEN+NIR

It was used to delineate the water bodies efficiently and their Spatio-temporal changes. The index uses green and near-infrared wavelengths. NDSI(Normalized Difference Snow Index was used to differentiate the snow-covered glaciers from water bodies which helped in the accurate mapping of the water bodies.NDSI is defined as,

NDSI = (G – SWIR1) / (G + SWIR1)

RESULT AND DISCUSSION

Based on regional analysis, we have chosen three glacial lakes which show significant Spatio-temporal changes. These three lakes are end-damned moraine lakes one (GL_A) of which was cited as a very high dangerous, Potentially critical lake, and very high-risk lake by Worni et.al (2013).These lakes are named according to their basins, GL_A - Alaknanda basin, GL_G -Goriganga Basin, SawragSarover(local name)-GL_S-Dhauliganga Basin. Watershed map (Figure 3), Relief map (Figure 4), Hill shade map (Figure 5) and Aspect map (Figure 6) has been created for the study area using arc GIS software.

These lakes showed significant Spatio-temporal changes throughout the area of interest. These glacial lakes are in fragile environments. These lakes showed an increase in their area from 1990 to 2020. This becomes an essential factor to monitor these lakes and their topological features that may lead to a disaster in the future. This growth may be due to the recession of the surrounding glaciers and the climatic factors influencing it. This stands as a major concern of preparedness for any forthcoming disasters in the surrounding regions of the Himalayan ranges.

Table 2. Information about selected glacial lakes

Lake	Local Name	LONG	LAT	Lake Type	Basin
GL_S	SWARG SAROVER	80.38759	30.44602	END MDL	DHAULIGANGA
GL_G	UNNAMED	80.17628	30.56382	END MDL	GORIGANGA
GL_A	UNNAMED	79.46	30.976	MDL	ALAKNANDA

GL_S

This is a moraine-dammed glacial lake situated at location coordinates 30°26'45.7"N 80°23'15.3" E. It pertains to the Dhauliganga basin. The amount of water contained in the lake varies with the time but overall showed an increase in its extent. The lake area has increased from 0.086742 to 0.106037 sq. km from 1994 to 2020. The huge loss in the glacier area (IN 5O103 04 030- GSI ID) in the period 1968 to 2016 contributed to the growth of this highest lake in the Dhauliganga basin. NDWI has been calculated for each lake and (Figure7) is showing the NDWI of GL_S lake. Figure 8 is showing the spatio-temporal changes and Figure 9 showing the growth of GL_S Lake.

Table 3. Temporal variations in the aerial extent of GL_S

Year	AREA (in ha)	AREA (in sq. km)
1994	8.6742	0.086742
2000	10.3601	0.103601
2010	7.2091	0.072091
2020	10.6037	0.106037

GL_G

This is a Moraine dammed glacial lake situated at the location coordinates 30°33'49.8"N 80°10'34.6" E. It pertains to the Goriganga basin. This glacial lake shows a progressive growth of the amount of contained water in it. The lake area has increased from 0.11612 to 0.219626 sq. km from 1994 to 2020. Nearly the lake has doubled in its area which is a matter of concern. Figure 10 is showing the spatio-temporal changes of GL_G block. (Figure11) is showing the NDWI and Figure 12 is representing the growth of GL_G Lake.

Table 4. Temporal variations in the aerial extent of glacial Lake GL_G

Year	Area (in ha)	Area (in sq. km)
1994	11.612	0.11612
2000	14.2439	0.142439
2010	20.0351	0.200351
2020	21.9626	0.219626

GL_A

This is a moraine-dammed glacial lake situated at the location coordinates 30°58'33.6"N 79°27'36.0" E. It pertains to the Alaknanda basin. This glacial lake shows a progressive and sudden tremendous growth especially from 2010 to 2020. The lake area has increased from 0.070755 to 0.168089 sq. km from 1994 to 2020. Additionally, this lake was cited as a very high dangerous, potentially critical lake, and very high-risk lake by, Worni et.al (2013). Spatio-temporal changes of the lake represented in Figure 13, where Figure 14 depicting the NDWI in different time period and Figure 15 representing the growth of the lake within the changes of the time period.

Table 5. Temporal variations in the aerial extent of glacial lake GL_A

Year	Area in ha	Area in sq. km
1994	7.0755	0.070755
2000	12.3626	0.123626
2010	11.9627	0.119627
2020	16.8089	0.168089

FUTURE WORK

Assessing the future Glacial lake Outburst Flood danger, flood paths, downstream impacts, GLOF risk assessment of these lakes may be subjected to future work.

CONCLUSION

Usage of GIS and Remote sensing techniques was highly helpful in carrying out studies like this in far inaccessible regions. It allows the possibility of mapping these high-altitude lakes, in understanding their growth and formation. Generally, Uttarakhand has only a few lakes that show significant Spatio-temporal changes. Even though the state is prone to highly dangerous disasters like the Kedarnathtragedy(2012), Chamoli disaster 2021, etc has a horrible impact (Srivastava et al., 2022). This emphasizes the preparedness of the state for natural disasters. Global climatic change has a paramount impact on the melting of glaciers and the origin, evolution of Glacial Lakes in the Himalayan territory. The corresponding impact of these is a threatening factor to the living beings that rely upon the Himalayan region for basic sources. The need of the hour is to monitor these glacial lakes, being prepared for hazards and effective mitigation.

REFERENCES

Ahmed, R., Wani, G. F., Ahmad, S. T., Mir, R. A., Almazroui, M., Jain, S. K., & Ahmed, P. (2021). Spatiotemporal dynamics of glacial lakes (1990–2018) in the Kashmir Himalayas, India using Remote Sensing and GIS. *Discov Water*, *1*(1), 7. doi:10.100743832-021-00007-1

Atlas: Glacial Lakes of Uttarakhand. (n.d.). https://www.iirs.gov.in/atlas-glacial-lakes-of-uttarakhand

Bajracharya, S. R. (2007). Impacts of climate change on Himalayan glaciers and glacial lakes: case studies on GLOF and associated hazards in Nepal and Bhutan. Kathmandu: International Centre for Integrated Mountain Development (ICIMOD).

Bhambri, R., Mehta, M., Dobhal, D., & Gupta, A. (2015). *Glacial lake inventory of Uttarakhand*. Academic Press.

Dou, X., Fan, X., Yunus, A. P., & Xiong, J. (2021). *Spatio-temporal evolution of glacial lakes in the Tibetan Plateau over the past 30 years*. doi:10.5194/essd-2021-354

Kulkarni, A. V., Rathore, B. P., Singh, S. K., & Bahuguna, I. M. (2011). Understanding changes in the Himalayan cryosphere using remote sensing techniques. *International Journal of Remote Sensing*, *32*(3), 601–615. doi:10.1080/01431161.2010.517802

Mal, S., Allen, S., Frey, H., Huggel, C., & Dimri, A. P. (2021). Sector wise Assessment of Glacial Lake Outburst Flood Danger in the Indian Himalayan Region. *Mountain Research and Development*. Advance online publication.

Mir, R. A., Jain, S. K., Thayyen, R. J., & Saraf, A. K. (2017). Assessment of recent glacier changes and its controlling factors from 1976 to 2011 in Baspa basin, western Himalaya. *Arctic, Antarctic, and Alpine Research*, *49*(4), 621–647. doi:10.1657/AAAR0015-070

Raj, K. B. G., & Kumar, K. V. (2016). Inventory of glacial lakes and its evolution in Uttarakhand Himalaya using time- series satellite data. *Photonirvachak (Dehra Dun)*, *44*(6), 959–976. doi:10.100712524-016-0560-y

Richardson, S., & Reynolds, J. (2000). An overview of glacial hazards in the Himalayas. *Quaternary International*, *65*, 31–47. doi:10.1016/S1040-6182(99)00035-X

Sattar, A., Goswami, A., Kulkarni, A., & Das, P. (2019). Glacier-Surface Velocity Derived Ice Volume and Retreat Assessment in the Dhauliganga Basin, Central Himalaya – A Remote Sensing and Modeling Based Approach. *Frontiers in Earth Science*. https://doi.org/7. doi:10.3389/feart.2019.00105

Srivastava, P., Namdev, P., & Singh, P. (2022). 7 February Chamoli (Uttarakhand, India) Rock-Ice Avalanche Disaster: Model-Simulated Prevailing Meteorological Conditions. *Atmosphere*, *267*. Advance online publication. https://doi.org/13. doi:10.3390/atmos13020267

Wadia Institute of Himalayan Geology. (2015). *Glacier lake inventory of Uttarakhand*. Author.

Watanabe, T., Lamsal, D., & Ives, J. D. (2009). Evaluating the growth characteristics of glacial a glacial lake and its degree of danger of outburst flooding Imja Glacier, Khumbu Himal, Nepal. *Norwegian J Geogr*, *63*(4), 255–267. doi:10.1080/00291950903368367

Worni, R., Stoffel, M., Huggel, C., Volz, C., Casteller, A., & Luckman, B. (2012). Analysis and dynamic modeling of a moraine failure and glacial lake outburst flood at Ventisquero Negro, Patagonian Andes (Argentina). *Journal of Hydrology (Amsterdam)*, *444*, 134–145. doi:10.1016/j.jhydrol.2012.04.013

APPENDIX

Figure 1.

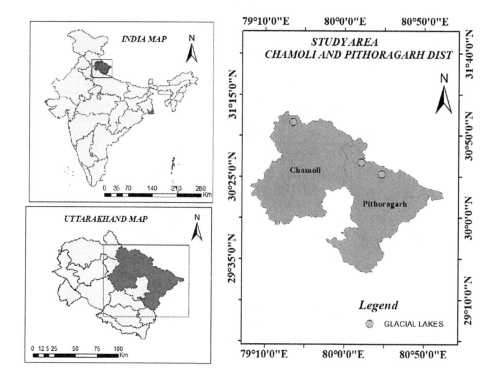

Figure 2.

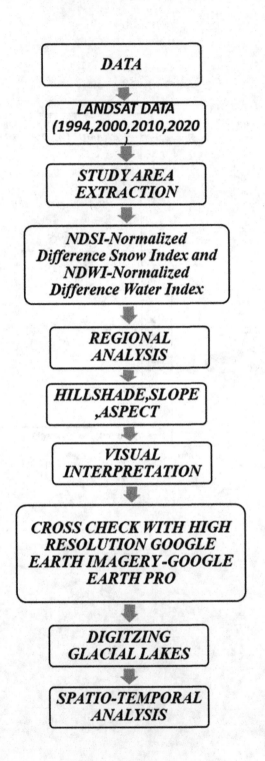

Figure 3.

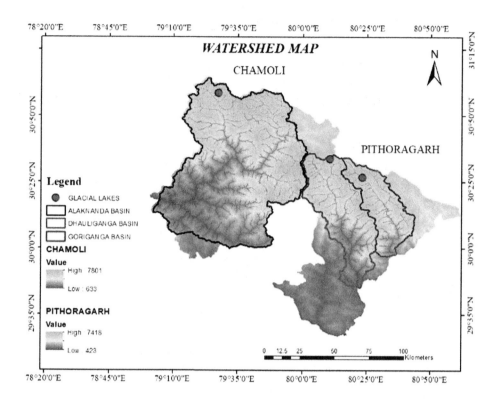

Figure 4.

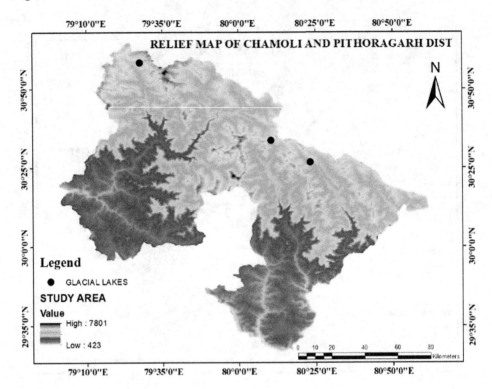

Figure 5.

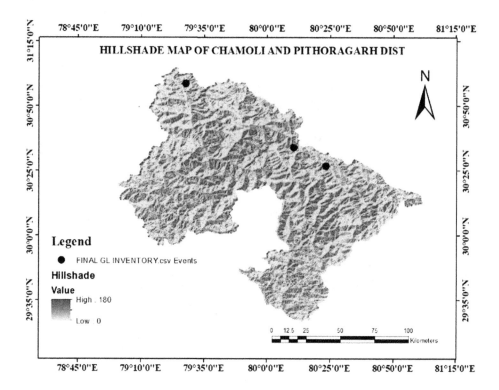

Figure 6.

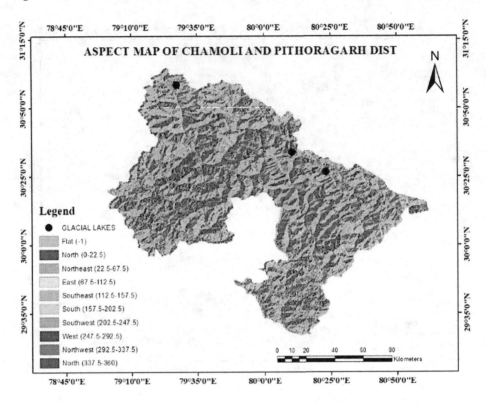

Figure 7.

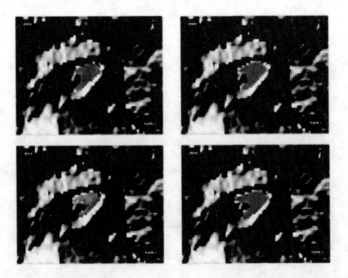

Figure 8.

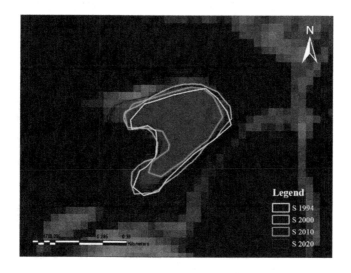

Figure 9.

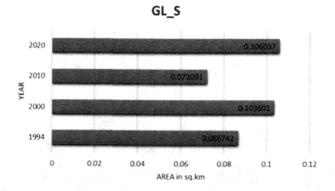

Figure 10.

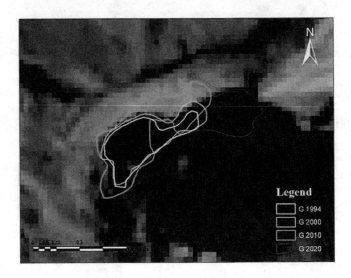

Figure 11.

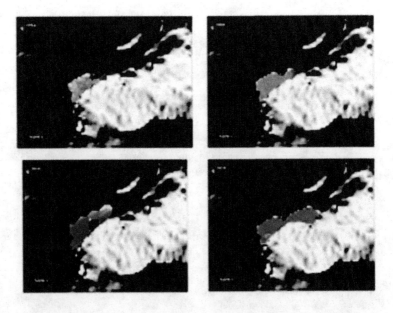

Figure 12.

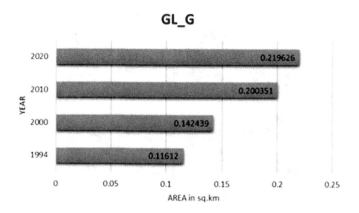

Figure 13.

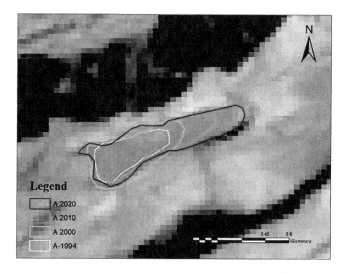

Figure 14.

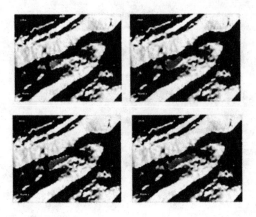

Figure 15.

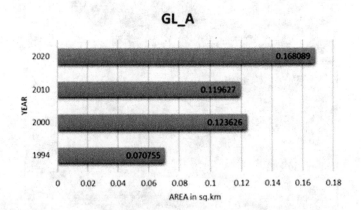

Chapter 15
Water Quality Prediction of Nainital Lake, Uttarakhand, India Using Artificial Neural Network Models

Manisha Koranga
Kumaon University, India

R. P. Pant
Graphic Era Hill University, India

Pushpa Pant
Motiram Baburam Government Post Graduate College, India

Ashutosh Kumar Bhatt
Uttarakhand Open University, India

Durgesh Pant
Uttarakhand Open University, India

Tarun Kumar
MIET Kumaun, India

ABSTRACT

Artificial neural networks have progressed in a rapid way in the field of soft computing, and it is widely used in forecasting. The work presented in this chapter is about the development of artificial neural network (ANN)-based models to forecast the water quality (WQ) in Nainital Lake, Uttarakhand, India. A dataset comprising pH, turbidity, and total dissolved solid (TDS) of time period 2018-2019 has been used and analyzed using MATLAB software. For experimentation purposes, four data partition strategies, 10 learning algorithms of back propagation neural network (BPNN), and different combinations of learning rates and training tolerance were evaluated. The performance of the model was evaluated using statistical methods such as MSE, RMSE, MAD, MAPE. The results of the experiment show the capability of the optimal ANN models to predict the WQ of Nainital Lake.

DOI: 10.4018/978-1-6684-2443-8.ch015

1. INTRODUCTION

Water is a crucial resource on the earth for the survival of living organisms. Besides it, water played a crucial role for several industries, irrigation, or many other fields. Worldwide approximately, 70% of water is utilized for farming and irrigation purposes, and 10% used for domestic purposes. The water level is decreasing very rapidly due to a speedy increase in population, which creates a worse situation in the future. Several scientific studies have reported that 80% of illnesses are based on poor water quality and sanitation conditions in developing countries (Kofi, 2003). Currently, water quality is a matter of serious concern because many water-borne diseases like cholera, diarrhea, dysentery, etc., affect a large population especially Rural area. India is one of the countries in the world most water-challenged developing. Uttarakhand is a Himalayan state and consists of Garhwal and Kumaon regions. Uttarakhand has special importance in Indian culture and traditions because it has the origin of several holy rivers, springs and lakes. Ganga and Yamuna both have their origin points reckoned to be sacred most in the country. Yamuna, Bhagirathi, and many other tributaries and distributaries (Semwal & Akolkar, 2006). Rivers, streams, springs, and lakes are the primary sources of water in the Kumaun division. More than 50% of the total population depends on these resources for their daily need of water (Singh & Rawat, 1985). Nainital district is called the Lake District of India, and the center of natural beauty in the Kumaun region. Therefore, it is a favorite tourist place of Uttarakhand and consists of seven lakes namely Nainital Lake, Sattal Lake, Sariyatal Lake, Khurpatal Lake, Naukuchiatal Lake, Bhimtal Lake, and Kamaltal Lake.

Nainital Lake is also known as Naini Lake and is the only source of drinking water supply for the population. But nowadays, the water of the Nainital lake is being polluted continuously due to many factors such as disposal of solid waste, anthropogenic activities and sewage effluents, etc. These factors affect the physicochemical and biological behavior of water, which affects the water quality of lakes (Alam et al., 2007; M. Alam et al., 2007; Chandra et al., 2006; Sharma & Kansal, 2011). Due to the high load of tourism activities and increasing population day by day, Lake is losing its rejuvenation and the self-purification capability and its water is becoming not suitable for domestic as well as agricultural purposes. Therefore, the need to monitor and maintain the quality of water becomes necessary for the safety of human beings.

The conventional method of water quality monitoring techniques consumes a lot of time and labor (Korostynska et al., 2013). So, there was a need for a technology-based water quality monitoring system for Nainital Lakes.

1.1 Objective

The research work focuses on the development of an optimal Artificial Neural Network model to predict the water quality of Nainital Lake which will work in an efficient and in accurate manner.

2. LITERATURE REVIEW

This research paper investigates the use of the Artificial Neural Network method to estimate water quality. ANN is quite popular due to its ability to model non-linear patterns, its self-adjusting nature and to provide an accurate result. Nowadays, ANN has been applied in a variety of prediction applications. Several parameters of water quality have been modelled using Artificial Neural Network, such as pH, temp, Total Dissolved Solids, turbidity, BOD by the researchers.

Seo and colleagues' (2016) proposed a technique to minimize the influence of components such as trend, periodicity and stochastic by developing the Ensemble ANN model with stratified sampling technique. They used 8 parameters temp, DO, pH, Electric Conductivity, Tn, TP and Chlorophyll. The result stated that 7 parameters have higher value of R Squared than 0.85 and 5 parameters have higher value of RMSE than 1.0.

Sarkar and Pandey (2015) present the use of Artificial Neural Network technique to estimate the concentration of Dissolved Oxygen at the downstream of Mathura City, India. They applied feed forward error back propagation Neural Network technique to develop three models by taking different combinations of input variables and input stations. They used monthly datasets of 6 parameters such as flow discharge, temp, pH, biochemical oxygen demand (BOD) and dissolved oxygen. Statistical tool has been used to evaluate the performance of ANN technique. The result stated that the predicted value of DO show outstanding accuracy by giving high correlation (up to 0.9) between measured and predicted value.

Palani and colleagues' (2008) used ANN approach for the simulation of regional seawater quality modeling. The aim of utilizing ANN approach is due to its ability of representing not only linear but also non-linear relationships. ANN has the capability of learning these relationships directly from the data used in modeling. They used 4 parameters namely, salinity, temp, dissolved oxygen and chlorophyll-alpha for the study. The result stated that for the training and overfitting test data, simulation accuracy (Nash- Sutcliffe coefficient of efficiency-R2) ranged between 0.8 and 0.9. This represents that ANN has great ability to simulate the water quality variable.

Sulaiman and colleagues' (2019) applied ANN technique due to its ability to classify the water quality. They used six input variables such as pH, Total Suspended

Solids (TSS), Dissolved Oxygen (DO), Chemical Oxygen Demand (COD), Biological Oxygen Demand (BOD) and Ammonia. After training and testing the network, the result stated that the model produces 80% of accuracy and 0.468 of RMSE value.

Zhang and colleagues' (2019) proposed a novel model to deal with the difficulties of ANN with a single layer and few numbers of units to represent complex inner relationships between multiple water quality variables. The novel model is based on Multilayer Artificial Neural Networks (MANN) and mutual information for predicting the trend of DO. The water quality data set of Baffle creek Australia has been used.

Li and colleagues' (2017) proposed a novel approach that combines particle Swarm optimization (PSO), chaos theory, self- adaptive strategy and back propagation neural network to evaluate the water quality of Weihe River, China. The performance of the model was evaluated using average absolute deviation (AAD), Root Mean Square error of prediction (RMSEP) and Squared correlation coefficient. The result stated that the proposed method has good prediction ability, high precision and good correlation for the evaluation of water quality.

Khayyun and colleagues' (2014) used ANN model for the prediction of forecasting of monthly TDS parameters in Euphrates River water, in Iraq. To accomplish the study, 6 sampling stations, 4 input variables comprising flow rates, the year, the month and distance of the sampling stations from the upstream of the river were utilized. In this proposed method, a computer program of multiple regression (MLR) is used to obtain a set of coefficients for a linear model. The performance of the model was evaluated using correlation coefficient, RMSE and MAPE. The result stated that performance of ANN model is less efficient than multiple regression model.

Latif and colleagues' (2020) proposed an ANN model to predict nitrate (NO3) concentration in the Feitsui reservoir, Taiwan. They used 5 water quality parameters of Ammonium (NH3), Nitrogen Dioxide (NO2), Dissolved Oxygen (DO), Nitrate (NO3) and phosphate (PO4) has been used. The performance of model evaluated using Statistical indicator i.e., Correlation Coefficient (R). The result stated that ANN is a correct model to predict accurate results.

Bisht and colleagues' (2017) have utilized soft computing-based ANN technique for the modelling the water quality of Ganga River by developing a prediction model by implementing six training functions. They used 5 years past data from 2001 to 2005 of five sampling stations and used 5 water quality parameters: temperature, BOD, TC, DO and pH. They developed a WQ prediction model, a neural network structure of 5-10-1, 0.1 as a training goal and various training functions by implementing feed forward error back propagation method. They used Mean Square Error as the method for assessing the performance and the result showed that the model developed with Conjugate Gradient with Polak-Ribiere Restarts predicted worst while the model with Levenberg-Marquardt backpropagation learning algorithm performed best.

3. MATERIAL AND METHOD USED

The data of 1.5 years of duration 2018-2019 used in this research work and it was procured from Jal Sansthan, Nainital, Uttarakhand and Sensor-based devices installed in Nainital lake by Uttarakhand Science Education and Research Center (USERC), Dehradun.

3.1 Study Area

Figure 1. Image of Nainital from google earth

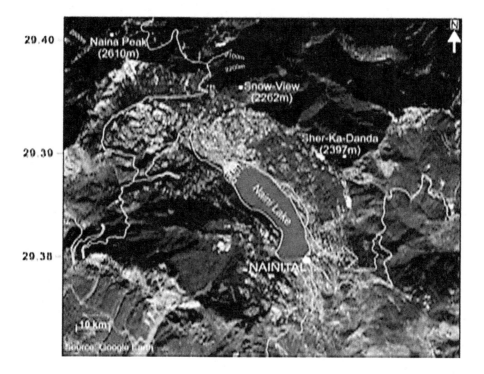

Natural Lake is known for its mesmerizing beauty. The characteristics of Nainital Lake are shown in Table 1. The lake supports a resident population of about 954,605 and about 7.45 lakh tourists annually within a small area of 11.73 km² (Gupta et al., 2010).

Table 1. Characteristics of Nainital Lake

Shape	Natural eye shaped or crescent shaped, warm holomictic lake
Latitude	29° 24' N
Longitude	79° 28' E
Maximum Depth	27.3m
Mean Depth	16.2m

3.2 Selection of Appropriate Inputs

We have selected a minimum of three input parameters namely, pH, Total Suspended Solids, and turbidity to predict the water quality and to construct a cost-effective system. The statistical information of input parameters is given in Table 2.

Table 2. Statistical Information of input parameters

Statistical Parameters	pH (pH)	Total Dissolved Solids (mg/L)	Turbidity (NTU)
Maximum Value	8.9	460.84	2.8
Minimum Value	8.1	430	1.1
Mean Value	8.362	440.249	1.34
Standard Deviation	0.152	6.048	0.215
Coefficient of Variation	1.8177	1.373768	16.044776

The figures 2, 3, 4 below illustrate the variation of parameters with respect to time (months).

Figure 2. pH

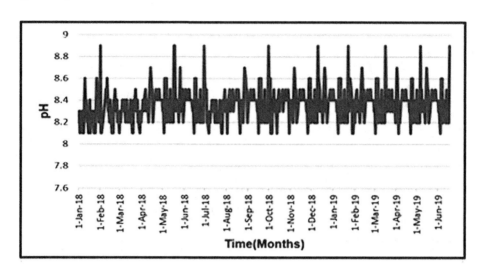

Figure 3. Total dissolved solid (TDS)

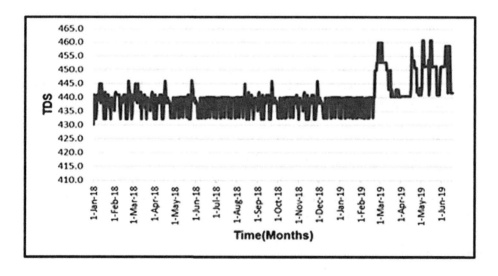

Figure 4. Turbidity

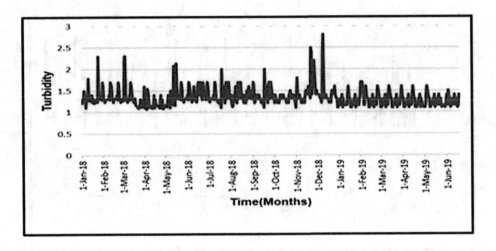

3.3 Artificial Neural Network Approach

3.3.1 *Basic Principle*

Artificial neural networks are the most popular machine learning mechanism that mimics the behavior of biological organisms. Artificial neural networks are inspired by the human brain, with neuron nodes interconnected like a web structure. An ANN model is a 3-layer structure comprising an input layer, a hidden layer and an output layer. Input for the network were three input variables which were represented by three neurons in the input layer. Output of the network was two outcomes (0 or 1) of water quality prediction. The output layer of the network consists of only one neuron that represents the quality of water. The number of neurons in the hidden layer was set to 25 for the experiment. ANN comprises a huge collection of neurons or nodes which are connected in some particular fashion that allow communication between the neurons or nodes, and works in parallel manner. Backpropagation neural network learning algorithm has been used for training purposes.

A I(3)-H(25)-O(1) framework of ANN model Structure considered for this implementation is shown in Figure 5.

Figure 5. Artificial neural network model with 3 input and 1 output

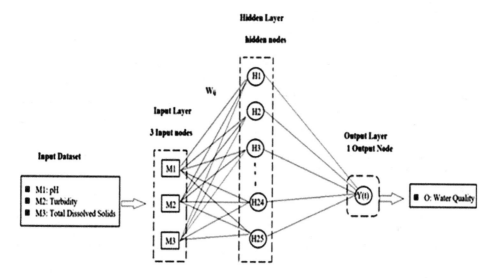

4. EXPERIMENT

4.1 Neural Network Training Parameters

The Table 3, shows the details of Neural Network training parameters and their corresponding values.

Table 3. Neural network training parameters and their corresponding values

Experiment Performed on	Neural Network Toolbox of MATLAB software
Total Dataset	530 tuples which is partitioned into two subsets, *viz.*, 'training set', and 'testing set'
Total Experiment Performed	1,440
Transfer Functions	Sigmoid Function and Linear transfer Function
Learning Rate (*lr*)	0.1, 0.01, 0.001
Training Tolerance (*e*) or Goal	0.1, 0.01, 0.001, 0.005
Data Partition Strategies (%)	75, 80, 85, 90 are named as '*a*', '*b*', '*c*' and '*d*'
Epochs	50000
Number of Neurons	25
Number of Hidden Layer	01
Backpropagation Learning Algorithms	*Gradient Descent with momentum term and adaptive learning rate (GDX), Gradient descent with adaptive learning rate (GDA), Resilient Backpropagation (RP), Fletcher-Reeves Conjugate Gradient (CGF), Polak-Ribiére Conjugate Gradient algorithm (CGP), Powell/Beale Conjugate Gradient algorithm (CGB), Scaled Conjugate Gradient (SCG), One Step Secant (OSS), and Levenberg-Marquardt (LM), Gradient descent with momentum term (GDM)*

4.2 Statistical Measures for Performance Evaluation

To assess the forecasting ability of ANN model following metrics have been used (Cyemezo et al., 2019).

1.   1. **Mean absolute deviation (MAD):** The sum of difference between actual expected output and model's prediction divided by total number of observations. It is calculated using the formula (1), where y_i is the original output and $\hat{y}_i$ is the predicted value and N is the total samples.

$$MAD = \frac{1}{N}\sum_{t=1}^{N}\left(y_i - \hat{y}_i\right) \qquad (1)$$

2.   2. **Mean square error (MSE):** The sum of squares of difference between actual expected output and model's prediction divided by total number of observations. It is calculated using the formula (2), where y_i is the original output and $\hat{y}_i$ is the predicted value and N is the total samples.

$$MSE = \frac{1}{N} \sum_{i=1}^{N} \left(y_i - \hat{y}_i \right)^2 \tag{2}$$

3.   3. **Root mean square error (RMSE):** The square root of MSE and scales the value of MSE close to the range of observed value. It is calculated using the formula (3), where y_i is the original output and $\hat{y}_i$ is the predicted value and N is the total samples.

$$RMSE = \sqrt{\frac{I}{N} \sum_{i=1}^{N} \left(y_i - \hat{y}_i \right)^2} = \sqrt{MSE} \tag{3}$$

4.   4. **Mean absolute percentage error (MAPE):** The mean or average of the absolute percentage errors of forecasts. Error is defined as actual expected output minus the model's prediction. Percentage errors are summed without regard to sign to calculate MAPE. It is calculated using the formula (4), where $y_{observed}$ is the original output and $y_{prediction}$ is the predicted value and N is the total samples.

$$MAPE = 100 \times \frac{I}{N} \sum \frac{\left| y_{observed} - y_{predicted} \right|}{y_{observed}} \tag{4}$$

5. RESULT AND DISCUSSION

In order to evaluate the best algorithm which provides fastest convergence in achieving the least value of indicators. The ANN models have been experimented for more reliable and accurate prediction of water quality using four training strategies adopted for partitions data into training and testing, different pairs of ANN parameters and using 10 ANN backpropagation training algorithms. In this experimentation work, we constructed 480 models per partition strategy, to obtain the optimum result each constructed model is run three times to get the best one among the 3 models, so that the total number of experimented models are (480x 3 = 1440) 1440.

Table 4 illustrates the least achieved values of MSE, RMSE, MAPE, MAD by evaluating different combinations of learning rate and training tolerance. In the table given below 'a', 'b','c' and 'd' represents data partition strategies used (%) *i.e.,* 75, 80, 85, 90 along with different learning algorithms.

Table 4. Least achieved values of MSE, RMSE, MAPE, MAD by evaluating different combinations of learning rate and training tolerance

Parameters (lr, e, n=25)	MSE	RMSE	MAPE	MAD
lr=0.1, e=0.1	0.000122 (c, LM)	0.011038(c,LM)	0.804764(c,LM)	0.009131(c,LM)
lr=0.1, e=0.01	8E-05(d,GDX)	0.008943(d,GDX)	0.30001(a,GDM)	0.00338(a,GDM)
lr=0.1, e=0.001	7.89E-05(c,GDA)	0.010038(a,CGP)	0.356985(a,CGP)	0.00407(a,CGP)
lr=0.1, e=0.005	7.28E-05(c,GDA)	0.008534(c,GDA)	0.30001(a,GDM)	0.00338(a,GDM)
lr=0.01, e=0.1	0.000272(c,LM)	0.016494(c,LM)	1.030908(c,LM)	0.01172(c,LM)
lr=0.01,e=0.01	6.42E-05(c,GDM)	0.00801(c,GDM)	0.328506(a,CGP)	0.003731(a,CGP)
lr=0.01, e=0.001	6.42E-05(c,GDM)	0.00801(c,GDM)	0.350052(a,CGB)	0.003999(a,CGB)
lr=0.01, e=0.005	0.000068(c,GDM)	0.008247(c,GDM)	0.135383(d,RP)	0.004771(c,GDA)
lr=0.001, e=0.1	0.000357(c,SCG)	0.018894(c,SCG)	1.141253(c,OSS)	0.013077(c,OSS)
lr=0.001, e=0.01	7.08E-05(c,GDA)	0.008416(c,GDA)	0.33241(a,GDA)	0.003742(a,GDA)
lr=0.001, e=0.001	7.09E-05(c,GDA)	0.008418(c,GDA)	0.316911(a,CGF)	0.003582(a,CGF)
lr=0.001, e=0.005	0.000088(a,GDX)	0.009383(a,GDX)	0.293126(a,GDX)	0.003345(a,GDX)

Figure 6-9, below shows the plotted graph showing the least achieved values of MSE, RMSE, MAPE and MAD taken from the above table evaluated using various learning algorithms by evaluating different learning rate and training tolerance. It was observed that the resultant values of most learning algorithms approach and lies in the scale between 0 and 0.005 which results in overlapping in case of MSE and RMSE. In MAPE, the resultant value fits into the scale between 0 and 10. In MAD, the resultant value fits into the scale between 0 and 0.1.

Figure 6. MSE performance of various prediction model at lr=0.01and e=0.01

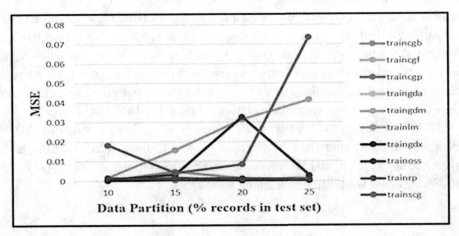

Figure 7. RMSE performance of various prediction model at lr=0.01and e=0.01

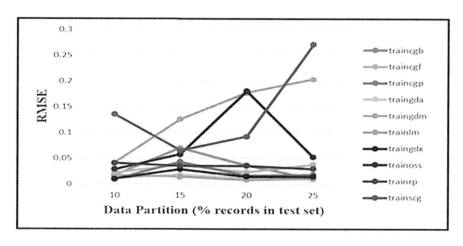

Figure 8. MAPE performance of various prediction model at lr=0.01and e=0.005

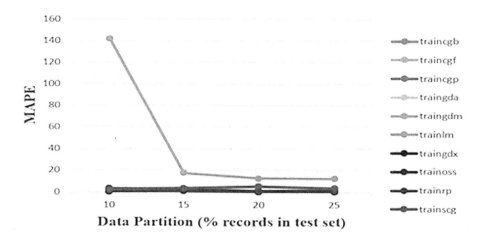

Figure 9. MAD performance of various prediction model at lr=0.001and e=0.005

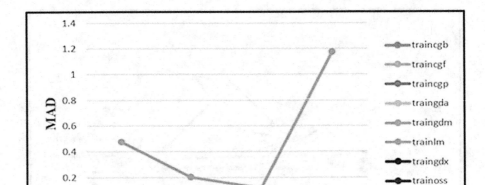

Table 5 illustrates the optimal values of Network parameters and their corresponding values of performance measures. It comprises the least value of performance measures which results in fast convergence.

Table 5. Compiled result of network parameters and optimal values of performance measures

Network Parameters	Optimal Values of Performance Measures			
Performance Measure	MSE	RMSE	MAPE	MAD
Minimum value recorded	6.42E-05	0.00801	0.135385	0.003345
Number of hidden layers (HL)	1	1	1	1
Number of neurons in Hidden layer	25	25	25	25
Learning rate (lr)	0.01	0.01	0.01	0.001
Training tolerance or Goal (e)	0.01,0.001	0.01,0.001	0.005	0.005
Data partition strategy	85% 15%	85% 15%	90% 10%	75% 25%
Learning Algorithm	Gradient descent with momentum (GDM)	Gradient descent with momentum (GDM)	Resilient Backpropagation (RP)	Gradient descent with momentum term and adaptive learning rate (GDX)

4. CONCLUSION

Artificial Neural Networks have a high ability to predict water quality. They are powerful enough to model complex relationships in a simple way as compared to another traditional model. In this research work, authors have developed ANN based models for the forecasting of Water Quality in Nainital Lake. Different partitions of training patterns and different combinations of ANN parameters using MATLAB have been sufficed for these experiments with ANN models. It has been observed that the *Gradient descent with momentum term (GDM)* algorithm will have the fastest convergence in achieving the least value of *MSE* and *RMSE* in the case of 85% 15% strategy. The *Resilient Back propagation (RP)* algorithm will have fastest convergence in achieving least value of *MAPE* while using data partition strategy 90% 10% and *Gradient Descent with momentum term and adaptive learning rate (GDX)* learning algorithm using data partition strategy 75% 25% will have fastest convergence in achieving least value of *MAD* as compared to other algorithms. The future work will explore new types of algorithms along with different data partition strategies that are more appropriate for time series prediction/forecasting.

CONFLICT OF INTEREST

Author and co-authors confirm that there is no conflict of Interest to publish this paper.

ACKNOWLEDGMENT

The author and co-authors thank the Jal Sansthan, Nainital and Uttarakhand Science Education and Research Centre (USERC) Dehradun, Uttarakhand, INDIA for their Support.

REFERENCES

Alam, J. B., Hossain, A., Khan, S. K., Banik, B. K., Islam, M. R., Muyen, Z., & Rahman, M. H. (2007). Deterioration of water quality of Surma river. *Environmental Monitoring and Assessment, 134*(1-3), 233–242. doi:10.100710661-007-9612-7 PMID:17294273

Alam, M. J. B., Islam, M. R., Muyen, Z., Mamun, M., & Islam, S. (2007). Water quality parameters along Rivers. *International Journal of Environmental Science and Technology, 4*(1), 159–167. doi:10.1007/BF03325974

Bisht, A. K., Singh, R., Bhutiani, R., Bhatt, A., & Kumar, K. (2017). Water quality modelling of the river Ganga using artificial neural networks with reference to the various training functions. *Environment Conservation Journal, 18*(1&2), 41–48. doi:10.36953/ECJ.2017.181206

Chandra, R., Singh, S., & Raj, A. (2006). Seasonal Bacteriological Analysis of Gola River Water Contaminated with Pulp Paper Mill Waste in Uttaranchal, India. *Environmental Monitoring and Assessment, 118*(1-3), 393–406. doi:10.100710661-006-1508-4 PMID:16897553

Cyemezo, P. C., Mugisha, E., & Niyigena, P. (2019). Forecasting Rwandan Agricultural Crop Yield Value and Identify Factors That Influence This Crop Yield. *International Journal of Scientific and Research Publications, 9*(10), 832–840. doi:10.29322/IJSRP.9.10.2019.p94106

Gupta, R., Bhagat, P., Joshi, M., Inaotombi, S., & Gupta, P. K. (2010). Heavy Metal Pollution status of Lake Nainital, Uttarakhand. *Indian Journal of Scientific Research, 1*(1), 15–19.

Khayyun, T., Al Obaidy, A. H., & Mustafa, A. (2014). Prediction of water quality of Euphrates River by using artificial neural network model (spatial and temporal study). *International Research Journal of Natural Sciences., 2*(3), 25–38.

Kofi, A. (2003). *Water-related diseases responsible for 80 per cent of all illnesses, deaths in developing World, says Secretary-General in Environment Day Message.* Available: https://digitallibrary.un.org/record/496690

Korostynska, O., Mason, A., & Al-Shamma'a, A. I. (2013). Monitoring Pollutants in Wastewater: Traditional Lab Based versus Modern Real-Time Approaches. In S. Mukhopadhyay & A. Mason (Eds.), *Smart Sensors for Real-Time Water Quality Monitoring. Smart Sensors, Measurement and Instrumentation, 4.* Springer. doi:10.1007/978-3-642-37006-9_1

Latif, S., Azmi, M., Ahmed, A. N., Fai, C. M., & El-Shafie, A. (2020). Application of Artificial Neural Network for Forecasting Nitrate Concentration as a Water Quality Parameter: A Case Study of Feitsui Reservoir, Taiwan. *International Journal of Design & Nature and Ecodynamics, 15*(5), 647–652. doi:10.18280/ijdne.150505

Li, M., Wu, W., Chen, B., Guan, L., & Wu, Y. (2017). Water Quality Evaluation using Back Propagation Artificial Neural Network based on Self-Adaptive Particle Swarm Optimization Algorithm and Chaos Theory. *Computational Water, Energy and Environmental Engineering, 6*(3), 229–242. doi:10.4236/cweee.2017.63016

Palani, S., Liong, S. Y., & Tkalich, P. (2008). An ANN Application for Water Quality Forecasting. *Marine Pollution Bulletin, 56*(9), 1586–1597. doi:10.1016/j.marpolbul.2008.05.021 PMID:18635240

Sarkar, A., & Pandey, P. (2015). River Water Quality Modelling Using Artificial Neural Network techniques. *Aquatic Procedia, 4*, 1070–1077. doi:10.1016/j.aqpro.2015.02.135

Semwal, N., & Akolkar, P. (2006). Water quality assessment of sacred Himalayan Rivers of Uttarakhand. *Current Science, 91*(4), 486–496.

Seo, W., Yun, S. H., & Choi, S. Y. (2016). Forecasting Water Quality Parameters by Artificial Neural Network model using preprocessing technique at the downstream of Cheongpyeong Dam. *Procedia Engineering, 154*, 1110–1115. doi:10.1016/j.proeng.2016.07.519

Sharma, D., & Kansal, A. (2011). Water quality analysis of River Yamuna using water quality index in the national capital territory, India (2000–2009). *Applied Water Science, 1*(3-4), 147–157. doi:10.100713201-011-0011-4

Singh, A. K., & Rawat, D. S. (1985). Depletion of oak forest threatening springs: An exploratory survey. *National Geographic Journal of India, 31*(1), 44–48.

Sulaiman, K., Ismail, L. H., Razi, M., Adnan, M. S., & Ghazali, R. (2019). Water Quality Classification Using an Artificial Neural Network (ANN). *IOP Conference Series. Materials Science and Engineering, 601*(1), 012005. doi:10.1088/1757-899X/601/1/012005

Zhang, Y., Fitch, P., Vilas, M. P., & Thorburn, P. J. (2019). Applying Multi-Layer Artificial Neural Network and Mutual Information to the Prediction of Trends in dissolved Oxygen. *Frontiers in Environmental Science, 7*, 46. doi:10.3389/fenvs.2019.00046

Compilation of References

Stearns, C. C., & Kannappan, K. (1995). *Method for 2-D affine transformation of images*. US Patent No. 5,475,803.

Yadav, S., & Sharma, N. (2018b). Homogenous ensemble of time-series models for indian stock market. *International Conference on Big Data Analytics*, 100–114. 10.1007/978-3-030-04780-1_7

Sankaran, S., Mishra, A., Ehsani, R., & Davis, C. (2010). A review of advanced techniques for detecting plant diseases. *Computers and Electronics in Agriculture*, *72*(1), 1–13. doi:10.1016/j.compag.2010.02.007

Yadav, S., & Sharma, K. P. (2018a). Statistical analysis and forecasting models for stock market. *2018 First International Conference on Secure Cyber Computing and Communication (ICSCCC)*, 117–121. 10.1109/ICSCCC.2018.8703324

Huang, J., Rathod, V., Sun, C., Zhu, M., Korattikara, A., Fathi, A., Fischer, I., Wojna, Z., Song, Y., & Guadarrama, S. (2017). Speed/accuracy trade-offs for modern convolutional object detectors. *Proceedings of the IEEE Computer Society Conference on Computer Vision and Pattern Recognition*. 10.1109/CVPR.2017.351

Sultana, N., & Sharma, N. (2018). Statistical models for predicting swine flu incidences in India. *2018 First international conference on secure cyber computing and communication (ICSCCC)*, 134–138. 10.1109/ICSCCC.2018.8703300

Chauhan, P., Sharma, N., & Sikka, G. (2021). The emergence of social media data and sentiment analysis in election prediction. *Journal of Ambient Intelligence and Humanized Computing*, *12*(2), 1–27. doi:10.100712652-020-02423-y

Fuentes, A., Yoon, S., Kim, S., & Park, D. (2017). A Robust Deep Learning-Based Detector for Real-Time Tomato Plant Diseases and Pests Recognition. *Sensors (Basel)*, *17*(9), 2022. doi:10.339017092022

Ren, S., He, K., Girshick, R., & Sun, J. (2016). Faster R-CNN: Towards Real-Time Object Detection with Region Proposal Networks. *IEEE Transactions on Pattern Analysis and Machine Intelligence*, *39*(6), 1137–1149. doi:10.1109/TPAMI.2016.2577031 PMID:27295650

Zubchenko, A. (2021). Data collection for machine learning: The complete guide. *Waverly.* https://waverleysoftware.com/blog/data-collection-for-machine-learning-guide/

Liu, W., Anguelov, D., Erhan, D., Szegedy, C., Reed, S., Fu, C., & Berg, A. C. (2016). SSD: Single Shot MultiBox Detector. *Proceedings of the European Conference on Computer Vision ECCV*, 21–37.

Singh, B., Kumar, P., Sharma, N., & Sharma, K. P. (2020). Sales forecast for Amazon sales with time series modeling. *2020 First International Conference on Diabetes Prediction Model 155 Power, Control and Computing Technologies (ICPC2T)*, 38–43. 10.1109/ICPC2T48082.2020.9071463

Dai, J., Li, Y., He, K., & Sun, J. R.-F. C. N. (2016). *Object Detection via Region based Fully Convolutional Networks.* arXiv:1605.06409v2.

Gurumoorthy, Parvezi, & Pavan. (2020). Data Preparation. *Devopedia.* Retrieved from https://devopedia.org/data-preparation

Everingham, M., Van Gool, L., Williams, C., Winn, J., & Zisserman, A. (2010). The Pascal Visual Object Classes (VOC) Challenge. *Int. Comput. Vis., 88*(2), 303–338. doi:10.100711263-009-0275-4

Verma, S., & Sharma, N. (2018). Statistical models for predicting chikungunya incidences in India. *2018 First International Conference on Secure Cyber Computing and Communication (ICSCCC)*, 139–142. 10.1109/ICSCCC.2018.8703218

Bird, S., Klein, E., & Loper, E. (2019). Learning to Classify Text. Natural Language Processing with Python. *NLTK.* Retrieved from https://www.nltk.org/book/ch06.html

Girshick, R. (2015). Fast r-cnn. *Proceedings of the IEEE International Conference on Computer Vision*, 1440–1448.

Dai, J., He, K., & Sun, J. (2015). *Instance-aware semantic segmentation via multi-task network cascades.* arXiv preprint arXiv:1512.04412.

Singh, N., Sharma, N., Sharma, A. K., & Juneja, A. (2019). Sentiment score analysis and topic modelling for gst implementation in India. In *Soft Computing for Problem Solving* (pp. 243–254). Springer. doi:10.1007/978-981-13-1595-4_19

Lu, J., Hu, J., Zhao, G., Mei, F., & Zhang, C. (2017). An in-field automatic wheat disease diagnosis system. *Computers and Electronics in Agriculture, 142*, 369–379. doi:10.1016/j.compag.2017.09.012

World Health Organization. (2016). *Global report on diabetes.* Retrieved from https://apps.who.int/iris/bitstream/handle/10665/204871/9789241565257_eng.pdf;jsessionid=71FB7458A7A77906729C4A96EEC4B3F7?sequence=1

Ali, A. (2018). K-Nearest Neighbor with Practical Implementation. *Medium.* Retrieved from https://medium.com/machine-learning-researcher/k-nearest-neighbors-in-machine-learning-e794014abd2a

SultanaN.SharmaN.SharmaK. P. (2019). Ensemble model based on NNAR and SVR for predicting influenza incidences. *Proceedings of the International Conference on Advances in Electronics, Electrical & Computational Intelligence (ICAEEC).* https://ssrn.com/abstract=3574620

Vidvan, T. (n.d.). *SVM in Machine Learning – An exclusive guide on SVM algorithms.* Retrieved from https://techvidvan.com/tutorials/svm-in-machine-learning/

Sharma, S., Juneja, A., & Sharma, N. (2018). Using deep convolutional neural network in computer vision for real-world scene classification. *2018 IEEE 8th International Advance Computing Conference (IACC)*, 284–289. 10.1109/IADCC.2018.8692121

Mahajan, A., Rastogi, A., & Sharma, N. (2020). Annual rainfall prediction using time series forecasting. In *Soft Computing: Theories and Applications* (pp. 69–79). Springer. doi:10.1007/978-981-15-4032-5_8

Magudeeswaran & Suganyadevi. (2013). Forecast of Diabetes using Modified Radial basis Functional Neural Networks. *International Journal of Computer Applications.*

Kamilaris, A., & Francesc, X. (2018). Deep learning in agriculture: A survey. *Computers and Electronics in Agriculture, 147*, 70–90. doi:10.1016/j.compag.2018.02.016

Saxena, Khan, & Singh. (2014). Classification Diagnosis of Diabetes Mellitus using K Nearest Neighbor Algorithm. *International Journal of Computer Science Trends and Technology, 2*(4).

Kavakiotis, I., Tsave, O., Salifoglou, A., Maglaveras, N., Vlahavas, I., & Chouvarda, I. (2017). Machine learning and data mining methods in diabetes research. *Computational and Structural Biotechnology Journal, 15*, 104–116. doi:10.1016/j.csbj.2016.12.005 PMID:28138367

Konstantinos, P. (2018). Deep learning models for plant disease detection and diagnosis. *Computers and Electronics in Agriculture, 145*, 311–318. doi:10.1016/j.compag.2018.01.009

Kulkarni Anand, H., & Ashwin Patil, R. K. (2012). Applying image processing technique to detect plant diseases. *Int J Mod Eng Res, 2*(5), 3661–3664.

Polat, K., & Günes, S. (2007). An expert system approach based on principal component analysis and adaptive neuro-fuzzy inference system to diagnosis of diabetes disease. *Digital Signal Processing, 17*(4), 702–710. doi:10.1016/j.dsp.2006.09.005

Sabah, B., & Navdeep, S. (2012). Remote area plant disease detection using image processing. *IOSR J Electron Commun Eng, 2*(6), 31–4.

Yue, C., Xin, L., Kewen, X., & Chang, S. (2008). An intelligent diagnosis to type 2 diabetes based on QPSO algorithm and WLS-SVM. *Proceedings of the 2008 IEEE International Symposium on intelligent Information Technology Application Workshops.* 10.1109/IITA.Workshops.2008.36

Çalişir, D., & Doğantekin, E. (2011). An automatic diabetes diagnosis system based on LDA-wavelet support vector machine classifier. *Expert Systems with Applications, 38*(7), 8311–8315. doi:10.1016/j.eswa.2011.01.017

Kaundal, R., & Amar, S. (2006). Machine learning technique in disease forecasting: A case study on rice blast prediction. *BMC Bioinformatics*. Advance online publication. doi:10.1186/1471-2105-7-485

Razavian, N., Blecker, S., Schmidt, A. M., Smith-McLallen, A., Nigam, S., & Sontag, D. (2015). Population-level prediction of type 2 diabetes from claims data and analysis of risk factors. *Big Data*, *3*(4), 277–287. doi:10.1089/big.2015.0020 PMID:27441408

Sladojevic, S., Arsenovic, M., Anderla, A., Culibrk, D., & Stefanovic, D. (2016). Deep Neural Networks Based Recognition of Plant Diseases by Leaf Image Classification. *Computational Intelligence and Neuroscience*. doi:10.1155/2016/3289801

Georga, E. I. I., Protopappas, V. C., Ardigo, D., Marina, M., Zavaroni, I., Polyzos, D., & Fotiadis, D. I. (2013). Multivariate prediction of subcutaneous glucose concentration in type 1 diabetes patients based on support vector regression. *IEEE Journal of Biomedical and Health Informatics*, *17*(1), 71–81. doi:10.1109/TITB.2012.2219876 PMID:23008265

Howse, J. (2013). *OpenCV ComputerVision with Python*. Packt Publishing.

Hawkins, D. M. (2004). The problem of over-fitting. *Journal of Chemical Information and Computer Sciences*, *44*(1), 1–12. doi:10.1021/ci0342472 PMID:14741005

Ozcift, A., & Gulten, A. (2011). Classifier ensemble construction with rotation forest to improve medical diagnosis performance of machine learning algorithms. *Computer Methods and Programs in Biomedicine*, *104*(3), 443–451. doi:10.1016/j.cmpb.2011.03.018 PMID:21531475

Aazhvaar, V. (2019). Artificial Intelligence in Indian Banking Sector: Challenges and Opportunities. *International Journal of Advanced Research*, *7*(5), 1581–1587.

ACCIS. (2021). *The Automated Cancer Information System*. Available at: https://accis.iarc.fr/

Adam, M., Wessel, M., & Benlian, A. (2021). AI-based Chatbots in Customer Service and their Effects on User Compliance. *Electronic Markets*, *31*(2), 427–445. doi:10.100712525-020-00414-7

Adetunji, J. (n.d.). *The Conversation*. https://theconversation.com/five-ways-artificial-intelligence-can-help-space-exploration-153664

Ahmed, R., Wani, G. F., Ahmad, S. T., Mir, R. A., Almazroui, M., Jain, S. K., & Ahmed, P. (2021). Spatiotemporal dynamics of glacial lakes (1990–2018) in the Kashmir Himalayas, India using Remote Sensing and GIS. *Discov Water*, *1*(1), 7. doi:10.100743832-021-00007-1

Airforgood. (2018). https://aiforgood.itu.int/challenges-and-opportunities-of-artificial-intelligence-for-good/

Akar, E., & Topçu, B. (2011). An examination of the factors influencing consumers' attitudes toward social media marketing. *Journal of Internet Commerce*, *10*(1), 35–67. doi:10.1080/15332861.2011.558456

Akay, M. F. (2009). Support vector machines combined with feature selection for breast cancer diagnosis. *Expert Systems with Applications*, *36*(2), 3240–3247. doi:10.1016/j.eswa.2008.01.009

Aksoy, E. (2017). Geography of Crime and Its Relation to Location: The City of Balıkesir (Turkey). *IOP Conf. Series: Materials Science and Engineering, 245*. 10.1088/1757-899X/245/7/072012

Alalwan, A. A., Rana, N. P., Dwivedi, Y. K., & Algharabat, R. (2017). Social media in marketing: A review and analysis of the existing literature. *Telematics and Informatics*, *34*(7), 1177–1190. doi:10.1016/j.tele.2017.05.008

Alam, J. B., Hossain, A., Khan, S. K., Banik, B. K., Islam, M. R., Muyen, Z., & Rahman, M. H. (2007). Deterioration of water quality of Surma river. *Environmental Monitoring and Assessment*, *134*(1-3), 233–242. doi:10.100710661-007-9612-7 PMID:17294273

Alam, M. J. B., Islam, M. R., Muyen, Z., Mamun, M., & Islam, S. (2007). Water quality parameters along Rivers. *International Journal of Environmental Science and Technology*, *4*(1), 159–167. doi:10.1007/BF03325974

Alam, M., & Khokhar, R. (2006). Impact of Internet on Customer Loyalty in Swedish Banks. *Journal of Economic Psychology*, *16*, 311–329.

Albert, B., Zhang, J., Noyvirt, A., Setchi, R., Sjaaheim, H., Velikova, S., & Strisland, F. (2016). Automatic EEG processing for the early diagnosis of traumatic brain injury. *Procedia Computer Science*, *96*, 703–712. doi:10.1016/j.procs.2016.08.253

Alkhathlan, L., & Khader Jilani, A. (2020). Machine Learning Techniques for Breast Cancer Analysis: A Systematic Literature Review. *International Journal of Computer Science and Network Security*, *20*(6), 83–90.

Alotaiby, T. N., Alshebeili, S. A., Alshawi, T., Ahmad, I., El-Samie, A., & Fathi, E. (2014). EEG seizure detection and prediction algorithms: A survey. *EURASIP Journal on Advances in Signal Processing*, *2014*(1), 1–21. doi:10.1186/1687-6180-2014-183

American Psychiatric Association. (2013). *DSM-5 Task Force Diagnostic and statistical manual of mental disorders: DSM-5*. Washington, DC: American Psychiatric Association.

Anckar, B. (2003). Consumer Intentions in Terms of Electronic Travel Distribution. *e-Service Journal*, *2*(2), 68–86. doi:10.2979/esj.2003.2.2.68

Anshari, M., Almunawar, M. N., Lim, S. A., & Al-Mudimigh, A. (2018). Customer Relationship Management and Big Data-Enabled: Personalization & Customization of Services. *Applied Computing and Informatics*, *15*(2), 94–101. doi:10.1016/j.aci.2018.05.004

Aragoncillo, L., & Orus, C. (2018). Impulse buying behaviour: an online-offline comparative and the impact of social media. *Spanish Journal of Marketing-ESIC*.

Atlas: Glacial Lakes of Uttarakhand. (n.d.). https://www.iirs.gov.in/atlas-glacial-lakes-of-uttarakhand

Bajracharya, S. R. (2007). Impacts of climate change on Himalayan glaciers and glacial lakes: case studies on GLOF and associated hazards in Nepal and Bhutan. Kathmandu: International Centre for Integrated Mountain Development (ICIMOD).

Bakhshi, S. I. (2016). Digitization and digital preservation of cultural heritage in India with special reference to IGNCA, New Delhi. *Asian J. Inf. Sci. Technol, 6*(2), 1–7.

Baltagi, B. H. (2006, May/June). Estimating an economic model of crime using panel data from North Carolina. *Journal of Applied Econometrics, 21*(4), 543–547.

Barrachina, M., & López, V. L. (2021). Machine Learning Techniques to Identify and Characterize Sleep Disorders Using Biosignals. In Advancing the Investigation and Treatment of Sleep Disorders Using AI. IGI Global.

Barrachina-Fernández, M., Maitín, A. M., Sánchez-Ávila, C., & Romero, J. P. (2021). Wearable Technology to Detect Motor Fluctuations in Parkinson's Disease Patients: Current State and Challenges. *Sensors (Basel), 21*(12), 4188. doi:10.339021124188 PMID:34207198

Bashiri, A., Ghazisaeedi, M., Safdari, R., Shahmoradi, L., & Ehtesham, H. (2017). Improving the prediction of survival in cancer patients by using machine learning techniques: experience of gene expression data: a narrative review. *Iranian Journal of Public Health, 46*(2), 165. PMID:28451550

Becker, A. (2019). Artificial intelligence in medicine: What is it doing for us today? *Health Policy and Technology, 8*(2), 198–205. doi:10.1016/j.hlpt.2019.03.004

Becker, A., Bar-Yehuda, R., & Geiger, D. (2000). Randomised Algorithms for the Loop Cutset Problem. *Journal of Artificial Intelligence Research, 12*, 219–234. doi:10.1613/jair.638

Beller, E., Clark, J., Tsafnat, G., Adams, C., Diehl, H., Lund, H., Ouzzani, M., Thayer, K., Thomas, J., Turner, T., Xia, J., Robinson, K., & Glasziou, P. (2018). Making progress with the automation of systematic reviews: Principles of the International Collaboration for the Automation of Systematic Reviews (ICASR). *Systematic Reviews, 7*(1), 77. doi:10.118613643-018-0740-7 PMID:29778096

Bennett, M., & Lai, K. (2005). The impact of the Internet on travel agencies in Taiwan. *Tourism and Hospitality Research, 6*(1), 8–23. doi:10.1057/palgrave.thr.6040041

Bhambri, R., Mehta, M., Dobhal, D., & Gupta, A. (2015). *Glacial lake inventory of Uttarakhand.* Academic Press.

Bhatt, A. K., & Pant, D. (2013). Automatic Apple Grading Model Development Based On Back Propagation Neural Network & Machine Vision, and Its Performance Evaluation. AI & Society: Journal of Knowledge, Culture and Communication, 30(1).

Bhatt, A. K., Pant, D., & Singh, R. (2012). An Analysis of the Performance of Artificial Neural Network Technique for Apple Classification. *AI & Society: Journal of Knowledge, Culture and Communication, 24*(115).

Bhatt, A. K., & Pant, D. (2015). Automatic apple grading model development based on back propagation neural network and machine vision, and its performance evaluation. *AI & Society*, *30*(1), 45–56. doi:10.100700146-013-0516-5

Bisht, A. K., Singh, R., Bhutiani, R., & Bhatt, A. K. (2017). Water Quality Modelling of the River Ganga using ANN with reference to the various training function. *Environment Conservation Journal, 18*(1&2), 41-48.

Bisht, A. K., Singh, R., Bhutiani, R., Bhatt, A., & Kumar, K. (2017). Water quality modelling of the river Ganga using artificial neural networks with reference to the various training functions. *Environment Conservation Journal, 18*(1&2), 41–48. doi:10.36953/ECJ.2017.181206

Biswal, S., Kulas, J., Sun, H., Goparaju, B., Westover, M. B., Bianchi, M. T., & Sun, J. (2017). *SLEEPNET: automated sleep staging system via deep learning*. arXiv preprint arXiv:1707.08262.

Boba, R. (2005). *Crime Analysis and Crime Mapping*. Sage Publications.

Bone, D., Goodwin, M. S., Black, M. P., Lee, C. C., Audhkhasi, K., & Narayanan, S. (2015). Applying machine learning to facilitate autism diagnostics: Pitfalls and promises. *Journal of Autism and Developmental Disorders, 45*(5), 1121–1136. doi:10.100710803-014-2268-6 PMID:25294649

Bonn, M. A., Furr, H. L., & Susskind, A. M. (1998). Using the internet as a pleasure travel planning tool: An examination of the sociodemographic and behavioral characteristics among internet users and nonusers. *Journal of Hospitality & Tourism Research (Washington, D.C.)*, *22*(3), 303–317. doi:10.1177/109634809802200307

Borghoff, U. M., Rödig, P., Schmitz, L., & Scheffczyk, J. (2006). *Long-term preservation of digital documents: Principles and practices*. Springer.

Brassy, J., Price, C., & Edwards, J. (2019). Developing a fully automated evidence synthesis tool for identifying, assessing and collating the evidence. *BMJ Evid Based Med*.

Bray, F., Laversanne, M., Weiderpass, E., & Soerjomataram, I. (2021). The ever-increasing importance of cancer as a leading cause of premature death worldwide. *Cancer*, *127*(16), 3029–3030. doi:10.1002/cncr.33587 PMID:34086348

Buhalis, D., & Licata, M. C. (2002). The future eTourism intermediaries. *Tourism Management*, *23*(3), 207–220. doi:10.1016/S0261-5177(01)00085-1

Burdea, G. C., & Coiffet, P. (2003). *Virtual reality technology* (2nd ed.). John Wiley & Sons, Inc. doi:10.1162/105474603322955950

Business-Standard. (n.d.). https://www.business-standard.com/about/what-is-artificial-intelligence#collapse

Cai, H., Sha, X., Han, X., Wei, S., & Hu, B. (2016, December). Pervasive EEG diagnosis of depression using Deep Belief Network with three-electrodes EEG collector. In *2016 IEEE International Conference on Bioinformatics and Biomedicine (BIBM)* (pp. 1239-1246). IEEE.

Cassel, D. (2017). *Remembering Shakey: The First Intelligent Robot*. SRI International Artificial Intelligence Center.

Cavadas, B., Branco, P., & Pereira, S. (2015). *Crime Prediction Using Regression and Resources Optimization*. doi:10.1007/978-3-319-23485-4_51

Chai, R., Naik, G. R., Nguyen, T. N., Ling, S. H., Tran, Y., Craig, A., & Nguyen, H. T. (2016). Driver fatigue classification with independent component by entropy rate bound minimization analysis in an EEG-based system. *IEEE Journal of Biomedical and Health Informatics, 21*(3), 715–724. doi:10.1109/JBHI.2016.2532354 PMID:26915141

Chandra, R., Singh, S., & Raj, A. (2006). Seasonal Bacteriological Analysis of Gola River Water Contaminated with Pulp Paper Mill Waste in Uttaranchal, India. *Environmental Monitoring and Assessment, 118*(1-3), 393–406. doi:10.100710661-006-1508-4 PMID:16897553

Chen, X., & Van Beek, P. (2001). Conflict-Directed Backjumping Revisited. *Journal of Artificial Intelligence Research, 14*, 53–81. doi:10.1613/jair.788

CI5 – Home. (2021). Available at: https://ci5.iarc.fr/Default.aspx

Constantinides, E., Romero, C. L., & Boria, M. A. G. (2008). Social media: a new frontier for retailers? In *European retail research* (pp. 1–28). Gabler Verlag. doi:10.1007/978-3-8349-8099-1_1

Cornwell, C., & Trumbull, W. N. (1994). Estimating the economic model of crime with panel data. *The Review of Economics and Statistics, 76*, 360–366.

Costanzo, M. C., Arcidiacono, C., Rodolico, A., Panebianco, M., Aguglia, E., & Signorelli, M. S. (2020). Diagnostic and interventional implications of telemedicine in Alzheimer's disease and mild cognitive impairment: A literature review. *International Journal of Geriatric Psychiatry, 35*(1), 12–28. doi:10.1002/gps.5219 PMID:31617247

Council of Europe. (n.d.). https://www.coe.int/en/web/artificial-intelligence/history-of-ai

Crimes in Boston. (2018). *Kaggle*. https://www.kaggle.com/AnalyzeBoston/crimes-in-boston

Cui, C., Chou, S. S., Brattain, L., Lehman, C. D., & Samir, A. E. (2019). Data engineering for machine learning in women's imaging and beyond. *AJR. American Journal of Roentgenology, 213*(1), 216–226. doi:10.2214/AJR.18.20464 PMID:30779668

Curtis-Ham, S., & Walton, D. (2017). Mapping crime harm and priority locations in New Zealand: A comparison of spatial analysis methods. *Applied Geography, 86*, 245–254. https://doi.org/10.1016/j.apgeog.2017.06.008

Cyemezo, P. C., Mugisha, E., & Niyigena, P. (2019). Forecasting Rwandan Agricultural Crop Yield Value and Identify Factors That Influence This Crop Yield. *International Journal of Scientific and Research Publications, 9*(10), 832–840. doi:10.29322/IJSRP.9.10.2019.p94106

Dara, F., & Devolli, A. (2016). Applying artificial neural networks (ANN) techniques to automated visual apple sorting. *Journal of Hygienic Engineering and Design, 17*, 55–63.

Datt, G., Bhatt, A. K., & Kumar, S. (2015). Disaster Management Information System Framework using Feed Forward Back Propagation. *Neural Networks*, *4*(3), 510–514. doi:10.17148/IJARCCE.2015.43122

Deloitte. (n.d.). https://www2.deloitte.com/us/en/pages/consulting/articles/the-future-of-ai.html

Dheeba, J., & Selvi, S. T. (2011). Classification of malignant and benign microcalcification using SVM classifier. In *2011 International Conference on Emerging Trends in Electrical and Computer Technology* (pp. 686-690). IEEE. 10.1109/ICETECT.2011.5760205

Diba, H., Vella, J. M., & Abratt, R. (2019). Social media influence on the B2B buying process. *Journal of Business and Industrial Marketing*, *34*(7), 1482–1496. doi:10.1108/JBIM-12-2018-0403

Dickson, M. A., Bausch, W. C., & Howarth, M. S. (1994). Classification of a broadleaf weed, a grassy weed, and corn using image processing techniques. *SPIE*, *2345*, 297–305.

Dou, X., Fan, X., Yunus, A. P., & Xiong, J. (2021). *Spatio-temporal evolution of glacial lakes in the Tibetan Plateau over the past 30 years*. doi:10.5194/essd-2021-354

El Naqa & Murphy. (2015). What Is Machine Learning? *Machine Learning in Radiation Oncology*, 3–11.

Elsabbagh, M., Divan, G., Koh, Y. J., Kim, Y. S., Kauchali, S., Marcín, C., Montiel-Nava, C., Patel, V., Paula, C. S., Wang, C., Yasamy, M. T., & Fombonne, E. (2012). Global prevalence of autism and other pervasive developmental disorders. *Autism Research*, *5*(3), 160–179. doi:10.1002/aur.239 PMID:22495912

Engemann, D. A., Raimondo, F., King, J. R., Rohaut, B., Louppe, G., Faugeras, F., Annen, J., Cassol, H., Gosseries, O., Fernandez-Slezak, D., Laureys, S., Naccache, L., Dehaene, S., & Sitt, J. D. (2018). Robust EEG-based cross-site and cross-protocol classification of states of consciousness. *Brain*, *141*(11), 3179–3192. doi:10.1093/brain/awy251 PMID:30285102

Erkan, I., & Evans, C. (2016). The influence of eWOM in social media on consumers' purchase intentions: An extended approach to information adoption. *Computers in Human Behavior*, *61*, 47–55. doi:10.1016/j.chb.2016.03.003

Evans, M. (1989). Consumer behaviour towards fashion. *European Journal of Marketing*, *23*(7), 7–16. doi:10.1108/EUM0000000000575

Fan, C. Y., Chang, P. C., Lin, J. J., & Hsieh, J. C. (2011). A hybrid model combining case-based reasoning and fuzzy decision tree for medical data classification. *Applied Soft Computing*, *11*(1), 632–644. doi:10.1016/j.asoc.2009.12.023

FBI, Crime in the United States 2013. (n.d.). https://www.fbi.gov/about-us/cjis/ucr/crime-in-the-u.s/2013/crime-in-the-u.s.-2013

Fröhlich, H. (2018). Premenopausal Breast Cancer: Potential Clinical Utility of a Multi-Omics Based Machine Learning Approach for Patient Stratification. *EPMA Journal, 9*(2), 175–86.

Gabbatiss, J. (2017, July 12). Is Violence Embedded in Our DNA? *Sapiens*. https://www.sapiens.org/biology/human-violence-evolution/

Gaur, R., & Chakraborty, M. (2009). Preservation and access to Indian manuscripts: A knowledge base of Indian cultural heritage resources for academic libraries. ICAL 2009 – Vision and Roles of the Future Academic Libraries, 90-98.

Gemein, L. A., Schirrmeister, R. T., Chrabąszcz, P., Wilson, D., Boedecker, J., Schulze-Bonhage, A., Hutter, F., & Ball, T. (2020). Machine-learning-based diagnostics of EEG pathology. *NeuroImage*, *220*, 117021. doi:10.1016/j.neuroimage.2020.117021 PMID:32534126

Geography of crime. (2021). *Bitesize*. https://www.bbc.co.uk/bitesize/guides/zytycdm/revision/2

Geron, A. G. (2017). Hands-On Machine Learning with Scikit-Learn and TensorFlow. O'Reilly Media, Inc.

Global Cancer Observatory. (2021). Available at: https://gco.iarc.fr/

Godey, B., Manthiou, A., Pederzoli, D., Rokka, J., Aiello, G., Donvito, R., & Singh, R. (2016). Social media marketing efforts of luxury brands: Influence on brand equity and consumer behavior. *Journal of Business Research*, *69*(12), 5833–5841. doi:10.1016/j.jbusres.2016.04.181

Goh, K. Y., Heng, C. S., & Lin, Z. (2013). Social media brand community and consumer behavior: Quantifying the relative impact of user-and marketer-generated content. *Information Systems Research*, *24*(1), 88–107. doi:10.1287/isre.1120.0469

Goodfellow, I. (2016). *Nips 2016 tutorial: Generative adversarial networks*. arXiv preprint arXiv:1701.00160.

Goodrich, K., & De Mooij, M. (2014). How 'social' are social media? A cross-cultural comparison of online and offline purchase decision influences. *Journal of Marketing Communications*, *20*(1-2), 103–116. doi:10.1080/13527266.2013.797773

Gupta, N. A. (2017). *Literature Survey on Artificial Intelligence*. https://www.ijert.org/research/a-literature-survey-on-artificial-intelligence-IJERTCONV5IS19015.pdf

Gupta, P., Chiang, S.-F., Sahoo, P., Mohapatra, S., You, J.-F., Onthoni, D., Hung, H.-Y., Chiang, J.-M., Huang, Y., & Tsai, W.-S. (2019). Prediction of Colon Cancer Stages and Survival Period with Machine Learning Approach. *Cancers (Basel)*, *11*(12), 2007. Advance online publication. doi:10.3390/cancers11122007 PMID:31842486

Gupta, R., Bhagat, P., Joshi, M., Inaotombi, S., & Gupta, P. K. (2010). Heavy Metal Pollution status of Lake Nainital, Uttarakhand. *Indian Journal of Scientific Research*, *1*(1), 15–19.

Guyer, D. E., Miles, G. E., Gaultney, L. D., & Schereiber, M. M. (1993). Application of machine vision to shape analysis in leaf and plant identification. *TASAE*, *36*(1), 163–171.

Halal, W. E. (2003). Artificial intelligence is almost here. *On the Horizon*, *11*(2), 37–38. doi:10.1108/10748120310486771

Hanahan, D., & Weinberg, R. A. (2011). Hallmarks of cancer: The next generation. *Cell, 144*(5), 646–674. doi:10.1016/j.cell.2011.02.013 PMID:21376230

Heinsfeld, A. S., Franco, A. R., Craddock, R. C., Buchweitz, A., & Meneguzzi, F. (2018). Identification of autism spectrum disorder using deep learning and the ABIDE dataset. *NeuroImage. Clinical, 17*, 16–23. doi:10.1016/j.nicl.2017.08.017 PMID:29034163

He, J., Baxter, S. L., Xu, J., Xu, J., Zhou, X., & Zhang, K. (2019). The Practical Implementation of Artificial Intelligence Technologies in Medicine. *Nat., 2019*(25), 30–36. doi:10.103841591-018-0307-0 PMID:30617336

He, K., Zhang, X., Ren, S., & Sun, J. (2016, October). Identity mappings in deep residual networks. In *European conference on computer vision* (pp. 630-645). Springer.

Hong, J. (2001). Goal Recognition through Goal Graph Analysis. *Journal of Artificial Intelligence Research, 15*, 1–30. doi:10.1613/jair.830

Hosseini, M., Agereh, S. R., & Khaledian, Y. (2017). Comparison of multiple statistical techniques to predict soil phosphorus. *Appl. Soil Ecol., 114*, 123–131. doi:10.1016/j.apsoil.2017.02.011

Houfani, D., Slatnia, S., Kazar, O., Zerhouni, N., Merizig, A., & Saouli, H. (2020). Machine Learning Techniques for Breast Cancer Diagnosis: Literature Review. In M. Ezziyyani (Ed.), *Advanced Intelligent Systems for Sustainable Development (AI2SD'2019). AI2SD 2019. Advances in Intelligent Systems and Computing* (Vol. 1103). Springer. doi:10.1007/978-3-030-36664-3_28

Huang, C., Wang, Q., Yang, D., & Xu, F. (2018). Topic mining of tourist attractions based on a seasonal context aware LDA model. *Intelligent Data Analysis, 22*(2), 383–405. doi:10.3233/IDA-173364

Huang, Y., Lan, Y., Thomson, S. J., Fang, A., Hoffmann, W. C., & Lacey, R. E. (2010). Development of soft computing and applications in agricultural and biological engineering. *Comput. Electron. Agric., 71*(2), 107–127. doi:10.1016/j.compag.2010.01.001

Hu, H., Niu, Z., Bai, Y., & Tan, X. (2015). Cancer classification based on gene expression using neural networks. *Genetics and Molecular Research, 14*(4), 17605–17611. doi:10.4238/2015.December.21.33 PMID:26782405

IARC Home. (2021). Available at: https://www.iarc.fr/

Irshad, M., Ahmad, M. S., & Malik, O. F. (2020). Understanding consumers' trust in social media marketing environment. *International Journal of Retail & Distribution Management, 48*(11), 1195–1212. doi:10.1108/IJRDM-07-2019-0225

Jha, G., & Ahuja, L., & Rana, A. (2020). Criminal Behaviour Analysis and Segmentation using K-Means Clustering. *8th International Conference on Reliability, Infocom Technologies and Optimization (Trends and Future Directions) (ICRITO)*, 1356-1360. doi: 10.1109/ICRITO48877.2020.9197791

Jiang, D., Liao, J., Duan, H., Wu, Q., Owen, G., Shu, C., Chen, L., He, Y., Wu, Z., He, D., Zhang, W., & Wang, Z. (2020). A machine learning-based prognostic predictor for stage III colon cancer. *Scientific Reports, Vol., 10*(1), 10333. doi:10.103841598-020-67178-0 PMID:32587295

Jiang, F., Jiang, Y., Zhi, H., Dong, Y., Li, H., Ma, S., Wang, Y., Dong, Q., Shen, H., & Wang, Y. (2017). Artificial intelligence in healthcare: Past, present and future. *Stroke and Vascular Neurology, 2*(4), 230–243. doi:10.1136vn-2017-000101 PMID:29507784

Kaggle. (2020). *Lung and Colon Cancer Histopathological Images.* Kaggle. Available online: https://www.kaggle.com/andrewmvd/lung-and-colon-cancer-histopathological-images

Kannan, A. (n.d.). *What are the different therapeutic interventions for depression?* https://www.whiteswanfoundation.org/disorders/mood-disorders/what-are-the-different-therapeutic-interventions-for-depression

Karabatak, M., & Ince, M. C. (2009). An expert system for detection of breast cancer based on association rules and neural network. *Expert Systems with Applications, 36*(2), 3465–3469. doi:10.1016/j.eswa.2008.02.064

Karlsson, B. F. F. (2003). Issues and Approaches in Artificial Intelligence Middleware Development for Digital Games and Entertainment Products. *CEP, 50740*, 540.

Kaur, H. (2015). Digital preservation of manuscripts: An Indian perspective with special reference to Punjab. *Proc. 4th International Symposium on Emerging Trends and Technologies in Libraries and Information Services (ETTLIS)*, 271-274. 10.1109/ETTLIS.2015.7048210

Kawthalkar, I., Jadhav, S., Jain, D., & Nimkar, A.V. (2020). A Survey of Predictive Crime Mapping Techniques for Smart Cities. *National Conference on Emerging Trends on Sustainable Technology and Engineering Applications (NCETSTEA)*, 1-6. 10.1109/NCETSTEA48365.2020.9119948

Khamis, H., Mohamed, A., & Simpson, S. (2013). Frequency–moment signatures: A method for automated seizure detection from scalp EEG. *Clinical Neurophysiology, 124*(12), 2317–2327. doi:10.1016/j.clinph.2013.05.015 PMID:23786794

Khan & Ali. (2017, Jan.). Digital preservation of manuscripts: Initiative in India. *J. Indian Libr. Assoc.*, 25-30.

Kharya, S., Agrawal, S., & Soni, S. (2014). Naive Bayes classifiers: A probabilistic detection model for breast cancer. *International Journal of Computer Applications, 92*(10).

Khayyun, T., Al Obaidy, A. H., & Mustafa, A. (2014). Prediction of water quality of Euphrates River by using artificial neural network model (spatial and temporal study). *International Research Journal of Natural Sciences., 2*(3), 25–38.

Khuda Bakhsh Oriental Public Library. (n.d.). http://kblibrary. bih.nic.in/

Kim, A. J., & Johnson, K. K. (2016). Power of consumers using social media: Examining the influences of brand-related user-generated content on Facebook. *Computers in Human Behavior, 58*, 98–108. doi:10.1016/j.chb.2015.12.047

Kim, S., Joshi, P., Kalsi, P. S., & Taheri, P. (2018). Crime Analysis Through Machine Learning. *IEEE 9th Annual Information Technology, Electronics and Mobile Communication Conference (IEMCON)*, 415-420. 10.1109/IEMCON.2018.8614828

Koelstra, R. A. L. (2012). *Affective and Implicit Tagging using Facial Expressions and Electroencephalography* (Doctoral dissertation). Queen Mary University of London.

Kofi, A. (2003). *Water-related diseases responsible for 80 per cent of all illnesses, deaths in developing World, says Secretary-General in Environment Day Message.* Available: https://digitallibrary.un.org/record/496690

Koklu, M., Kursun, R., Taspinar, Y. S., & Cinar, I. (2021). Classification of Date Fruits into Genetic Varieties Using Image Analysis. *Mathematical Problems in Engineering, 2021*, 1–13. Advance online publication. doi:10.1155/2021/4793293

Koranga, M., Pant, P., Pant, D., Bhatt, A. K., & Pant, R. P. (2021). SVM Model to predict the Water Quality based on Physicochemical Parameters. *International Journal of Mathematical, Engineering and Management Sciences.*

Korostynska, O., Mason, A., & Al-Shamma'a, A. I. (2013). Monitoring Pollutants in Wastewater: Traditional Lab Based versus Modern Real-Time Approaches. In S. Mukhopadhyay & A. Mason (Eds.), *Smart Sensors for Real-Time Water Quality Monitoring. Smart Sensors, Measurement and Instrumentation, 4.* Springer. doi:10.1007/978-3-642-37006-9_1

Kosmicki, J. A., Sochat, V., Duda, M., & Wall, D. P. (2015). Searching for a minimal set of behaviors for autism detection through feature selection-based machine learning. *Translational Psychiatry, 5*(2), e514–e514. doi:10.1038/tp.2015.7 PMID:25710120

Kourou, K., Exarchos, T. P., Exarchos, K. P., Karamouzis, M. V., & Fotiadis, D. I. (2015). Machine Learning Applications in Cancer Prognosis and Prediction. *Computational and Structural Biotechnology Journal, 13*, 8–17. doi:10.1016/j.csbj.2014.11.005 PMID:25750696

Kovaˇcevi'c., M., Bajat, B., & Gaji'c, B. (2009). Soil type classification and estimation of soil properties using support vector machines. *Geoderma, 154*, 340–347.

Kulkarni, A. V., Rathore, B. P., Singh, S. K., & Bahuguna, I. M. (2011). Understanding changes in the Himalayan cryosphere using remote sensing techniques. *International Journal of Remote Sensing, 32*(3), 601–615. doi:10.1080/01431161.2010.517802

Kumar, A., Bezawada, R., Rishika, R., Janakiraman, R., & Kannan, P. K. (2016). From social to sale: The effects of firm-generated content in social media on customer behavior. *Journal of Marketing, 80*(1), 7–25. doi:10.1509/jm.14.0249

Kumari, N., Bhatt, A. K., Dwivedi, R. K., & Belwal, R. (2020). Automatic Grading of Mangoes based on surface defect detection using a combined approach of Image Segmentation. *Environment Conservation Journal, 21*(3), 17-23.

Kumari, N., Bhatt, A. K., Dwivedi, R. K., & Belwal, R. (2020). Hybrid Approach of Image Segmentation in classification of fruit mango using BPNN and discriminate analyzer. *Multimedia Tools and Application, 79*(37-38).

Kumari, N., Bhatt, A. K., Dwivedi, R. K., & Belwal, R. (2020). Non-destructive classification of fruit mango based on extracted color–geometric features and used sample size in training phase of machine learning. *Journal of Xidian University, 14*(4), 3066-3074.

Kumari, M., & Singh, V. (2018). Breast Cancer Prediction system. *Procedia Computer Science, 132*, 371–376. doi:10.1016/j.procs.2018.05.197

Kumari, N., Dwivedi, R. K., Bhatt, A. K., & Belwal, R. (2021). Automated fruit grading using optimal feature selection and hybrid classification by self-adaptive chicken swarm optimization: Grading of mango. *Neural Computing & Applications*. Advance online publication. doi:10.100700521-021-06473-x

Kumari, N., Kr. Bhatt, A., Kr. Dwivedi, R., & Belwal, R. (2021). Hybridized approach of image segmentation in classification of fruit mango using BPNN and discriminant analyzer. *Multimedia Tools and Applications, 80*(4), 4943–4973. doi:10.100711042-020-09747-z

Kumar, P., & Pawaiya, R. (2010). Advances in Cancer Diagnostics. *Brazilian Journal of Veterinary Pathology, 3*, 141–152.

Labor-Statistics. (n.d.). *United States Department of Labor - Bureau of Labor Statistics: Police and detectives*. https://www.bls.gov/ooh/protective-service/police-and-detectives.htmtab-1. Accessed:21-01-2015

Lamorski, K., Pachepsky, Y., Slawin'ski, C., & Walczak, R. T. (2008). Using support vector machines to develop pedotransfer functions for water retention of soils in Poland. *Soil Sci. Soc. Amer. J., 72*(5), 1243–1247. doi:10.2136ssaj2007.0280N

Larrañaga, P., Calvo, B., Santana, R., Bielza, C., Galdiano, J., Inza, I., Lozano, J. A., Armañanzas, R., Santafé, G., Pérez, A., & Robles, V. (2006). Machine Learning in Bioinformatics. *Briefings in Bioinformatics, 7*(1), 86–112. doi:10.1093/bib/bbk007 PMID:16761367

Latif, S., Azmi, M., Ahmed, A. N., Fai, C. M., & El-Shafie, A. (2020). Application of Artificial Neural Network for Forecasting Nitrate Concentration as a Water Quality Parameter: A Case Study of Feitsui Reservoir, Taiwan. *International Journal of Design & Nature and Ecodynamics, 15*(5), 647–652. doi:10.18280/ijdne.150505

Li, H., Leng, W., Zhou, Y., Chen, F., Xiu, Z., & Yang, D. (2014). Evaluation Models for Soil Nutrient Based on Support Vector Machine and Artificial Neural Networks. *Sci. World J., 478569.*

Liakos, K., Busato, P., Moshou, D., Pearson, S., & Bochtis, D. (2018). Machine Learning in Agriculture: A Review. *Published in Sensors, 18*(8), 2674. doi:10.339018082674 PMID:30110960

Li, B., Sharma, A., Meng, J., Purushwalkam, S., & Gowen, E. (2017). Applying machine learning to identify autistic adults using imitation: An exploratory study. *PLoS One, 12*(8), e0182652. doi:10.1371/journal.pone.0182652 PMID:28813454

Li, M., Wu, W., Chen, B., Guan, L., & Wu, Y. (2017). Water Quality Evaluation using Back Propagation Artificial Neural Network based on Self-Adaptive Particle Swarm Optimization Algorithm and Chaos Theory. *Computational Water, Energy and Environmental Engineering*, *6*(3), 229–242. doi:10.4236/cweee.2017.63016

Lindsey-Mullikin, J., & Borin, N. (2017). Why strategy is key for successful social media sales. *Business Horizons*, *60*(4), 473–482. doi:10.1016/j.bushor.2017.03.005

Li, Q., Li, S., Hu, J., Zhang, S., & Hu, J. (2018). Tourism review sentiment classification using a bidirectional recurrent neural network with an attention mechanism and topic-enriched word vectors. *Sustainability (Switzerland)*, *10*(9), 3313. Advance online publication. doi:10.3390u10093313

Liu, R., Gupta, S., & Patel, P. (2021). The Application of the Principles of Responsible AI on Social Media Marketing for Digital Health. *Information Systems Frontiers*. Advance online publication. doi:10.100710796-021-10191-z PMID:34539226

Liu, Y., Wang, H., Zhang, H., & Liber, K. (2016). A comprehensive support vector machine-based classification model for soil quality assessment. *Published in Soil Tillage Res.*, *155*, 19–26. doi:10.1016/j.still.2015.07.006

Logistic Regression. (2021, May 5). https://www.saedsayad.com/logistic_regression.htm

Lord, C., Elsabbagh, M., Baird, G., & Veenstra-Vanderweele, J. (2018). Seminar Autism spectrum disorder. *Lancet*, *392*(10146), 508–520. doi:10.1016/S0140-6736(18)31129-2 PMID:30078460

Lord, C., Risi, S., Lambrecht, L., Cook, E. H. Jr, Leventhal, B. L., DiLavore, P. C., Pickles, A., & Rutter, M. (2000). The Autism Diagnostic Observation Schedule—Generic: A standard measure of social and communication deficits associated with the spectrum of autism. *Journal of Autism and Developmental Disorders*, *30*(3), 205–223. doi:10.1023/A:1005592401947 PMID:11055457

Lord, C., Rutter, M., & Le Couteur, A. (1994). Autism Diagnostic Interview-Revised: A revised version of a diagnostic interview for caregivers of individuals with possible pervasive developmental disorders. *Journal of Autism and Developmental Disorders*, *24*(5), 659–685. doi:10.1007/BF02172145 PMID:7814313

Malone, T. W., Yates, J., & Benjamin, R. I. (1987). Electronic markets and electronic hierarchies. *Communications of the ACM*, *30*(6), 484–497. doi:10.1145/214762.214766

Mal, S., Allen, S., Frey, H., Huggel, C., & Dimri, A. P. (2021). Sector wise Assessment of Glacial Lake Outburst Flood Danger in the Indian Himalayan Region. *Mountain Research and Development*. Advance online publication.

Marcano-Cedeño, A., Quintanilla-Domínguez, J., & Andina, D. (2011). WBCD breast cancer database classification applying artificial metaplasticity neural network. *Expert Systems with Applications*, *38*(8), 9573–9579. doi:10.1016/j.eswa.2011.01.167

MarrB. (2021). https://bernardmarr.com/the-7-biggest-ethical-challenges-of-artificial-intelligence/

Marrese-Taylor, E., Velásquez, J. D., Bravo-Marquez, F., & Matsuo, Y. (2013). Identifying customer preferences about tourism products using an aspect-based opinion mining approach. *Procedia Computer Science*, *22*, 182–191. doi:10.1016/j.procs.2013.09.094

Masnikosa, V. P. (1998). The fundamental problem of an artificial intelligence realization. *Kybernetes*, *27*(1), 71–80. doi:10.1108/03684929810200549

Masud, M., Sikder, N., Nahid, A. A., Bairagi, A. K., & AlZain, M. A. (2021). A Machine Learning Approach to Diagnosing Lung and Colon Cancer Using a Deep Learning-Based Classification Framework. *Sensors (Basel)*, *21*(3), 748. doi:10.339021030748 PMID:33499364

Matsumura, R., Harada, K., Domae, Y., & Wan, W. (2019). Learning based industrial bin-picking trained with approximate physics simulator. *Advances in Intelligent Systems and Computing*, *867*, 786–798. doi:10.1007/978-3-030-01370-7_61

Max, T. (2016). *The Future of Life: Benefits and Risks of Artificial Intelligence*. The Future of Life Institute. https://futureoflife.org/background/benefits-risks-of-artificial-intelligence/

Ma, Y., Chen, B., Li, R., Wang, C., Wang, J., She, Q., Luo, Z., & Zhang, Y. (2019). Driving fatigue detection from EEG using a modified PCANet method. *Computational Intelligence and Neuroscience*, *2019*, 2019. doi:10.1155/2019/4721863 PMID:31396270

MC, L. (2013). Lombardo, Michael V, Baron-Cohen S. Autism. *Lancet*, *383*(9920), 896–910. PMID:24074734

McCarthy, J., Minsky, M. L., Rochester, N., & Shannon, C. E. (2006). A Proposal for the Dartmouth Summer Research Project on Artificial Intelligence, August 31, 1955. *AI Magazine*, *27*(4), 12. doi:10.1609/aimag.v27i4.1904

McCarthy, J., Minsky, M. L., Rochester, N., & Shannon, C. E. (2006). A Proposal for the Dartmouth Summer Research Project on Artificial Intelligence. *AI Magazine*, *27*, 12.

McClendon, L., & Meghanathan, N. (2015, March). Using Machine Learning Algorithms to Analyze Crime Data. *Machine Learning and Applications: An International Journal*, *2*(1), 1–12. Advance online publication. doi:10.5121/mlaij.2015.2101

Medjahed, S. A., Saadi, T. A., & Benyettou, A. (2013). Breast cancer diagnosis by using k-nearest neighbor with different distances and classification rules. *International Journal of Computers and Applications*, *62*(1).

Megan, B. (n.d.). *Women still handle main household task in US*. Gallup Mag, Politics. https://news.gallup.com/poll/283979/women-handle-main-household-tasks.aspx

Metaxiotis, K., Ergazakis, K., Samouilidis, E., & Psarras, J. (2003). Decision Support through Knowledge Management: The role of the Artificial Intelligence. *Information Management & Computer Security*, *11*(5), 216–221. doi:10.1108/09685220310500126

Mir, I. A. (2012). Consumer attitudinal insights about social media advertising: A South Asian perspective. *The Romanian Economic Journal*, *15*(45), 265–288.

Mir, R. A., Jain, S. K., Thayyen, R. J., & Saraf, A. K. (2017). Assessment of recent glacier changes and its controlling factors from 1976 to 2011 in Baspa basin, western Himalaya. *Arctic, Antarctic, and Alpine Research*, *49*(4), 621–647. doi:10.1657/AAAR0015-070

Mishra, P., & Jagdish, S. (2021). *How India fared in Global gender gap report*. Mint. https://www.livemint.com/news/india/how-india-fared-in-global-gender-gap-report-2021-11617726598143.html

Moore, A. (2017). *Carnegie Mellon Dean of Computer Science on the Future of AI*. Available online: https://www.forbes.com/sites/peterhigh/2017/10/30/carnegie-mellon-dean-of-computer-science-onthe-future-of-ai/#3a283c652197

Moore, A., & High, P. (2017). Future of AI. *Forbes*. https://www.forbes.com/sites/peterhigh/2017/10/30/carnegie-mellon-dean-of-computer-science-onthe-future-of-ai/#3a283c652197

Mülle, V. C., & Bostrom, N. (2016). Future Progress in Artificial Intelligence: A Survey of Expert Opinion. In Fundamental Issues of Artificial Intelligence (pp. 555–572). Springer.

Müller, J. M., Pommeranz, B., Weisser, J., & Voigt, K. I. (2018). Digital, Social Media, and Mobile Marketing in industrial buying: Still in need of customer segmentation? Empirical evidence from Poland and Germany. *Industrial Marketing Management*, *73*, 70–83. doi:10.1016/j.indmarman.2018.01.033

Mythili, M. S., & Shanavas, A. M. (2014). A study on Autism spectrum disorders using classification techniques. *International Journal of Soft Computing and Engineering*, *4*(5), 88–91.

Naeem, M. (2021). Do social media platforms develop consumer panic buying during the fear of Covid-19 pandemic. *Journal of Retailing and Consumer Services*, *58*, 102226. doi:10.1016/j.jretconser.2020.102226

Nash, J. (2019). Exploring how social media platforms influence fashion consumer decisions in the UK retail sector. *Journal of Fashion Marketing and Management*, *23*(1), 82–103. doi:10.1108/JFMM-01-2018-0012

Nextgov. (2021). https://www.nextgov.com/emerging-tech/2021/10/future-artificial-intelligence/186123/

NileshB. (n.d.).Self Driving Cars with Convolutional Neural Network. https://neptune.ai/blog/self-driving-cars-with-convolutional-neural-networks-cnn

Nordcan 2.0. (2021). Available at: https://nordcan.iarc.fr/en/database

Palani, S., Liong, S. Y., & Tkalich, P. (2008). An ANN Application for Water Quality Forecasting. *Marine Pollution Bulletin*, *56*(9), 1586–1597. doi:10.1016/j.marpolbul.2008.05.021 PMID:18635240

Pant, H., Lohani, M. C., Bhatt, A., Pant, J., & Joshi, A. (2020). Soil Quality Analysis and Fertility Assessment to Improve the Prediction Accuracy using Machine Learning Approach. *International Journal of Advanced Science and Technology, 29*(3), 10032-10043.

Pant, H., Lohani, M. C., Bhatt, A., Pant, J., & Singh, M. K. (2020). Rule Descriptions for Soil Quality and Soil Fertility Assessment using Fuzzy Control System. *International Journal of Recent Technology and Engineering, 8*(6), 1341-1346.

Pant, J., Pant, P., Bhatt, A., Pant, H., & Pandey, N. (2019). Feature Selection towards Soil Classification in the context of Fertility classes using Machine Learning. *International Journal of Innovative Technology and Exploring Engineering, 8*(12), 4000-4004.

Pant, J., Pant, P., Pant, R. P., Bhatt, A., Pant, D., & Juyal, A. (2021). Soil Quality Prediction For Determining Soil Fertility In Bhimtal Block Of Uttarakhand (India) Using Machine Learning. *International Journal of Analysis and Applications, 19*, 91–109. doi:10.28924/2291-8639-19-2021-91

Paquette, H. (2013). *Social media as a marketing tool: A literature review.* Academic Press.

Pavlopoulou, A., Spandidos, D. A., & Michalopoulos, I. (2015). Human cancer databases. *Oncology Reports, 33*(1), 3–18. doi:10.3892/or.2014.3579 PMID:25369839

Peng, Y., & Zhang, X. (2007). Integrative Data Mining in Systems Biology: From Text to Network Mining. *Artificial Intelligence, 41*(2), 83–86. doi:10.1016/j.artmed.2007.08.001 PMID:17888638

Pham, T., Ma, W., Tran, D., Nguyen, P., & Phung, D. (2014, July). Multi-factor EEG-based user authentication. In *2014 International Joint Conference on Neural Networks (IJCNN)* (pp. 4029-4034). IEEE. 10.1109/IJCNN.2014.6889569

Plitt, M., Barnes, K. A., & Martin, A. (2015). Functional connectivity classification of autism identifies highly predictive brain features but falls short of biomarker standards. *NeuroImage. Clinical, 7*, 359–366. doi:10.1016/j.nicl.2014.12.013 PMID:25685703

Politico Magazine. (2019). *What are the biggest problems women faced today.* https://www.politico.com/magazine/story/2019/03/08/women-biggest-problems-international-womens-day-225698/

Pratap, A., & Kanimozhiselvi, C. S. (2014). Predictive assessment of autism using unsupervised machine learning models. *International Journal of Advanced Intelligence Paradigms, 6*(2), 113–121. doi:10.1504/IJAIP.2014.062174

Puspita, M. N., Kusuma, W. A., Kustiyo, A., & Heryanto, R. (2016). A classification system for jamu efficacy based on formula using support vector machine and k-means algorithm as a feature selection. *ICACSIS 2015 - 2015 International Conference on Advanced Computer Science and Information Systems, Proceedings,* 215–220. 10.1109/ICACSIS.2015.7415176

Pütter, M. (2017). The impact of social media on consumer buying intention. *Marketing, 3*(1), 7–13.

Quebec Declaration. (2015). https://www.international.icomos.org/quebec2008/quebec_declaration/pdf/GA16_Quebec_Declaration_Final_EN.pdf

Rajiv, M. (n.d.). *Common Problems Faced By Homemakers Who Stay Indoors - How Physiotherapy Can Be Of Help?* Lybrate. Mag. https://www.lybrate.com/topic/common-problems-faced-by-homemakers-who-stay-indoors-how-physiotherapy-can-be-of-help/de3def568eb692f805b619e3d53ff7a3

Raj, K. B. G., & Kumar, K. V. (2016). Inventory of glacial lakes and its evolution in Uttarakhand Himalaya using time- series satellite data. *Photonirvachak (Dehra Dun)*, *44*(6), 959–976. doi:10.100712524-016-0560-y

Raj, S., & Masood, S. (2020). Analysis and detection of autism spectrum disorder using machine learning techniques. *Procedia Computer Science*, *167*, 994–1004. doi:10.1016/j.procs.2020.03.399

Ramani, R. G., & Sivaselvi, K. (2017). Autism spectrum disorder identification using data mining techniques. *International Journal of Pure and Applied Mathematics*, *117*(16), 427–436.

Raynor, W.J. (2000). The International Dictionary of Artificial Intelligence. *AMACOM, 14.*

Richardson, S., & Reynolds, J. (2000). An overview of glacial hazards in the Himalayas. *Quaternary International*, *65*, 31–47. doi:10.1016/S1040-6182(99)00035-X

Rieger, O. Y. (n.d.). *Preservation in the age of large-scale digitization: A white paper.* https://www.clir.org/pubs/ reports/pub141/

Roy, Y., Banville, H., Albuquerque, I., Gramfort, A., Falk, T. H., & Faubert, J. (2019). Deep learning-based electroencephalography analysis: A systematic review. *Journal of Neural Engineering*, *16*(5), 051001. doi:10.1088/1741-2552/ab260c PMID:31151119

RSNA. (n.d.). https://www.rsna.org/education/ai-resources-and-training/ai-image-challenge

Ruiz, L. A., Moltó, E., Juste, F., & Aleixos, N. (1995). *Aplicación de métodos ópticos para la inspección automática de productos hortofrutícolas.* VI Congreso de la Sociedad Española de Ciencias Hortícolas, Barcelona, Spain.

Ruzich, E., Allison, C., Smith, P., Watson, P., Auyeung, B., Ring, H., & Baron-Cohen, S. (2015). Measuring autistic traits in the general population: A systematic review of the Autism-Spectrum Quotient (AQ) in a nonclinical population sample of 6,900 typical adult males and females. *Molecular Autism*, *6*(1), 1–12.

Sahoo, J., & Mohanty, B. (2015). Digitization of Indian manuscripts heritage: Role of the National Mission for Manuscripts. *Int. Fed. Libr. Assoc. Inst.*, *41*(3), 237–250. doi:10.1177/0340035215601447

Sakr, S., Elshawi, R., Ahmed, A. M., Qureshi, W. T., Brawner, C. A., Keteyian, S. J., & Al-Mallah, M. H. (2017). *Comparison of machine learning techniques to predict all-cause mortality using fitness data: the Henry ford exercIse testing (FIT) project. In BMC medical informatics and decision making* (Vol. 17). BMC.

Sarkar, A., & Pandey, P. (2015). River Water Quality Modelling Using Artificial Neural Network techniques. *Aquatic Procedia*, *4*, 1070–1077. doi:10.1016/j.aqpro.2015.02.135

Sartoretto, F., & Ermani, M. (1999). Automatic detection of epileptiform activity by single-level wavelet analysis. *Clinical Neurophysiology, 110*(2), 239–249. doi:10.1016/S0013-4694(98)00116-3 PMID:10210613

Sathyadevan, S., Devan, M. S., & Gangadharan, S. S. (2014). Crime analysis and prediction using data mining. *First International Conference on Networks & Soft Computing (ICNSC2014),* 406-412. 10.1109/CNSC.2014.6906719

Sattar, A., Goswami, A., Kulkarni, A., & Das, P. (2019). Glacier-Surface Velocity Derived Ice Volume and Retreat Assessment in the Dhauliganga Basin, Central Himalaya – A Remote Sensing and Modeling Based Approach. *Frontiers in Earth Science.* https://doi.org/7. doi:10.3389/feart.2019.00105

ScienceL. (2014). https://www.livescience.com/49007-history-of-artificial-intelligence.html

ScikitLearn. (n.d.). *Toy Dataset.* https://scikit-learn.org/stable/datasets/toy_dataset.html

Semwal, N., & Akolkar, P. (2006). Water quality assessment of sacred Himalayan Rivers of Uttarakhand. *Current Science, 91*(4), 486–496.

Seo, W., Yun, S. H., & Choi, S. Y. (2016). Forecasting Water Quality Parameters by Artificial Neural Network model using preprocessing technique at the downstream of Cheongpyeong Dam. *Procedia Engineering, 154,* 1110–1115. doi:10.1016/j.proeng.2016.07.519

Shareef, M. A., Mukerji, B., Dwivedi, Y. K., Rana, N. P., & Islam, R. (2019). Social media marketing: Comparative effect of advertisement sources. *Journal of Retailing and Consumer Services, 46,* 58–69. doi:10.1016/j.jretconser.2017.11.001

Sharma, D., & Kansal, A. (2011). Water quality analysis of River Yamuna using water quality index in the national capital territory, India (2000–2009). *Applied Water Science, 1*(3-4), 147–157. doi:10.100713201-011-0011-4

Sharmita, K. (2021, Nov. 19). Women entrepreneurs in India boosting start-up ecosystem amid challenges, gender inequality. *The Hindustan times.*

Simonyan, K., & Zisserman, A. (2014). *Very deep convolutional networks for large-scale image recognition.* arXiv preprint arXiv:1409.1556.

Singer, J., & Gent, I.P., & Smaill. (2000). A Backbone Fragility and the Local Search Cost Peak. *Journal of Artificial Intelligence Research, 12,* 235–270.

Singh, A. (2012). Digital preservation of cultural heritage resources and manuscripts: An Indian Government initiative. *Int Fed. Libr. Assoc. Inst., 38*(4), 289–296. doi:10.1177/0340035212463139

Singh, A. K., & Rawat, D. S. (1985). Depletion of oak forest threatening springs: An exploratory survey. *National Geographic Journal of India, 31*(1), 44–48.

Singh, J., & Keer, N. (2020). Overview of Telemedicine and Sleep Disorders. *Sleep Medicine Clinics, 15*(3), 341–346. doi:10.1016/j.jsmc.2020.05.005 PMID:32762967

Sirintrapun, S. J., & Lopez, A. M. (2018). Telemedicine in Cancer Care. American Society of Clinical Oncology Educational Book, 38(1), 540-545. doi:10.1200/EDBK_200141

Smith, R. (2020). *Telehealth market to hit $53.1 billion by 2026.* Insurance Business America. https://www.insurancebusinessmag.com/us/news/breaking-news/telehealth-market-to-hit-53-1-billion-by-2026--report-213866.aspx

Song, S., & Yoo, M. (2016). The role of social media during the pre-purchasing stage. *Journal of Hospitality and Tourism Technology, 7*(1), 84–99. doi:10.1108/JHTT-11-2014-0067

Srivastava, P., Namdev, P., & Singh, P. (2022). 7 February Chamoli (Uttarakhand, India) Rock-Ice Avalanche Disaster: Model-Simulated Prevailing Meteorological Conditions. *Atmosphere, 267.* Advance online publication. https://doi.org/13. doi:10.3390/atmos13020267

Srivastava, V., & Srivastava, M. K. (2021). Modelling Enablers of Customer-Centricity in Convenience Food Retail. In P. K. Singh, Z. Polkowski, S. Tanwar, S. K. Pandey, G. Matei, & D. Pirvu (Eds.), *Innovations in Information and Communication Technologies (IICT-2020). Advances in Science, Technology & Innovation (IEREK Interdisciplinary Series for Sustainable Development).* Springer. doi:10.1007/978-3-030-66218-9_21

Srivastava, V., & Tyagi, A. (2013). The study of impact of after sales services of passenger cars on customer retention. *International Journal of Current Research and Review, 5*(1), 127.

Stanford. (2021). *Cancer types.* Available at: https://stanfordhealthcare.org/medical-conditions/cancer/cancer/cancer-types.html

Starmer, J. (2018, June 11). *Logistic Regression Details Pt 2: Maximum Likelihood* [Video]. YouTube. https://www.youtube.com/watch?v=BfKanl1aSG0

Stefanuk, V. L., & Zhozhikashvili, A. V. (2002). Productions and Rules in Artificial Intelligence. *Kybernetes, 31,* 817–826.

Stephen, A. T. (2016). The role of digital and social media marketing in consumer behavior. *Current Opinion in Psychology, 10,* 17–21. doi:10.1016/j.copsyc.2015.10.016

Sternberg, R. J. A. (2019). Theory of Adaptive Intelligence and Its Relation to General Intelligence. *Journal of Intelligence from MDPI, 7*(4), 23. doi:10.3390/jintelligence7040023 PMID:31581505

Stone, P., Littman, M. L., Singh, S., & Kearns, M. (2001). ATTac-2000: An Adaptive Autonomous Bidding Agent. *Journal of Artificial Intelligence Research, 15,* 189–206. doi:10.1613/jair.865

Street, W. H., Wolberg, W. H., & Mangasarian, O. L. (1993). Nuclear feature extraction for breast tumor diagnosis. *IS&T/SPIE 1993 International Symposium on Electronic Imaging: Science and Technology, 1905,* 861-870.

Suen, J. P., & Eheart, J. W. (2003). Evaluation of neural networks for modelling nitrate concentration in rivers. *Journal of Water Resources Planning and Management, 129*(6), 505–510. doi:10.1061/(ASCE)0733-9496(2003)129:6(505)

Sulaiman, K., Ismail, L. H., Razi, M., Adnan, M. S., & Ghazali, R. (2019). Water Quality Classification Using an Artificial Neural Network (ANN). *IOP Conference Series. Materials Science and Engineering*, *601*(1), 012005. doi:10.1088/1757-899X/601/1/012005

Sun, W., Zheng, B., & Qian, W. (2016). Computer aided lung cancer diagnosis with deep learning algorithms. In Medical imaging 2016: computer-aided diagnosis. International Society for Optics and Photonics.

Tang, K. Y., Chang, C. Y., & Hwang, G. J. (2021). Trends in Artificial Intelligence-Supported e-Learning: A systematic Review and Co-Citation Network Analysis 1998-2019. *Interactive Learning Environments*, 1–19. doi:10.1080/10494820.2021.1875001

Tanveer, M., Richhariya, B., Khan, R. U., Rashid, A. H., Khanna, P., Prasad, M., & Lin, C. T. (2020). Machine Learning Techniques for the Diagnosis of Alzheimer's Disease: A Review. *ACM Transactions on Multimedia Computing Communications and Applications*, *16*(1), 1–35. doi:10.1145/3344998

Tao, Y., Morrow, C. T., Heinemann, P. H., & Sommer, J. H. (1990). Automated machine vision inspection of potatoes. ASAE Paper No. 90-3531.

Tay, D. P. H., & Ho, D. K. H. (1992). Artificial Intelligence and the Mass Appraisal of Residential Apartments. *J. Prop. Valuat. Invest*, *10*(2), 525–540. doi:10.1108/14635789210031181

Taylor, E. B. (1871). *Primitive Culture*. John Murray.

Terrence, W. D. (1997). *The Co-Evolution of Language and the Brain-The Symbolic Species*. W. W. Norton.

Thabtah, F. F. (2017a). *Autistic spectrum disorder screening data for adult data set*. UCI machine learning repository.

Thabtah, F. F. (2017b). *Autistic spectrum disorder screening data for children data set*. UCI machine learning repository.

Thabtah, F. F. (2017c). *Autistic spectrum disorder screening data for adolescent data set*. UCI machine learning repository.

Thabtah, F. (2017, May). Autism spectrum disorder screening: Machine learning adaptation and DSM-5 fulfillment. In Proceedings of the 1st International Conference on Medical and health. *Informatics (MDPI)*, *2017*, 1–6.

Thabtah, F. (2019a). Machine learning in autistic spectrum disorder behavioral research: A review and ways forward. *Informatics for Health & Social Care*, *44*(3), 278–297. doi:10.1080/175381 57.2017.1399132 PMID:29436887

Thabtah, F. (2019b). An accessible and efficient autism screening method for behavioural data and predictive analyscs. *Health Informatics Journal*, *25*(4), 1739–1755. doi:10.1177/1460458218796636 PMID:30230414

Thabtah, F., Kamalov, F., & Rajab, K. (2018). A new computational intelligence approach to detect autistic features for autism screening. *International Journal of Medical Informatics*, *117*, 112–124. doi:10.1016/j.ijmedinf.2018.06.009 PMID:30032959

The Cancer Genome Atlas Program - National Cancer Institute. (2021). Available at: https://www.cancer.gov/about-nci/organization/ccg/research/structural-genomics/tcga

Thomas, J. (2016). *Making the kitchen a women place*. https://www.livemint.com/Leisure/VZTcuPvgxIymhqJe4FKkDP/Making-the-kitchen-a-womans-place.html

Toppireddy, H. K. R., Saini, B., & Mahajan, G. (2018). Crime Prediction & Monitoring Framework Based on Spatial Analysis. In *Procedia Computer Science* (Vol. 132, pp. 696–705). Elsevier B.V. doi:10.1016/j.procs.2018.05.075

Tsai, M.-J., & Tao, Y.-H. (2021). Deep Learning Techniques for the Classification of Colorectal Cancer Tissue. *Electronics (Basel)*, *10*(14), 1662. doi:10.3390/electronics10141662

Unay, D., & Gosselin, B. (2005). Artificial neural network-based segmentation and apple grading by machine vision. *Proceedings - International Conference on Image Processing, ICIP, 2*(January), 630–633. 10.1109/ICIP.2005.1530134

Understanding confusion matrix. (2021, May 5). *Towardsdatascience*. https://towardsdatascience.com/understanding-the-confusion-matrix-and-how-to-implement-it-in-python-319202e0fe4d

Urigüen, J. A., & Garcia-Zapirain, B. (2015). EEG artifact removal—State-of-the-art and guidelines. *Journal of Neural Engineering*, *12*(3), 031001. doi:10.1088/1741-2560/12/3/031001 PMID:25834104

Vaishali, R., & Sasikala, R. (2018). A machine learning based approach to classify Autism with optimum behaviour sets. *IACSIT International Journal of Engineering and Technology*, *7*(4), 18.

Varghese, Z. Y., Morrow, C.T., Heinemann, P.H., Sommer III, J.H., Tao, Y., & Crassweller, R.M. (1991). *Automated inspection of golden delicious mangos using color computer vision*. ASAE Paper No. 91-7002.

Wadia Institute of Himalayan Geology. (2015). *Glacier lake inventory of Uttarakhand*. Author.

Wall, D. P., Dally, R., Luyster, R., Jung, J. Y., & DeLuca, T. F. (2012a). *Use of artificial intelligence to shorten the behavioral diagnosis of autism*. Academic Press.

Wall, D. P., Kosmicki, J., Deluca, T. F., Harstad, E., & Fusaro, V. A. (2012b). Use of machine learning to shorten observation-based screening and diagnosis of autism. *Translational Psychiatry*, *2*(4), e100–e100. doi:10.1038/tp.2012.10 PMID:22832900

Wang, S., Wang, Y., Du, W., Sun, F., Wang, X., Zhou, C., & Liang, Y. (2007). A Multi-Approaches-Guided Genetic Algorithm with Application to Operon Prediction. *Artificial Intelligence*, *41*(2), 151–159. doi:10.1016/j.artmed.2007.07.010 PMID:17869072

Watanabe, T., Lamsal, D., & Ives, J. D. (2009). Evaluating the growth characteristics of glacial a glacial lake and its degree of danger of outburst flooding Imja Glacier, Khumbu Himal, Nepal. *Norwegian J Geogr*, *63*(4), 255–267. doi:10.1080/00291950903368367

WHO. (2021). *Cancer*. Available at: https://www.who.int/news-room/fact-sheets/detail/cancer

Wirt, N. (2018). Hello Marketing, What Can Artificial Intelligence Help You. *International Journal of Market Research*, *60*(5), 435–438. doi:10.1177/1470785318776841

Wolpaw, J. R., Birbaumer, N., Heetderks, W. J., McFarland, D. J., Peckham, P. H., Schalk, G., Donchin, E., Quatrano, L. A., Robinson, C. J., & Vaughan, T. M. (2000). Brain-computer interface technology: A review of the first international meeting. *IEEE Transactions on Rehabilitation Engineering*, *8*(2), 164–173. doi:10.1109/TRE.2000.847807 PMID:10896178

Wongpinunwatana, N., Ferguson, C., & Bowen, P. (2000). An Experimental Investigation of the effects of Artificial Intelligence Systems on the Training of Novice Auditors. *Managerial Auditing Journal*, *15*(6), 306–318. doi:10.1108/02686900010344511

Worni, R., Stoffel, M., Huggel, C., Volz, C., Casteller, A., & Luckman, B. (2012). Analysis and dynamic modeling of a moraine failure and glacial lake outburst flood at Ventisquero Negro, Patagonian Andes (Argentina). *Journal of Hydrology (Amsterdam)*, *444*, 134–145. doi:10.1016/j.jhydrol.2012.04.013

Wu, W., Li, A. D., He, X. H., Ma, R., Liu, H.-B., & Lv, J.-K. (2018). A comparison of support vector machines, artificial neural network and classification tree for identifying soil texture classes in southwest China. *Comput. Electron. Agric.*, *144*, 86–93. doi:10.1016/j.compag.2017.11.037

Xie, Y., Meng, W. Y., Li, R. Z., Wang, Y.W., Qian, X., Chan, C., Yu, Z.F., & Fan, X.X. (2021). Early lung cancer diagnostic biomarker discovery by machine learning methods. *Translational Oncology*, *14*(1). doi:10.1016/j.tranon.2020.100907

Xu, Y., Fu, C., Kennedy, E., Jiang, S., & Owusu-Agyemang, S. (2017). The impact of street lights on spatial-temporal patterns of crime in Detroit, Michigan. *Cities*. doi:10.1016/j.cities.2018.02.021

Yadav, M., & Rahman, Z. (2018). The influence of social media marketing activities on customer loyalty: A study of e-commerce industry. *Benchmarking*, *25*(9), 3882–3905. doi:10.1108/BIJ-05-2017-0092

Yadav, S., Timbadia, M., Yadav, A., Vishwakarma, R., & Yadav, N. (2017). Crime pattern detection, analysis & prediction. *International conference of Electronics, Communication and Aerospace Technology (ICECA)*, 225-230. 10.1109/ICECA.2017.8203676

Yang, G., Lin, Y., & Bhattacharya, P. (2010). A driver fatigue recognition model based on information fusion and dynamic Bayesian network. *Information Sciences*, *180*(10), 1942–1954. doi:10.1016/j.ins.2010.01.011

Yang, M. H., Xu, D. Y., Chen, S. C., Li, H., & Shi, Z. (2019). Evaluation of machine learning approaches to predict soil organic matter and pH using Vis-NIR spectra. *Sensors (Basel)*, *19*(2), 263. doi:10.339019020263 PMID:30641879

Ye, Q., Law, R., Gu, B., & Chen, W. (2011). The influence of user-generated content on traveler behavior: An empirical investigation on the effects of e-word-of-mouth to hotel online bookings. *Computers in Human Behavior*, 27(2), 634–639. doi:10.1016/j.chb.2010.04.014

Yi, S. J., Pittman, C. A., Price, C. L., Nieman, C. L., & Oh, E. S. (2021). Telemedicine and Dementia Care: A Systematic Review of Barriers and Facilitators. *Journal of the American Medical Directors Association*, 22(7), 1396–1402. doi:10.1016/j.jamda.2021.03.015 PMID:33887231

Yu, K. H., Lee, T. M., Yen, M. H., Kou, S. C., Rosen, B., Chiang, J. H., & Kohane, I. S. (2020). Reproducible Machine Learning Methods for Lung Cancer Detection Using Computed Tomography Images: Algorithm Development and Validation. *Journal of Medical Internet Research*, 22(8), e16709. doi:10.2196/16709 PMID:32755895

Zafar, A. U., Qiu, J., Li, Y., Wang, J., & Shahzad, M. (2019). The impact of social media celebrities' posts and contextual interactions on impulse buying in social commerce. *Computers in Human Behavior*, 106178.

Zawacki-Richter, O., Marín, V. I., Bond, M., & Gouverneur, F. (2019). Systematic Review of Research on Artificial Intelligence Applications in Higher Education – Where are the Educators? *International Journal of Educational Technology in Higher Education*, 16(1), 39. Advance online publication. doi:10.118641239-019-0171-0

Zeynali, M., & Seyedarabi, H. (2019). EEG-based single-channel authentication systems with optimum electrode placement for different mental activities. *Biomedical Journal*, 42(4), 261-267.

Zhang, Y., Fitch, P., Vilas, M. P., & Thorburn, P. J. (2019). Applying Multi-Layer Artificial Neural Network and Mutual Information to the Prediction of Trends in dissolved Oxygen. *Frontiers in Environmental Science*, 7, 46. doi:10.3389/fenvs.2019.00046

Zhou, X., Liu, B., Wu, Z., & Feng, Y. (2007). Integrative Mining of Traditional Chines Medicine Literature and MEDLINE for Functional Gene Networks. *Artificial Intelligence*, 41(2), 87–104. doi:10.1016/j.artmed.2007.07.007 PMID:17804209

About the Contributors

Abhay Saxena is Dean of School of Technology, Management and Communication and Professor, Computer Science at Dev Sanskriti Vishwavidyalya, Hardwar, Uttrakhand, India. He holds Doctoral Degree of Computer Science in the area of Artificial Neural Networks (ANN). He is a visiting Professor for Budapest Business School, Hungary, National Formosa University Taiwan. He had been appointed as a Honorary Research fellow for two years by University of Malaysia (UNIMAS). He had also delivered Technical talks in Swinburne University, Malaysia, University of Malaysia, Yunlin University, Taiwan along with his contribution and participation in national and international workshop, conferences across India and abroad. In his 28 years of Teaching and Industry experience, he had authored twelve books on discrete areas of Core computing, i.e., Computer Networks, DBMS, E-commerce, Web technology, .Net Framework, Life management and Human values, Internet of things for futuristic computing (2018) and Vedic Informatics (2109). His upcoming two books are Artificial Intelligence for the societal development and Global well-being (IGI global publication May 2022) and Block Chain (2021 December).

Ashutosh Kumar Bhatt is working in Dept. of CSE BIAS, Bhimtal, Uttarakhand, India. He has done his Ph.D. in CSE in the field of Machine Learning. He is having a teaching experience of 20 years. He has a good number of reputed research publications. His Interest area: Neural Networks, Web Applications. He has guided many scholars.

Rajeev Kumar is Associate Professor CCSIT, Teerthanker Mahaveer University, Moradabad, Uttar Pradesh, India. He is Visited international countries London, United Kingdom and Mauritius as professional activities. Under his supervision awarded 4 scholar their Ph.D. and 5 Scholar is Ongoing their research work. He is awarded 3 times Best project supervisor award; He is delivered a guest lecture, keynote speaker, chaired a session in many National and International conferences, Faculty Development program and workshop; He is completed one Research Project from DST in Bhimtal. He has organized many IEEE international conferences and workshop. He is authored and coauthored more than 85 papers in refereed international journal (SCI and Non- SCI) and conferences like IEEE, Springer, American Institute of Physics, New York Science international Journal New York City (USA), American Science Journal, BioInfo science Journal, Academic science of international journal (USA), International Journal of researcher, American Journal of Physics (USA) and many international Conferences and National Conferences, like IIT Roorkee (International Conference), etc.

* * *

Anal Acharya is currently Assistant Professor in Computer Science Department in St. Xavier's College Kolkata. He has several publications in international journals and conferences to his credit.

Anni Arnav is associated with School of Management, Presidency University as Associate Professor.

Mercedes Barrachina studied a BSc and MSc in Telecommunications Engineering and developed her master thesis in the German Aerospace Center in Germany. She also completed a BSc in Economics and she is completing now her PhD in Biomedical Engineering in Universidad Politécnica de Madrid (Spain). She is working as Senior Manager in IBM and she has led different technological projects in many different countries such as Japan, United Arab Emirates, Russia, Peru, Switzerland or France. She has also a strong background working with Big Data and Data Analytics. She has attended different courses related to Data Science, Machine Learning, Blockchain and Innovation in prestigious international schools (IE Business School (Spain), MIT (Boston, USA), Berkeley (San Francisco, USA).

Bulu Basak is currently working as a Faculty in Geoinformatics at South Asian Institute for Advanced Research and Development (SAIARD). Miss Basak completed her schooling from her Village Dalimpur, Falakata, Alipurduar. She pursued her M.Tech in Geoinformatics from Maulana Abul Kalam Azad University of Technology And M.Sc in Geography from Presidency University. Previously Miss Basak worked as GIS business developer at Creatronics as well. Beside this, she Interned under the Department of Science and Technology, Government of West Bengal with a Project Name: "Targeting Rice Fallow Areas (TRFA) Using High Resolution Satellite Data in the State of West Bengal. Miss Basak published her paper in International Conference on Advanced Computing Applications, ICACA 2021 on GeoLens: Geospatial Location Exploration Using Mobile Crowdsensing in Tourism 4.0: A Case Study of Kunjanagar Eco-Park, Falakata, West Bengal. Mis Basak was also involved in some Short Term Projects like Socio-Economic Condition of Slum Dwellers: A Case Study of Kelabagan Slum Area, Ward no 39, Kolkata, West Bengal also. She has vast range of experiences in Software Skills like Arc GIS, ENVI, QGIS, Google Earth Explorer, ERDAS Imagine, Python, PostgreSQL, Google Earth Engine, AutoCAD, NVivo, SPSS, NetDraw, Microsoft Office, etc.

Neeraj Bisht is an Assistant Professor in the Department of Commuter Application at the Birla Institute of Applied Sciences in Bhimtal, India. He has a wealth of teaching expertise spanning more than two decades. Artificial intelligence, blockchain technology, and green computing are some of the topics that he is interested in researching.

Shilpi Bisht is Assistant Professor at Birla Institute of Applied Sciences, Bhimtal, Uttarakhand, India. She is PhD in Mathematics, CSIR-UGC NET Qualified and M. Sc.-Gold Medalist from Lucknow University. Area of her research interests include Spline solutions, Energy Efficient Computing, Blockchain and Artificial Intelligence. She has published many SCI and Scopus indexed research articles.

Debabrata Datta is an Assistant Professor in the department of Computer Science of St. Xavier's College (Autonomous), Kolkata, India. He has more than 15 years of teaching experience both at the undergraduate and postgraduate levels of Computer Science and Applications. His main research interest is in the domain of data analysis. He is a Life Member of Institution of Electronics and Telecommunication Engineers. Prof. Datta has more than 30 publications in different reputed international journals and conferences. He has also contributed chapters in the books published by different internationally acclaimed publishers. He has been working as a technical committee member of different international journals for the last five years. He has also worked as a reviewer of many book chapters. He has attended different technical seminars, conferences and workshops. Prof. Datta has taught the following topics in the undergraduate and the postgraduate levels: ü Data Warehousing and Data Mining ü Cryptography and Network Security ü Socket Programming ü Computer Networks ü Object Oriented Programming ü Database Management Systems ü Data Structures.

Soumili Dey pursued B.Sc. and M.Sc in Computer Science from St. Xavier's College (Autonomous), Kolkata, India. She has various publications in different reputed journals.

Shahid Gulzar was born in small and backward hamlet of south –Kashmir (Bogund-Kulgam)-Kashmir on 06th May 1987.Though study and bought up in conflict zone which was not easy. Did high schooling from neighbourhood, later took admission in Sri Pratap College Srinagar (Kashmir University) where completed B.SC.Very keen to work with an organization working for Socio-economic development. Joined VOSEP local Kashmir based Organization, where I got enhanced my technical skills on grass root level. Interacted and worked with different SHG's, rural communities in remote areas with a flexible approach to problem solving. Enjoyed rigorous thinking of socio-economic planning and regional development; this influenced my decision to peruse geospatial applications in regional development as major. loved regional development because it blends abstract theory to real world applications. Double M.sc degrees, M.sc geography-Rajasthan University, M.sc Geospatial applications in regional development-Central university Karnataka, Diploma in computer Application, Certificate in geospatial applications in rural development –NIRD Hyderabad and many other short-term courses. During course work learned many things and its applications on grass root level. Apart worked as mapping Engineer with Cowi India Private limited, RAMteCH Software solutions & Directorate land records Kashmir, Department of Environment, forest and remote sensing J&K govt. Working with different esteemed organizations not only enhanced my technical skills but improved my knowledge too. Presently working as faculty (SAIARD/IIGST) -Kolkata, core areas are Climate Change, Argo-geomatics, Rural Development, with 6 years of industrial experience . Lives in Kashmir both personal and professional are governed around political calendar of region. A region ridden with decades of Conflict, working on grass root level is not so easy. Though it is challenging but Knowledge, understanding and proven leadership qualities can be valuable tool in positive change. Regional planning modals can bring positive change in environment, Healthcare, income generation and domestic policy.

Sunil Kumar is a Ph.D. in Computer Science from Gurukula Kangri Vishwavidyalaya, Haridwar, India. He was awarded MCA degree by Indira Gandhi National Open University, New Delhi. His career in academies spans over 29 years. Presently he is working as Assistant Professor in Sir J. C. Bose Technical Campus, Kumaun University, Nainital. His research interests include machine learning and computer networks. Dr. Sunil's publications in national and international journals and in the form of book chapters have been widely appreciated and cited.

Rahul Kumar Mishra received MCA Degree from KNIT Sultanpur in 1992 and MBA from IGNOU, New Delhi in 2012. He is Ph.D. in Computer Science & Engineering. His research interest includes Database Management Systems, Real-Time Systems, and Distributed Real-Time Database Systems. He has published 20 research papers in International National journals and presented 7 papers at different Conferences. He has written a number of books on various Computing and Management Topics. Currently he is engaged in writing books on Artificial Intelligence for Humans, Data Science for Business, and Internet of Things for Business Professionals in collaboration with his associates. Recently, he has published patients on 'Cancer Detection Techniques in Big Data and 'IOT with Deep Learning-Based Automatic Eye Cataract Detection Using Matlab Approach'. He has completed a project (MODROB) of 13.5 lakh from AICTE in 2010. A number of Ph.D. research scholars of computer science and applications are enrolled under his supervision & more than five Ph.D. degrees have been awarded under his valuable guidance. Over a span of 27 years, he has been associated with both industry and academia. He has worked on multiple projects in diverse areas such as Software Consulting, Software Development, Configuration Management, Software Quality Assurance, etc. He is also having an assignment as pro-vice-chancellor and Director, Admissions and is playing a vital role in the overall growth of IFTM University.

Biswajit Roy Chowdhury, faculty member in the Department of Geography of Vidyasagar College (affiliated to University of Calcutta), Kolkata, India, has obtained his master degree in Geography from Calcutta University in the year 2008 with a specialization in Urban and Transport Geography. He is also awarded Honorary Doctorate from UN Rescue Services, Sweden. Along with teaching he has engaged in number of academic and administrative activities. He has significantly contributed in the field of Environmental science. He has a keen interest in studying the various aspects of urban environment. Besides that he has a deep research experience in various fields of Geography especially in Transport planning, Regional science, RS and GIS etc. Recently he is trying to introduce a new dimension in his subject i.e. Medical Geography and also collide this field with the environmental science. He had number of national and international research publications on these various aspects. Considering all his achievements and outstanding contribution in the field of research, the Search Committee of the Confederation of Indian Universities, New Delhi and the International Foundation for Environment and Ecology has recommended the name for the Junior Scientist of the Year 2017 Award. Besides that on behalf of Asian Society for Scientific Research and Jha Scientific Research Lab he was also awarded for the Youngest Researchers Award 2018 and Young Innovator Award 2018 for the whole Eastern Regions of India. Till now he wrote 11 books, out of which 7 books were published by the School Education Dept., Govt. of West Bengal. He is also engaged with different research and academic bodies like, Institute of Landscape, Ecology and Ekistics, Bangio Bhugol Mancha, Foundation of Practicing geographers, Break through Science Society of India, International Benevolent Research Foundation, CEED, New Delhi etc. Along with these academic activities he has a keen interest in studying literature and as an active member of Paschim Banga Kabita Academy he devoted himself through the writing of poems in both Bengali and Hindi languages and recite them in different cultural programmes. Not only that Dr. Roy Chowdhury is also engaged with various social activities and he also takes an important parts in various intellectual reformations in Bengal. He is the founder Chairman, of South Asian Institute for Advanced Research and Development (SAIARD) and International Institute of Geospatial Science and Technology (IIGST).

Aditi Saxena, a B.Tech. II year E.I student of Banasthali University, Rajasthan. She is passionate in technology driven devices designing and instrumentation. She owns couple of copyrights and design patent. She is looking to carry out her Masters in Cyber Forensic world.

Amit Saxena is currently associated with Birla Institute of Management and Technology (BIMTECH) Greater Noida.He works in the area of Human Resources and People Management. He holds a Post Graduate Degree in Management. He has attended many national and international level conferences, workshops, and seminars. He has published 4 research papers in reputed journals with copyrights and patents.

Hari Om Sharan, serving as Dean – Academic Affairs & FET at Rama University Uttar Pradesh, Kanpur (India), has more than 15 years of experience in academic as well in research, his research area is AI, Security and HPC. Dr. Sharan received his Ph.D in DNA Computing: A Novel Approach towards the solution of NP-Complete Problems, and his UG (B.Tech) & PG (M.Tech) in Computer Science and Engineering, He has done International certification in Data Science and Artificial Intelligence Machine Learning Deep Learning and its Application. Dr. Sharan also published three (03) books on Mobile Network Technology. Dr. Sharan developed short term course on Artificial Intelligence Machine Learning Deep Learning and its Application, and published 14 patents (National/International) & copyrights mostly in Computer Science and Engineering to serve the nation in the field of research. Dr. Sharan authored and coauthored more than 60 papers in refereed international journal & many international Conferences and National Conferences & serve as editor/Reviewer of different international journals, Springer International Conferences.

Ajay Narayan Shukla is working as Assistant Professor in DIT University, Dehradun. He has published research papers in the Scopus/Web of Science journals. he has also presented research papers in the various conferences of repute. His current area of research is Algorithms, machine learning.

Vishal Srivastava is associated with School of Commerce, Jain (Deemed-to-be University) as Associate Professor.

Laura Valenzuela studied a BSc in Biomedical Engineering, specializing in medical devices, biomaterials and biomechanics, with a final project about machine learning. She has completed a MSc in Biomedical Engineering focusing on business and projects management, and she has developed her master thesis in collaboration with Hospital Universitario La Paz (Madrid). She has attended different courses related to mobile applications and programming, but also others focused on neuroscience and on Covid19. Her main interest is to apply new technologies in neuroscience to help as much as possible in that field.

Index

Ensure Quality Research is Introduced to the Academic Community

Become an Evaluator for IGI Global Authored Book Projects

Premier Reference Source

Stabilizing Currency and Preserving Economic Sovereignty Using the Grondona System

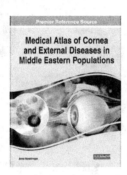

Premier Reference Source

Medical Atlas of Cornea and External Diseases in Middle Eastern Populations

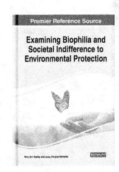

Premier Reference Source

Examining Biophilia and Societal Indifference to Environmental Protection

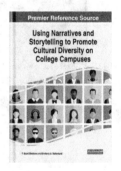

Premier Reference Source

Using Narratives and Storytelling to Promote Cultural Diversity on College Campuses

The overall success of an authored book project is dependent on quality and timely manuscript evaluations.

Applications and Inquiries may be sent to:
development@igi-global.com

Applicants must have a doctorate (or equivalent degree) as well as publishing, research, and reviewing experience. Authored Book Evaluators are appointed for one-year terms and are expected to complete at least three evaluations per term. Upon successful completion of this term, evaluators can be considered for an additional term.

If you have a colleague that may be interested in this opportunity, we encourage you to share this information with them.

Increase Your Manuscript's Chance of Acceptance

IGI Global Author Services

Learn More or Get Started Here:
www.igi-global.com/editorial-service-partners/

Copy Editing & Proofreading

Professional, native English language copy editors improve your manuscript's grammar, spelling, punctuation, terminology, semantics, consistency, flow, formatting, and more.

Scientific & Scholarly Editing

A Ph.D. level review for qualities such as originality and significance, interest to researchers, level of methodology and analysis, coverage of literature, organization, quality of writing, and strengths and weaknesses.

Figure, Table, Chart & Equation Conversions

Work with IGI Global's graphic designers before submission to enhance and design all figures and charts to IGI Global's specific standards for clarity.

- Professional Service

- Quality Guarantee & Certificate

- Timeliness

- Affordable Pricing

What Makes IGI Global Author Services Stand Apart?

Services/Offerings	IGI Global Author Services	Editage	Enago
Turnaround Time of Projects	3-5 Business Days	6-7 Busines Days	6-7 Busines Days
Pricing	Fraction of our Competitors' Cost	Up to 2x Higher	Up to 3x Higher

For Questions, Contact IGI Global's Customer Service Team at cust@igi-global.com or 717-533-8845

IGI Global
PUBLISHER of TIMELY KNOWLEDGE
www.igi-global.com

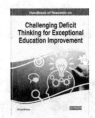

Printed in the United States
by Baker & Taylor Publisher Services